A Roman drainage culvert, Great Fire destruction debris and other evidence from hillside sites north-east of London Bridge

Excavations at Monument House and 13–21 Eastcheap, City of London

GW01186381

MoLAS Archaeology Studies Series

1 A 14th-century pottery site in Kingston upon Thames, Surrey: excavations at 70–76 Eden Street, Pat Miller and Roy Stephenson
ISBN 1 901992 07 1

2 Excavations at 72–75 Cheapside/83–93 Queen Street, City of London, Julian Hill and Aidan Woodger
ISBN 1 901992 08 X

3 Bankside: excavations at Benbow House, Southwark, London SE1, Anthony Mackinder and Simon Blatherwick
ISBN 1 901992 12 8

4 A Romano-British cemetery on Watling Street: excavations at 165 Great Dover Street, Southwark, London, Anthony Mackinder
ISBN 1 901992 11 X

5 Excavations at 25 Cannon Street, City of London: from the Middle Bronze Age to the Great Fire, Nicholas J Elsden
ISBN 1 901992 22 5

6 The London Millennium Bridge: excavation of the medieval and later waterfronts at Peter's Hill, City of London, and Bankside, Southwark, Julian Ayre and Robin Wroe-Brown
ISBN 1 901992 25 X

7 An excavation in the western cemetery of Roman London: Atlantic House, City of London, Sadie Watson
ISBN 1 901992 26 8

8 The Roman tower at Shadwell, London: a reappraisal, David Lakin, with Fiona Seeley, Joanna Bird, Kevin Rielly and Charlotte Ainsley
ISBN 1 901992 27 6

9 Early modern industry and settlement: excavations at George Street, Richmond, and High Street, Mortlake, in the London Borough of Richmond upon Thames, Barney Sloane and Stewart Hoad, with John Cloake, Jacqueline Pearce and Roy Stephenson
ISBN 1 901992 35 7

10 Roman burials, medieval tenements and suburban growth: 201 Bishopsgate, City of London, Dan Swift
ISBN 1 901992 41 1

11 Investigating the maritime history of Rotherhithe: excavations at Pacific Wharf, 165 Rotherhithe Street, Southwark, Kieron Heard with Damian Goodburn
ISBN 1 901992 40 3

12 Medieval and later urban development at High Street, Uxbridge: excavations at the Chimes Shopping Centre, London Borough of Hillingdon, Heather Knight and Nigel Jeffries
ISBN 1 901992 37 3

13 Pre-Boudican and later activity on the site of the forum: excavations at 168 Fenchurch Street, City of London, Lesley Dunwoodie
ISBN 1 901992 53 5

14 Roman and medieval development south of Newgate: excavations at 3–9 Newgate Street and 16–17 Old Bailey, City of London, Ken Pitt
ISBN 1 901992 58 6

15 The Doulton stoneware pothouse in Lambeth: excavations at 9 Albert Embankment, London, Kieron Tyler with John Brown, Terence Paul Smith and Lucy Whittingham
ISBN 1 901992 63 2

16 Becoming Roman: excavation of a Late Iron Age to Romano-British landscape at Monkston Park, Milton Keynes, Raoul Bull and Simon Davis
ISBN 1 901992 67 5

17 A Roman drainage culvert, Great Fire destruction debris and other evidence from hillside sites north-east of London Bridge: excavations at Monument House and 13–21 Eastcheap, City of London, Ian Blair and David Sankey
ISBN 1 901992 69 1

A Roman drainage culvert, Great Fire destruction debris and other evidence from hillside sites north-east of London Bridge

Excavations at Monument House and 13–21 Eastcheap, City of London

Ian Blair and David Sankey

MoLAS Archaeology Studies Series 17

Museum of London Archaeology Service

Published by the Museum of London Archaeology Service
Copyright © Museum of London 2007

The Ordnance Survey mapping included in this publication is provided
by the City of London under licence from the Ordnance Survey
© Crown copyright. Unauthorised reproduction infringes Crown copyright
and may lead to prosecution or civil proceedings.
City of London 100023243-2007

A CIP catalogue record for this book is available from the British Library

Production and series design by Tracy Wellman
Typesetting and design by Sue Cawood
Reprographics by Andy Chopping
Copy editing by Carol Fellingham Webb
Series editing by Sue Hirst/Susan M Wright
Post-excavation and series management by Peter Rowsome

Printed by the Lavenham Press

Front cover: recording the interior of the Monument House Roman culvert (S3),
looking south

CONTRIBUTORS

Monument House

Principal author	Ian Blair
Documentary sources	Tony Dyson
Sedimentary analysis	Jane Corcoran
Ceramic building material	Ian M Betts
Architectural worked stone	Mark Samuel
Ceiling plaster	Terence P Smith
Clay tobacco pipes	Jacqui Pearce
Roman pottery	Robin P Symonds
Medieval and post-medieval pottery	Lyn Blackmore
Accessioned finds	Jackie Keily, Geoff Egan
Plant remains	Lisa Gray
Animal bone	Alan Pipe
Human bone	Bill White

13–21 Eastcheap

Principal author	David Sankey
Ceramic building material	Susan Pringle
Clay tobacco pipes	Kieron Heard
Roman pottery	Beth Richardson with Louise Rayner
Medieval and post-medieval pottery	Roy Stephenson
Accessioned finds	Jackie Keily
Animal bone	Alan Pipe, Jane Liddle

Conclusions	Peter Rowsome
Graphics	Peter Hart-Allison, Faith Vardy
Photography	Andy Chopping, Maggie Cox
Project managers	Sophie Jackson, Robin Nielsen, Peter Rowsome
Editor	Peter Rowsome

CONTENTS

List of figures viii

List of tables x

Summary xi

Acknowledgements xii

Introduction   **1**

1.1   Location and circumstances of fieldwork 1

1.2   Archaeological and historical background 1

1.3   Organisation of this report 4

1.4   Textual and graphical conventions in this report 4

The archaeological evidence from   **2**
Monument House

2.1   Geology and prehistory (period 1) 6

Natural topography of the area 6

2.2   The Roman sequence (periods 2 and 3) 6

Early Roman occupation and quarrying, c AD 50–
125 (period 2 phase 1) 6

Activity after c AD 125 (period 2 phase 2) 7

Infrastructure and building of the 3rd century AD
(period 3 phase 1) 8

Late Roman abandonment (period 3 phase 2) 16

2.3   The early medieval and medieval sequence up to
c 1500 (periods 4 and 5) 17

Documentary evidence 17

Late Saxon and early medieval occupation to the late
13th century (period 4) 22

Later medieval development in the 14th and 15th
centuries (period 5) 25

2.4   Post-medieval occupation up to and including the
Great Fire (period 6) 28

Properties north of Cat Lane and the St Botolph
burial ground 28

The Great Fire horizon 35

2.5   The post-Great Fire and modern sequence (periods
7 and 8) 48

Documentary evidence 48

Rebuilding after the Great Fire (period 7) 49

Reconstruction in the 19th century (period 8) 52

The archaeological evidence from   **3**
13–21 Eastcheap

3.1   Geology and prehistory (period 1) 54

Natural topography of the area 54

3.2   The Roman sequence (periods 2–4) 54

Early Roman occupation, c AD 50–125 (period 2
phase 1) 54

Late 1st-century AD development (period 2 phase 2) . 54

Early 2nd-century AD occupation (period 2 phase 3) . 55

A Hadrianic fire horizon of *c* AD 125 (period 3
phase 1) 57

Post-Hadrianic rebuilding up to *c* AD 200 (period 3
phase 2) 57

Late Roman change from *c* AD 200 until the 5th
century AD (period 4) 59

3.3 The early medieval and medieval sequence up to
c 1500 (period 5) 61

Activity south of Eastcheap 61

3.4 Post-medieval and modern evidence after *c* 1500
(period 6) 61

Further development along Eastcheap 61

Thematic aspects amd conclusions   **4**   4.1 The Roman culvert (S3) and terraced Building 2
at Monument House 62

The function and significance of the culvert (S3)
and Building 2 62

The importance of the Camulodunum form 306
bowl 63

Sedimentation in the Roman culvert 65

4.2 Conclusions 65

Research findings 65

Future research questions 66

Specialist appendices   **5**   5.1 The Roman pottery 67

5.2 The medieval and post-medieval pottery 67

5.3 Accessioned finds 69

Introduction 69

Characteristics of the site assemblages 69

Catalogue of illustrated finds from the two sites 69

French and German summaries   71

Bibliography   73

Index   77

FIGURES

Fig 1   Location of the study area in the City of London . . 2

Fig 2   Location of the Monument House and 13–21 Eastcheap excavations and selected nearby sites referred to in the report 2

Fig 3   Areas of archaeological excavation at Monument House 2

Fig 4   Areas of archaeological investigation at 13–21 Eastcheap 3

Fig 5   Graphical conventions used in this report 5

Fig 6   Camulodunum 186 amphora <P1> and fine micaceous reduced ware cup <P2> 7

Fig 7   Fragmentary remains of Building 1 (period 2 phase 2) at Monument House 8

Fig 8   Necked jar in Verulamium region coarse white-slipped ware <P3> and London oxidised ware lid <P4> 8

Fig 9   Excavating the complete pot <P3> and inverted lid <P4>, a foundation deposit associated with Building 1 at Monument House 9

Fig 10   Terraced building (B2) and culvert (S3) (period 3 phase 1) at Monument House 9

Fig 11   Aerial view of culvert (S3) at Monument House . . 10

Fig 12   The culvert (S3) access shaft fully excavated 11

Fig 13   Two sections of culvert (S3) butted against a cross-wall 11

Fig 14   Interior of culvert (S3) 12

Fig 15   View looking south along culvert (S3) 12

Fig 16   Culvert (S3), looking south from the central silt trap 12

Fig 17   Central silt trap in culvert (S3) 13

Fig 18   Southern silt trap in culvert (S3) 13

Fig 19   Finds associated with culvert (S3) construction backfills: enamelled belt plate <S1> and enamelled disc brooch <S2>, obverse and reverse; rim fragment from an 'Airlie' cup <S3> and a colourless glass bowl <S4> 14

Fig 20   Robber cut for the central wall of Building 2 at Monument House 15

Fig 21   The western tile pier for the south wall of Building 2 at Monument House 15

Fig 22   Unusual sherd of Nene Valley colour-coated ware <P5> with ring and dot stamped decoration and rouletting 16

Fig 23   Copper-alloy spoon <S5> from a cosmetic set . . 17

Fig 24   Documented properties in the vicinity of Monument House and 13–21 Eastcheap 22

Fig 25   Sunken building (B3), Structure 5 and pitting in Open Area 4 (period 4) at Monument House . . . 23

Fig 26   North–south section through cellared building (B3) 24

Fig 27   Rhenish greyware globular jar <P6>, London-type ware waisted baluster jug <P7> and Kingston-type ware frying pan <P8> 25

Fig 28   Cat Lane (R1) and properties to the south and north (period 5) at Monument House 26

Fig 29   Chalk-lined cesspit (S8) 27

Fig 30   Basket-handled bowl with stabbed decoration <P9> and jug decorated with applied strips <P10> . 28

Fig 31   Corroded woolcombs <S6> from fragments A<450> and A<397>; X-ray of A<397> 29

Fig 32   Building complex Building 6 and Building 7 enclosing courtyard Open Area 7 (period 6) at Monument House 30

Fig 33   Building 7 rooms A and B, Building 6 and well (S7) and courtyard (OA7) at Monument House . . 31

Fig 34   Chalk-lined cesspit (S8) incorporated into Building 6 32

Fig 35   Ornate fireplace mantelpiece A<36> 32

Fig 36   Deep two-handled jar <P11> and squat, rounded two-handled jar <P12> 33

Fig 37   Removing sunken pot <P12> from the sump in Building 7 room A 33

Fig 38   The remains of the staircase walls and limestone floor slabs in Building 7 room B at Monument House 34

Fig 39   The blocked window in the east wall of Building 7 room B 34

Fig 40   Frechen stoneware bottle with applied medallion dated 1645 <P13> 35

Fig 41   Early 16th-century Spanish floor tiles <T1> (A[+] A<361> and A[119] A<63>) and <T2> (A[107] A<57>) 36

Fig 42   Mid 16th-century Antwerp floor tile <T3> (A[104] A<119>) 36

Fig 43   Early to mid 17th-century London floor tiles: <T4>– <T12> 37

Fig 44   Mid 16th-century Dutch wall tiles <T13>–<T19> . . 39

Fig 45   Late Tudor decorative ceiling plaster from Great Fire debris A[119] in Open Area 9: <WP1>– <WP3> 40

Fig 46   Window catch <S7> 42

Fig 47   Mounted locks <S8> and <S9> 42

Fig 48   Padlock cases and keys: case <S10>; cases <S11> and <S12> with associated keys <S16> and <S17>; case <S13>; keys <S14> and <S15> . . . 43

Fig 49   Sliding bolt <S18>, handle <S19> and strap with terminal <S20> 44

Fig 50   Cast-iron vessel <S21> 44

Fig 51   Patten <S22> and reconstruction showing use . . . 45

Fig 52   Round grate <S23> 45

Fig 53   Waffle tongs <S24> and reconstruction showing use 45

Fig 54   Goffering iron <S25> and reconstruction with straight handle 46

Fig 55 Bone and iron tool <S26> 46
Fig 56 Rapier <S27> 46
Fig 57 Iron lid <S28> 47
Fig 58 Glass wine bottle seal showing a mitre and the
initial 'P' <S29> 47
Fig 59 Complete clay pipes <S30> (A<438>, A<437>
and A<436>) 48
Fig 60 Ogilby and Morgan's map of 1676 with the
Monument House and 13–21 Eastcheap sites
highlighted 49
Fig 61 Post-Great Fire development (period 7) at
Monument House 50
Fig 62 'Wren's House' at 32 Botolph Lane 51
Fig 63 Horwood's map of 1813 with the Monument
House and 13–21 Eastcheap sites highlighted . . . 52
Fig 64 Decorated type OS12 clay pipe <S31> 52
Fig 65 Building 1 (period 2 phase 1) at 13–21 Eastcheap . 55
Fig 66 Building 2 and external activity up to c AD 125
(period 2 phase 2) at 13–21 Eastcheap 56
Fig 67 Pad base from glass beaker <S33> 56
Fig 68 Early 2nd-century AD buildings (period 2 phase 3)
at 13–21 Eastcheap 57
Fig 69 Copper-alloy seal box <S36> and unguent jar <S34> . 58
Fig 70 Post-Hadrianic activity (period 3 phase 2) at 13–
21 Eastcheap 58
Fig 71 Copper-alloy circular plate mount with rivets
<S37> and a possible scabbard runner or strap tag
<S38> 59
Fig 72 Annular glass bead <S32> and melted window
glass <S39> 59
Fig 73 A 3rd-century AD pottery assemblage <P14>–
<P27> from drain backfill B[113] in Open Area 6 . 60
Fig 74 Mica-dusted lamp <S35> 61
Fig 75 The alignment of the Roman culvert recorded at
Monument House 63
Fig 76 Camulodunum form 306 bowls <P28>–<P35> . . 64

TABLES

Table 1 Camulodunum form 306 bowls as a percentage of the total pottery assemblage at Monument House and selected other sites 64

Table 2 Camulodunum form 306 bowls as a percentage of the total pottery assemblage in contexts where it is present at Monument House and selected other sites 64

Table 3 Details of the illustrated Roman pottery from sites A (Monument House) and B (13–21 Eastcheap) 68

Table 4 Details of the illustrated medieval and post-medieval pottery from site A (Monument House) . . 68

SUMMARY

This report comprises findings from two sites located to the north-east of London Bridge, between the waterfront and Cornhill to the north.

Monument House lay on steeply sloping ground c 120m from the bridgehead. The earliest extant activity was represented by several large, 1st-century AD gravel quarries. These were backfilled and the site levelled to allow construction of late 1st- or early 2nd-century AD timber buildings.

In the late 2nd or early 3rd century AD a large masonry building was constructed on the hillside, with an integral drainage culvert running southwards beneath it. An access shaft at the northern end of the culvert contained a timber silt trap at its base. Two smaller silt traps inside the culvert included a timber dated to AD 176–221. Ritual bowls were recovered from fills of the culvert, which may have led from a public building to the north or formed part of a drainage system carrying waste water from the forum-basilica southwards to the Thames. The terraced building and culvert remained in use until the mid 4th century AD and were sealed by 'dark earth'.

Reoccupation of the site was represented by two successive 10th-century AD sunken-floored buildings. The post and stave walls of the later structure were destroyed by an 11th-century fire. Later properties included two adjoining 15th-century buildings on the south and east sides of a courtyard. These may have formed part of Lombardes Place. The lower terrace building to the south flanked Cat Lane, a narrow alleyway which ran along the north side of the upper burial ground of St Botolph church.

The cellars of the buildings were remodelled in the late 16th century with the addition of brick floors and new staircase access to the courtyard. The buildings were destroyed in the Great Fire and the associated finds assemblage contains many rare items, including a large group of ironwork, a highly ornate fireplace mantelpiece, and both floor and wall tiles.

A large, enclosed courtyard established after the Great Fire was associated with a fine house at 32 Botolph Lane, rebuilt in 1670 by Arnold and Samuel Beake, members of a wealthy family of Dutch merchants. The house was demolished in 1906 but its courtyard survived until redevelopment in 1998.

13–21 Eastcheap is located c 100m further north, towards the higher ground of Cornhill. Early Roman hillside terracing was found here, but there was no surviving evidence of associated buildings or the Boudican fire horizon seen on nearby sites. Fragmentary remains of post-Boudican features and late 1st-century AD earth-and-timber buildings were found. The pottery and other finds were domestic in character and included a complete glass jar, possibly an unguent vessel. Some of the buildings were covered by a refuse midden which included large quantities of oyster shell.

A substantial layer of burnt debris may have been associated with the 'Hadrianic' fire of c AD 125. Post-Hadrianic rebuilding included timber-lined drains and the Kentish ragstone foundations of masonry buildings. Large assemblages of pottery and animal bone were recovered from 3rd- and 4th-century AD fills of drains and pits.

The sequence following the Roman period was severely truncated, although some isolated medieval pits survived, many containing 'dark earth' and residual Roman finds. Animal bone from the pits may relate to Eastcheap's role as a centre of butchery during the later medieval period.

ACKNOWLEDGEMENTS

The Museum of London Archaeology Service (MoLAS) would like to thank Berkeley Homes Ltd (Essex) for its generous funding of the archaeological fieldwork and publication of the findings from Monument House, and particularly Mike Sampson, Steve Rusbridge and Steven Bangs for their help and support. Site attendances were provided by Blanchills. The archaeological investigation at 13–21 Eastcheap was kindly funded by Taylor Woodrow Developments Ltd, with attendances by Demolition Services Ltd.

We would also like to thank Kathryn Stubbs, Senior Planning and Archaeology Officer of the City of London, for her input and support of the aims at both projects. Many other people showed an active interest in the sites, particularly Ellen Barnes, the English Heritage Inspector of Ancient Monuments for London, who provided advice on how best to preserve the Roman culvert unexpectedly found at Monument House. Thanks go to Waterman Partnership, who carried out design alterations to the proposed piling to allow the culvert to be preserved in situ. We would also like to thank the staff from the City Engineer's Department who kindly carried out the CCTV survey of the Roman culvert in advance of excavation, with additional financial support from Thames Water.

Desk-based assessment of the Monument House site was by Kevin Wooldridge, and subsequent evaluation phases were supervised by Julian Bowsher, Lesley Dunwoodie and Peter Rowsome. Angus Stephenson project-managed the initial stages of the archaeological work. Louise Rayner and Fiona Seeley (Roman pottery), Kieron Heard (clay tobacco pipes), Elizabeth Goodman (conservation), Kevin Rielly (animal bone), Anne Davis (plant remains) and Ian Tyers (dendrochronology) carried out assessment work or offered specialist advice.

Desk-based assessment of 13–21 Eastcheap was carried out by Robin Nielsen, and followed by an auger survey by Niall Roycroft and evaluation by Tony MacKinder. Specialists who contributed to the assessment included Angela Wardle (non-ceramic finds), Kevin Rielly (animal bone), John Giorgi (plant remains), Ian M Betts (building material) and Fiona Seeley (Roman pottery). Michael Hammerson assessed the Roman coins from both sites.

Special thanks are due to the members of the MoLAS excavation team at both sites for their efforts in often difficult conditions. Site photography was by Maggie Cox and Andy Chopping. Surveying was undertaken by the MoLAS survey team. The summary was translated into French by Elisabeth Lorans and into German by Manuela Struck. The index was compiled by Margaret Binns.

1

Introduction

1.1 Location and circumstances of fieldwork

This publication reports on archaeological excavations at two sites located to the north-east of London Bridge, on the terraced slope between Cornhill to the north and the north bank of the Thames. The two sites have been prefixed A and B for the purposes of this report. Site A is Monument House, 30–35 Botolph Lane and 29–31 Monument Street, London EC3 (site code BPL95), located *c* 120m to the east-north-east of the Roman and medieval London bridge. The site is located on the east side of Botolph Lane, to the north of Monument Street, with its approximate centre located at Ordnance Survey national grid reference TQ 330200 807400. Approximately 100m to the north, site B is 13–21 Eastcheap, London EC3, bounded by Eastcheap to the south and Philpot Lane to the east (site code ESC97). The national grid reference for the centre of the site is TQ 33020 80850 (Fig 1; Fig 2). Both sites were subject to planning conditions stating that archaeological excavation was required prior to redevelopment.

A 1994 proposal for redevelopment of the Monument House site was followed by a desk-based assessment, and subsequent evaluation work confirmed the presence of archaeological remains. Berkeley Homes Ltd acquired the site in 1997 and a second site evaluation was undertaken. The main excavation took place between March and July 1998, following the demolition of 19th- and 20th-century buildings (Fig 3).

A remarkably well-preserved Roman culvert was discovered during the excavations and Berkeley Homes Ltd agreed to redesign the new building's foundations to preserve the structure in situ beneath it. The culvert was lined with Terram and filled with Buckland sand, topped with sandbags to support its vaulted roof. A time capsule was placed in the culvert beneath One Tree Park prior to its infilling.

A proposal for redevelopment of 13–21 Eastcheap was granted conditional planning permission in 1997, followed by a desk-based assessment, auger survey and evaluation work. A revised proposal for redevelopment was approved in 1998. Preservation of archaeological deposits was recommended at 13–15 Eastcheap, making the inclusion of new basements impractical in this area. Excavations took place in September 1998, followed by a watching-stopping brief until January 1999 (Fig 4).

1.2 Archaeological and historical background

There have been few prehistoric finds from the vicinity of the sites, although evidence of a Mesolithic marsh has been found along the north bank of the Thames immediately to the east and west of the Roman bridgehead (Brigham and Woodger 2001) and Late Bronze Age pottery has been recovered at several sites nearby.

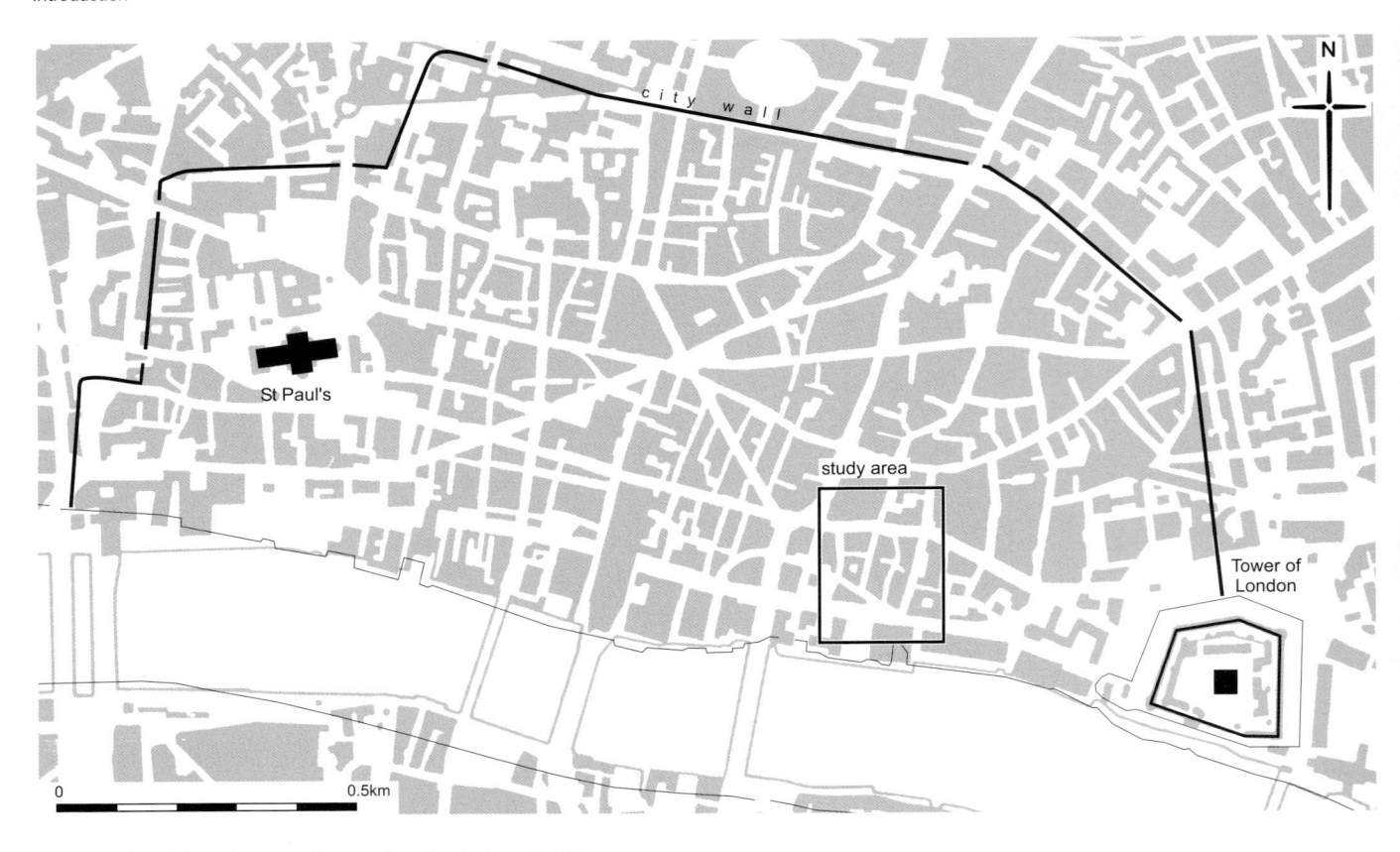

Fig 1 Location of the study area in the City of London (scale 1:12,500)

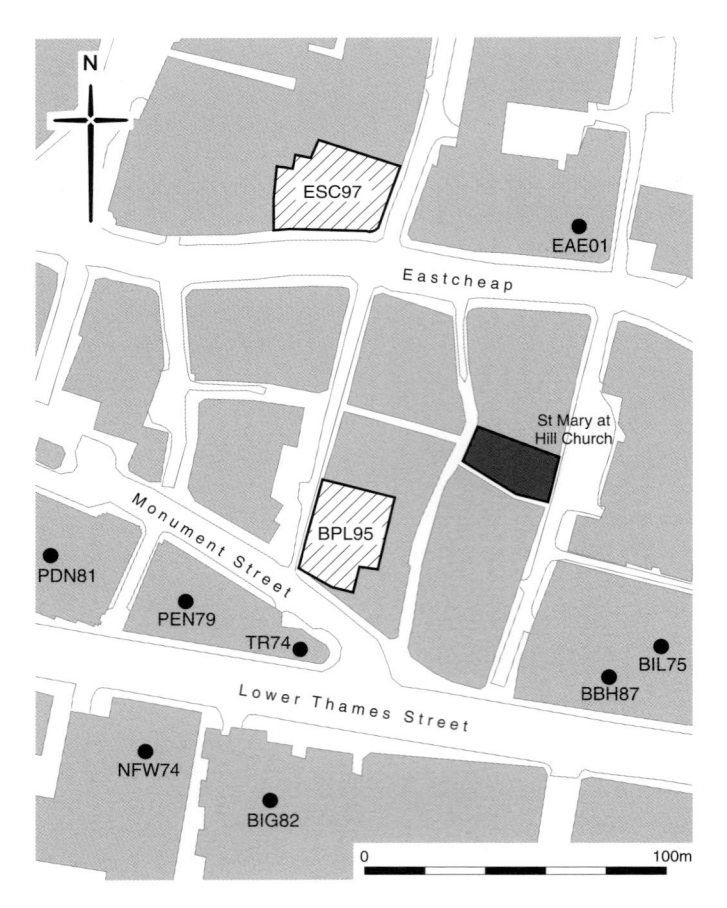

Fig 2 Location of the Monument House and 13–21 Eastcheap excavations and selected nearby sites referred to in the report (scale 1:2000)

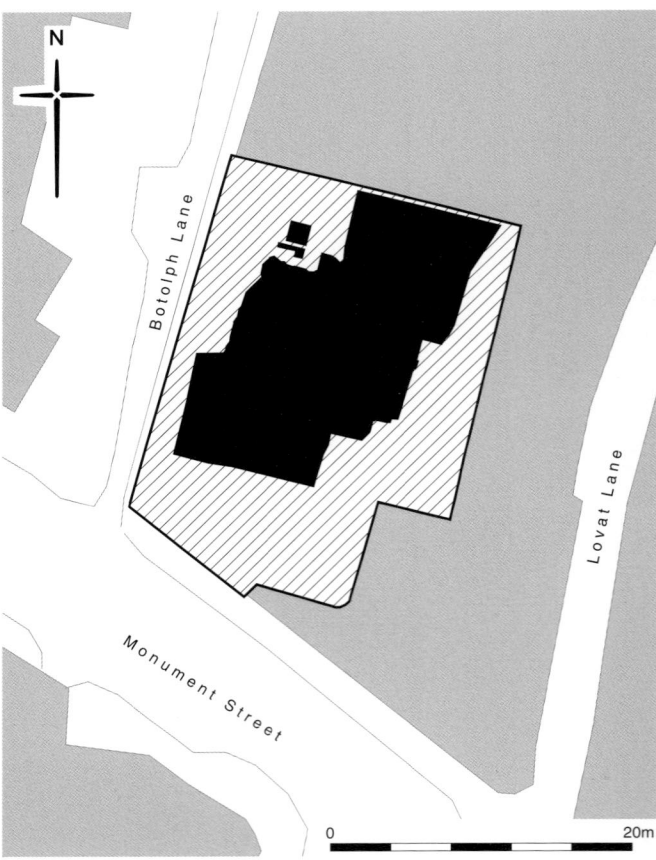

Fig 3 Areas of archaeological excavation at Monument House (scale 1:500)

The establishment of the Roman bridgehead in *c* AD 50 (Watson et al 2001, 30–43) was followed by construction of waterfronts immediately to the east. The hillside to the north was terraced to facilitate the construction of riverside warehouses and buildings (Milne 1985; Perring 1991). The north–south-aligned bridgehead road met the new settlement's main east–west axial road in a T-junction near the crest of Cornhill (Dunwoodie 2004; Hill and Rowsome in prep).

Early Roman timber waterfronts and warehouses have been recorded at sites downstream of the bridge, less than 50m to the south of Monument House, including Billingsgate Buildings (TR74) (Jones 1980), Peninsular House (PEN79) and Pudding Lane (PDN81) (Milne 1985). A similar sequence has been recorded immediately upstream of the bridge at Regis House (KWS94) (Brigham and Watson 1996; Brigham et al 1996).

The early settlement was destroyed in the Boudican revolt of AD 60–1 and took more than a decade to recover from this setback, although some roads, waterfronts and other infrastructure were rebuilt in the early years of the decade. Excavations at Plantation Place (FER97) have identified the north-eastern part of a military camp enclosed by V-shaped ditches, established south-east of Cornhill in the decade following the revolt (Dunwoodie et al in prep). The western side of this military enclosure may have been located just to the east of the 13–21 Eastcheap excavation area (ibid and Chapter 3.2).

The town grew quickly from the AD 70s onwards, with the first forum on Cornhill built in about AD 75. Roman occupation has been recorded at several sites near 13–21 Eastcheap, including 41 Eastcheap (EAE01) *c* 60m to the east, where evidence includes intensive early Roman occupation and both Boudican and Hadrianic fire horizons (Pitt in prep).

In the late 1st and early 2nd century AD reclamation work extended the line of the waterfront southwards. Construction of a much larger forum-basilica on Cornhill was progressed but this period of sustained expansion was halted in *c* AD 125 by the 'Hadrianic' fire. Subsequent development may have been less intense in peripheral areas of the town but continued to be robust along the main roads (Hill and Rowsome in prep).

The forum-basilica continued in use into the 3rd century AD, by which time Londinium's landward defensive walls had been built. Several large late Roman buildings have been found to the north of the waterfront downstream from the bridgehead. A building at Pudding Lane incorporated a bathing suite and the 3rd-century AD Billingsgate bathhouse (BIL75 and BBH87) lay further east (Rowsome 1996), both sited on the hillside's lower terrace to tap into the spring water flowing through the natural gravels.

Regression of the tidal range of the Thames (Brigham 1990) and general economic and political change (Perring 1991) contributed to decline of the waterfront and led to the late 3rd-century AD establishment of a riverside defensive wall (Hill et al 1980; Williams 1993). Following the withdrawal of the Roman legions in the early 5th century AD, the focus of settlement moved to Lundenwic to the west (Vince 1990), with the decline of the Roman town marked by a horizon of 'dark earth' at many sites (Yule 1990).

The bridgehead became the renewed focus for settlement when King Alfred reoccupied the walled area in AD 886. Billingsgate (BIG82), to the south of the Monument House site, was established as a landing place for boats (Steedman et al 1992). The remains of 10th- and 11th-century buildings have been recorded at several neighbouring sites (Horsman et al 1988).

Eastcheap may have been one of the first axial streets in the Late Saxon town and is first mentioned in documents between 1098 and 1108. Several churches in the vicinity are documented from the late 12th century. Philpot Lane was named *venella Sancti Andree Hubert* by *c* 1270 (Lobel 1989, 83) and renamed after Sir John Philpot, mayor, who died in 1384. The Tabard Inn was established to the north-west by 1464, by which time Eastcheap was the City's meat market.

The area north of Thames Street around Botolph Lane was intensively developed throughout the medieval period. In 1393 the upper burial ground of St Botolph Billingsgate was dedicated and consecrated on land south of Cat Lane, on the south part of the Monument House site. Substantial medieval tenements were established to the north of the lane. The 1553–9 'copperplate map' of the City and documentary information indicate that the area was densely built up in the mid 16th century (Lobel 1989; see Fig 24).

The Great Fire of 1666 is reputed to have started in the King's bakery in Pudding Lane (Milne 1986). The extent of the

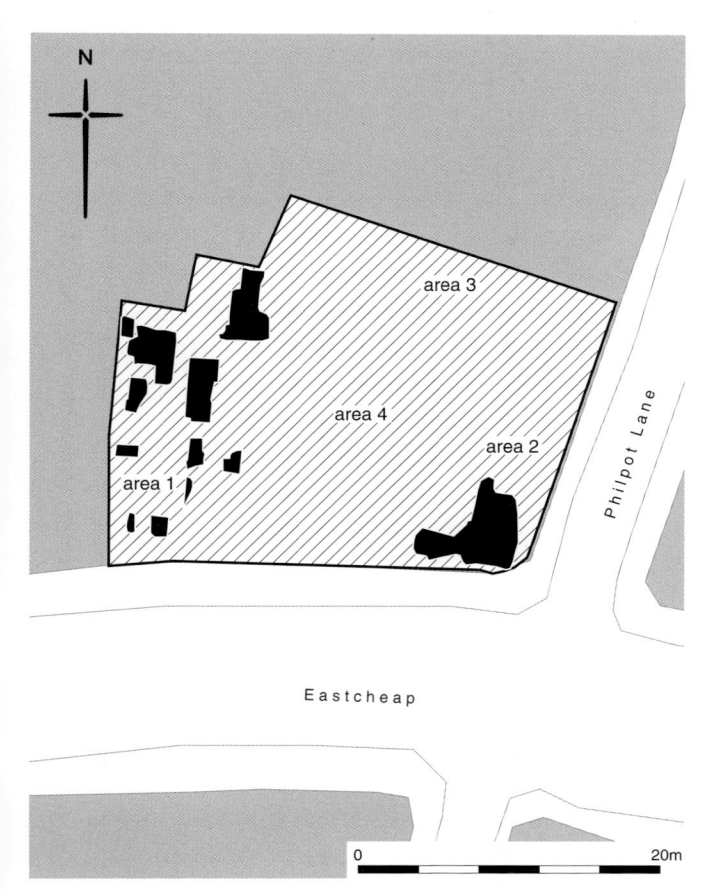

Fig 4 *Areas of archaeological investigation at 13–21 Eastcheap (scale 1:500)*

resulting destruction is shown on the Leake survey of 1667, and archaeological evidence of the Great Fire has been found on many nearby sites. The Ogilby and Morgan map of 1676 is the first to depict London's buildings in plan and shows that the whole area had been redeveloped (see Fig 60). Later maps show that the late 17th-century street plan was retained until recent times (see Fig 63).

1.3 Organisation of this report

Chapter 2 presents the archaeological sequence recorded at Monument House, which was the larger of the two excavations, followed by the sequence from 13–21 Eastcheap in Chapter 3. The archaeological sequences from the two sites form separate chronological narratives, with periods defined through analysis of the stratigraphy in relation to its ceramic dating and documentary evidence where available. Periods are subdivided into phases where appropriate.

The assigned periods are unique to the evidence from each site and cannot be equated. The Monument House chronological narrative (Chapter 2) contains eight periods. Natural topography (period 1) is followed by 1st- and 2nd-century AD evidence for quarrying and timber buildings (period 2). In the 3rd century AD a major redevelopment sees the construction of a drainage culvert and associated stone building, both of which go out of use by the end of the 4th century (period 3). Saxon and medieval evidence (periods 4 and 5) is followed by post-medieval building up to and including the Great Fire (period 6), post-Fire rebuilding (period 7) and 19th-century development (period 8).

The 13–21 Eastcheap sequence (Chapter 3) consists of natural topography (period 1), evidence for terracing and timber buildings up to the Hadrianic fire (period 2), post-Hadrianic rebuilding (period 3), late Roman change and abandonment (period 4), Saxon and medieval evidence (period 5), and post-medieval activity (period 6).

Thematic aspects of the investigations are presented in Chapter 4 and include essays on the most notable finds assemblages. The conclusions summarise the work and discuss how the findings will inform future research aims.

Chapter 5 presents a small selection of specialist appendices unsuitable for integration with the chronological narrative. Other specialist material is integrated, though more extensive research reports form part of the site archive. All of the specialist work took place in accordance with Museum of London and MoLAS standard methodologies, details of which are also available in the archive.

The archives, held under the site codes BPL95 for Monument House and ESC97 for 13–21 Eastcheap, are deposited with the London Archaeological Archive and Research Centre (LAARC) at Mortimer Wheeler House, 46 Eagle Wharf Road, London N1 7ED, and may be consulted by prior arrangement with the Archive Manager.

1.4 Textual and graphical conventions in this report

The basic unit of cross-reference throughout the archive that supports this report is the context, a unique number given to each recognised archaeological event (such as a layer, wall, pit cut, road surface). Context numbers in the text are shown thus: [100] and prefixed by a letter code, A (for Monument House) or B (for 13–21 Eastcheap).

The chronological periods are made up of land-use entities, Buildings (B), Open Areas (OA), Roads (R) and Structures (S), numbered from 1 onwards for each site sequence. Buildings are subdivided into rooms (A, B and so on) where the evidence allows it.

Museum of London accession numbers given to significant artefacts are shown thus: <100>, again with the letter prefix A (for Monument House) or B (for 13–21 Eastcheap).

Each category of illustrated finds has been assigned to a single alpha-numerical sequence across both sites (see below). Roman, medieval and later pottery form, fabric and decoration codes and tile fabric numbers follow standard Museum of London reference collection coding. A list of the codes and their expansions is available from the LAARC as part of the research archive and also posted on the Museum of London website. Illustrated finds are identified by the following letter prefixes:

<P100> pottery;
<S100> accessioned finds including glass;
<T100> tile;
<WP100> wall plaster.

Details of horizontal stratification, wall construction, areas of truncation and variations in ground level have not normally been included on the site plans, which are interpretative. The graphical conventions used on the period plans are shown in Fig 5.

Weights and measures quoted in the text are where appropriate in the units used before metrication. The documentary evidence is reported with the original imperial measurements (yards, and feet and inches, the latter abbreviated to ft and in), along with conversions when appropriate (1ft equals 0.305m; 12in to 1ft, 3ft to 1 yard). Sums of money are quoted in the text as cited in £, s and d, where 12 pence (d) made one shilling (s) and 20 shillings (or 240d) one pound (£), since modern equivalents would be misleading. A sense of the value of money in the 16th and the first half of the 17th century, a period of price inflation, can be gained from http://www.nationalarchives. gov.uk/currency/; for example, in 1550 12d represented a typical day's wages for a craftsman in the building trade. County names in the text refer to historic counties.

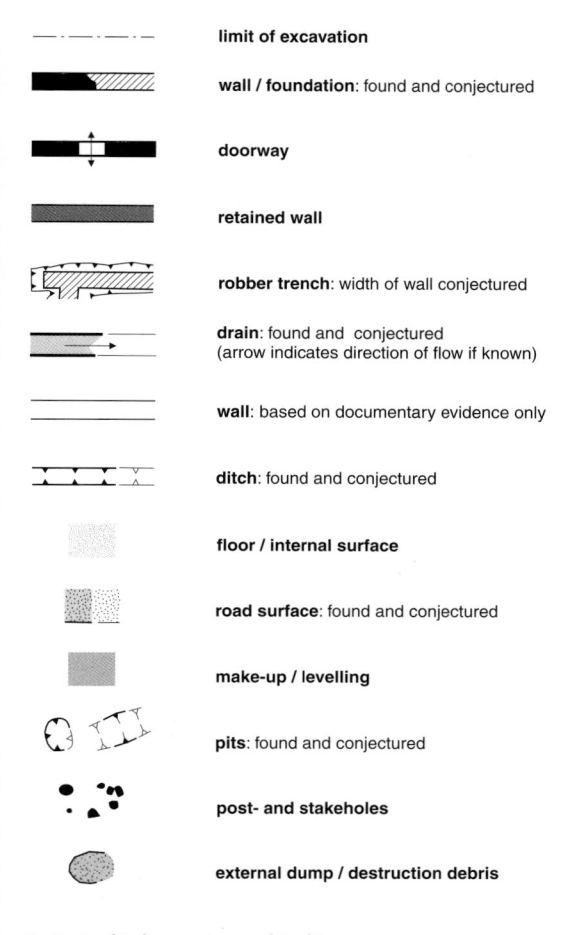

— · — · — · — **limit of excavation**

wall / foundation: found and conjectured

doorway

retained wall

robber trench: width of wall conjectured

drain: found and conjectured
(arrow indicates direction of flow if known)

wall: based on documentary evidence only

ditch: found and conjectured

floor / internal surface

road surface: found and conjectured

make-up / levelling

pits: found and conjectured

post- and stakeholes

external dump / destruction debris

Fig 5 *Graphical conventions used in this report*

2

The archaeological evidence from Monument House

2.1 Geology and prehistory (period 1)

Natural topography of the area

The natural geology in the area of the site is London Clay overlain by the Second Thames Terrace gravels. The gravel terraces were deposited during the Pleistocene era and have been completely eroded by the action of the River Thames between Monument Street and the present-day embankment. The natural slope of the river terrace in the Billingsgate area is still reflected by Botolph Lane, which slopes steeply down from Eastcheap to Monument Street.

Natural deposits (OA1)

Although cellars and pits had truncated the surface of the terrace gravels, enough survived to provide a north–south profile of natural across the site (not illustrated). To the north the gravel surface lay at 9.71m OD, only 0.5m lower than the present street level in Botolph Lane. Midway across the area the gravels were recorded at 8.53m OD, falling to 6.60m OD in the south-east corner of the site. The steep drop to the south may indicate the edge of a natural terrace across the site. The surface of the gravels was lowest in the south-west at 5.94m OD. The surface of London Clay was observed beneath the gravel at c 5m OD.

2.2 The Roman sequence (periods 2 and 3)

Early Roman occupation and quarrying, c AD 50–125 (period 2 phase 1)

Fragmentary building remains (S1), redeposited fire debris and levelling

The earliest extant archaeological deposits were layers of gravel and brickearth dumped to raise the level of the southern gravel terrace. To the north, two small, truncated areas of scorched brickearth between 6.7 and 6.8m OD may represent the remains of a floor slab, Structure 1 (not illustrated).

Pottery from the most extensive dump deposit is dated c AD 60–80 by an early Roman micaceous sandy ware (ERMS) jar with horizontal burnished lines, a bead-rimmed jar with low shoulder (Marsh and Tyers 1978, fig 234, nos IIA9–11) in unsourced sand-tempered ware (SAND), and a Camulodunum 186 (CADIZ) amphora, stamped below the handle in circular stamp with the initials A F R S, <P1> A[709] (Fig 6).

The deposits also contained fragments of roofing tile, brick, daub and tegula mammata, the last possibly from a tiled floor. A number of tiles were badly overfired, suggesting they were derived from a building destroyed in the Boudican fire or were wasters used as hard-core.

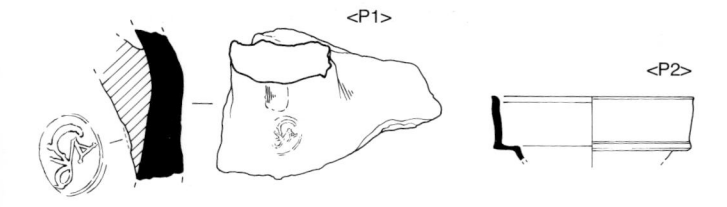

Fig 6 Camulodunum 186 amphora <P1>, stamped below handle with initials A R F S, and fine micaceous reduced ware cup <P2> (scale 1:4)

The mixed levelling make-ups were overlain by an extensive layer of carbonised grain which sloped south-eastwards from 7.29m OD to 6.24m OD and may have been dumped waste from a fire in a nearby warehouse or granary. Spatial sampling of the deposit was undertaken to try to identify storage or processing areas. Full analysis of the cereal remains was not carried out, but assessment showed the samples to contain very large quantities of well-preserved charred grain, along with chaff and weed seeds. The majority of the grain and chaff was provisionally identified as wheat (*Triticum* spp), with the glume wheats spelt (*T spelta*) and emmer (*T dicoccum*) predominating. Smaller quantities of barley (*Hordeum vulgare*) and oat (*Avena* spp) grains were also present in most of these samples. Occasional seeds of wild plants came from common arable weeds including corn cockle (*Agrostemma githago*), corn gromwell (*Lithospermum arvense*), sun spurge (*Euphorbia helioscopia*) and brome grass (*Bromus* sp). Similar deposits of dumped grain have been found nearby at Pudding Lane (Straker 1984) and Regis House (Davis in prep). A detailed study of Roman charred grain deposits, including the associated weed seeds, will include these findings (Giorgi in prep).

Pottery from the same deposit was dated *c* AD 50–140 but could have been burnt in the Boudican fire of AD 60. Only tiny groups of animal bone were present, derived from the major domesticates, chicken (*Gallus gallus*), ox (*Bos taurus*), sheep/goat, including sheep (*Ovis aries*), and pig (*Sus scrofa*). Each species was mainly represented by elements of good meat-bearing quality, particularly the vertebrae and upper limbs.

Quarrying (OA2)

The east side of Structure 1 was truncated by a series of large, intercutting quarry pits dug to extract gravel (not illustrated). Most of the pits contained backfills of dirty gravel and silt which had been tipped from the north. The fills contained large amounts of domestic refuse that was probably from a local source and used to consolidate the pits and level the area.

The pottery is dated pre-AD 70 by the absence of Highgate Wood ware C (HWC) and samian ware such as Dragendorff form 37 bowls and Dragendorff form 33 cups. The assemblage is dated post-AD 60 by the presence of a Highgate Wood ware B (HWB) bowl with curved walls and flat, hooked or folded rim (Marsh and Tyers 1978, fig 241, nos IVF1–6) and a Verulamium region white ware (VRW) pinch-mouthed flagon (ibid, fig 233, no. IC1). The group also contained the rim of a

large flagon/amphora in north French/south-east English oxidised ware (NFSE).

Other finds included three fragments of Roman vessel glass, overfired roofing tiles and small groups of animal bone. The bone was a diverse assemblage of the major domesticates, together with small numbers from fish, including herring family (Clupeidae), carp family (Cyprinidae) and plaice or flounder (Pleuronectidae), plus a small passerine bird and a house mouse (*Mus domesticus*).

External make-ups and a timber structure (S2)

External dumping across the southern half of the site further consolidated the Open Area 2 pits to form a level terrace platform on which to build. Fragmentary evidence for the earliest timber structures included two east–west beam slots, a possible hearth consisting of charcoal debris, and patchy floor surfaces of sandy gravel and brickearth. The bases of the slots were at 7.99m OD and 7.15m OD which, if they were part of a single structure, indicates a stepped profile down to the south, reflecting the underlying slope.

The pottery from the make-ups is dated post-AD 70 by the presence of a necked jar and a beaker with barbotine dot decoration in Highgate Wood ware C (HWC), and a Knorr form 78 cup in la Graufesenque samian (SAMLG). This group contained an early cup <P2> in fine micaceous reduced ware (FMIC) whose form is most similar to Camulodunum form 57, although it also has affinities with Camulodunum forms 58, 59 and 60 (Hawkes and Hull 1947, pl LIII) (Fig 6). The deposits also contained roofing tiles, bricks and fragments of daub, some burnt, which may be redeposited remains of pre-Boudican buildings.

Activity after *c* AD 125 (period 2 phase 2)

Clay and timber building (B1)

Building 1 was severely truncated and only survived in a small area on the eastern part of the site (Fig 7). The earliest deposit consisted of a burnt mixed brickearth construction make-up between 8.15m and 8.35m OD. A complete necked jar in Verulamium region coarse white-slipped ware (VCWS) <P3> had been placed on surface A[515], with a London oxidised ware (LOXI) lid <P4> inverted on its rim (Fig 8; Fig 9). The LOXI lid is dated to *c* AD 90.

The fill of the pot contained few diagnostic finds and appears to have been almost entirely composed of fragmented mortar. Carbonised material included 14 wheat grains, a few glume bases and charcoal fragments. The pot, located beneath the floor of Building 1, may be a deliberate foundation deposit. A mixed make-up had been spread around and over the vessel, followed by an apparently random scatter of stakeholes. A burnt mortar surface and associated occupation were probably part of a floor in a separate room to the south and contained pottery dated to *c* AD 120–60. Immediately to the west a north–south-aligned group of stakeholes could represent the

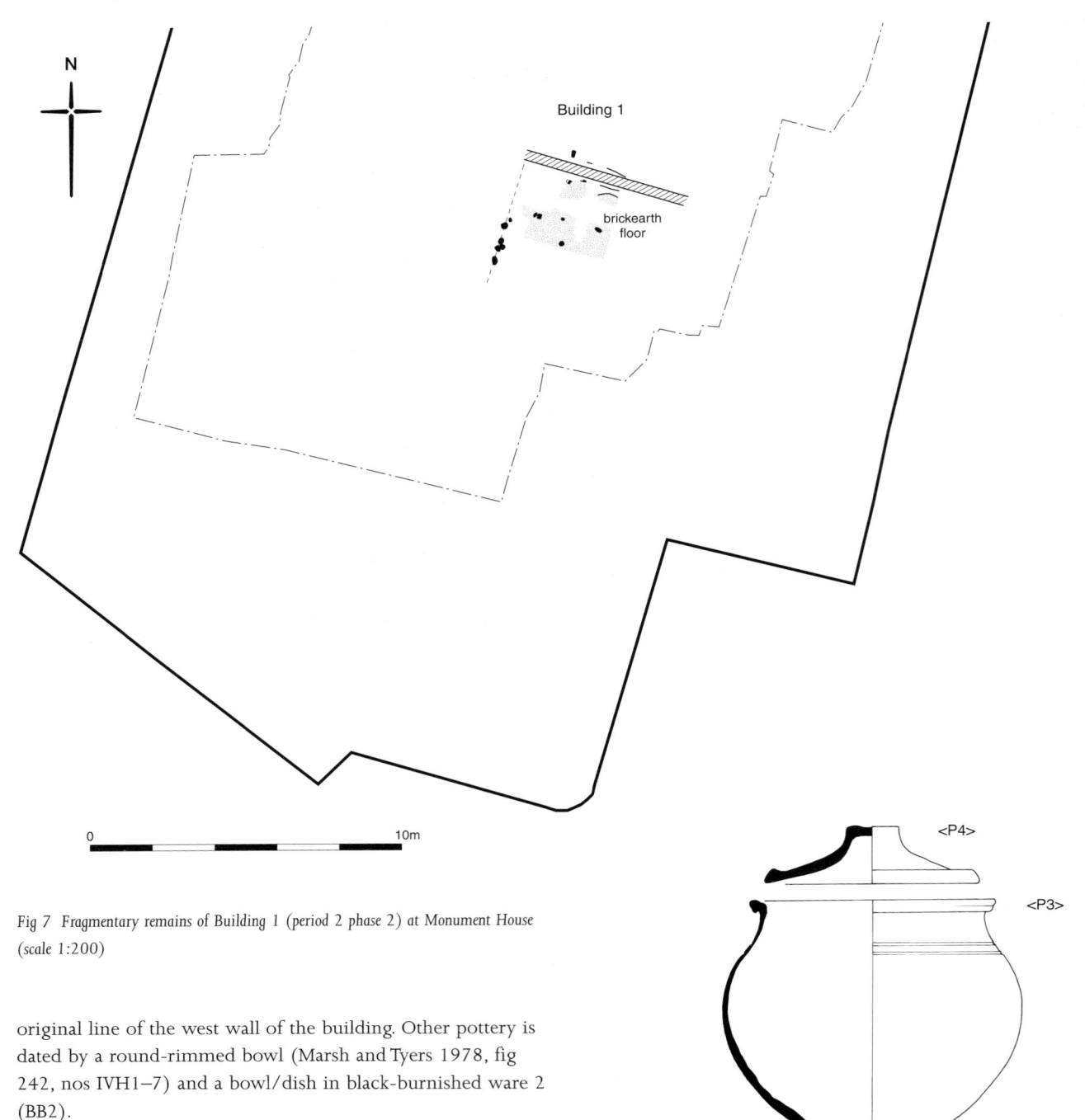

Fig 7 *Fragmentary remains of Building 1 (period 2 phase 2) at Monument House (scale 1:200)*

Fig 8 *Necked jar <P3> in Verulamium region coarse white-slipped ware and London oxidised ware lid <P4> (scale 1:4)*

original line of the west wall of the building. Other pottery is dated by a round-rimmed bowl (Marsh and Tyers 1978, fig 242, nos IVH1–7) and a bowl/dish in black-burnished ware 2 (BB2).

Modification of Building 1

A brickearth and gravel make-up was laid in the north end of Building 1 and cut by an east–west-aligned beam slot. The slot would originally have held a timber base plate, probably beneath an internal partition wall built to subdivide a larger room (not illustrated). The make-up deposit contained pottery dated to c AD 140–60. The pottery is dated by a Verulamium region coarse white-slipped ware (VCWS) ring-necked flagon with cupped mouth (Marsh and Tyers 1978, fig 232, nos IB7–9), accompanied by a central Gaulish samian (SAMCG) Dragendorff form 27 cup, and a jar and a bowl, both with acute lattice decoration in black-burnished ware 2 (BB2). The only accessioned find was a complete, plain copper-alloy ring A<292>, presumably part of a fitting or handle.

Infrastructure and building of the 3rd century AD (period 3 phase 1)

Terraced masonry building (B2) and culvert (S3)

INTRODUCTION
During the 3rd century AD a major redevelopment took place, with Building 1 replaced by the large masonry structure Building 2, whose walls were terraced into the hillside on two levels (Fig 10). The new building included an integral Roman

Fig 9 Excavating the complete pot <P3> and inverted lid <P4>, a foundation deposit associated with Building 1 at Monument House

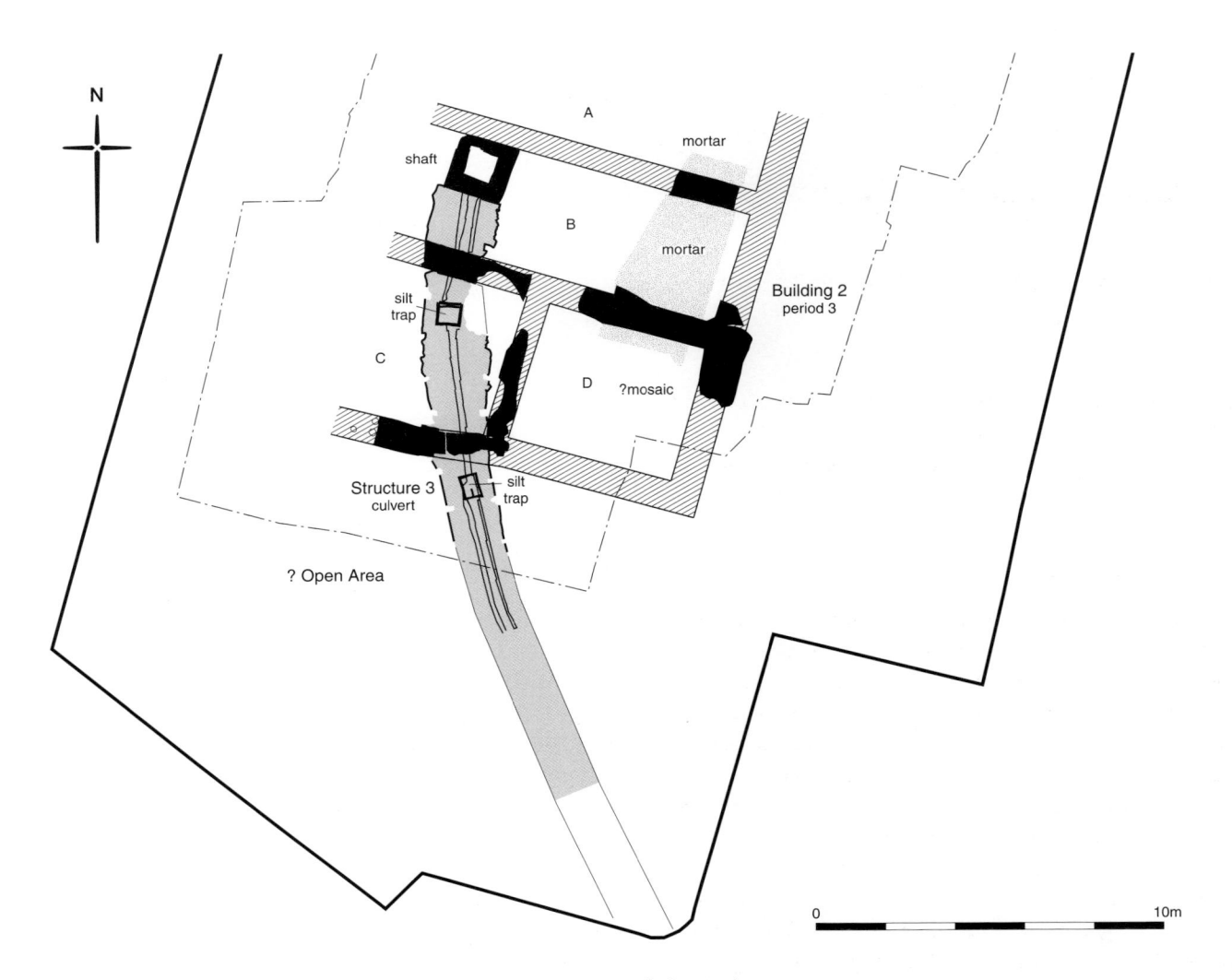

Fig 10 Terraced building (B2) and culvert (S3) (period 3 phase 1) at Monument House (scale 1:200)

drainage culvert (S3) which ran southwards beneath it. The culvert was recorded over a distance of 20m and incorporated a square access shaft at its upper (northern) end.

Although the access shaft was aligned with the walls of Building 2, the culvert had a pronounced curve towards the south-east (Fig 11). It is likely that the curvature of the structure was intended to allow water to be discharged into a channel or inlet into the Thames downstream of the site. The curve may also have slowed water flow, making it less damaging to the internal fabric of the culvert (discussion in Chapter 4.1).

METHOD OF CONSTRUCTION OF THE DRAINAGE CULVERT AND ACCESS SHAFT

The access shaft and culvert were trench-built, with some of the excavated spoil packed behind the lining and over the roof of the culvert, which would have helped to protect the structure from frost damage. Regularly spaced pairs of post voids along the external edges of the culvert indicate that two lines of substantial timber posts were set in place prior to the walls of the culvert being built around them. The posts, which provided shoring to support the sides of the construction cut and served as form-work during the construction of the culvert, were set at c 1m centres and would have originally been braced by horizontal timbers. The decayed remains of one of these beams

were found in a regular linear slot across the roof of the southern end of the culvert. The uniformity of the slot indicates that the beam was in place prior to the mortar surface of the roof being poured and levelled against it.

THE ACCESS SHAFT

The square access shaft at the northern end of the culvert was the highest surviving Roman masonry found on site, truncated at 7.66m OD. The primary floor level within Building 2 indicates that the shaft was constructed from c 8.50m OD. The shaft measured 0.90m square internally and was 3.36m deep, although its conjectured original depth is c 4.20m.

The mid section of the access shaft was built entirely of tile with a neatly corbelled entrance into the adjoining culvert (Fig 12). The tiles were mostly tegulae, with the flanges laid to give the outward appearance of thicker bonding bricks, bonded with a hard *opus signinum*-type mortar to provide water resistance. The use of roof tiles instead of bonding bricks may simply reflect the material available at the time, but the 'hydraulic' cement used in the access shaft and the culvert to the south was essential to prevent the lining being eroded where the vertical inflow of water met the outflow into the culvert. In contrast to the tile build of the central part of the shaft, the upper and lower sections of the lining were

Fig 11 Aerial view of culvert (S3) at Monument House, looking south

Fig 12 *The culvert (S3) access shaft fully excavated to reveal the large silt trap at its base, looking south*

Fig 13 *Two sections of culvert (S3) butted against a cross-wall, looking east (0.5m scale)*

constructed of courses of Kentish ragstone bonded with softer lime mortar, with tile present only as horizontal string courses in the upper part.

The lower section of the shaft below the opening into the culvert contained a wooden silt trap, designed to catch the majority of the heavier water-borne silt before it entered the culvert (Fig 12). The silt trap was made of two tiers of well-preserved oak planks. The lining was 0.68m deep, with the larger basal planks being 0.38m deep and the base of the silt trap at c 4.30m OD. Although the jointing at the corners of the silt trap was not seen, it was probably half-lapped. The shaft was an essential maintenance feature, allowing access to the silt trap at its base and to the north end of the adjoining culvert. The main function of the shaft, however, was to allow a large volume of waste water from a source close to the contemporary ground surface to the north to be channelled beneath Building 2.

THE SUBTERRANEAN CULVERT

To the south of the access shaft, two sections of culvert were built, separated by an east–west foundation for the central wall of Building 2 (Fig 13). Narrow butt joints between the builds may have been deliberately left open to allow any water trapped behind the lining to percolate into the culvert. The internal dimensions of the culvert varied from 1.83m high x 0.65m

wide at its north end (Fig 14) to a more restricted 1.30m x 0.65m where the roof of the culvert stepped down, approximately 9m to the south (Fig 15).

The roof of the culvert was constructed over a curved timber former, with tiles fanned out on edge to form the vault to the structure. Impressions of longitudinal planks were visible throughout the structure. Several nails were found projecting from the roof vault in the north section of the culvert. These indicate that the carpenters had left the nail heads standing proud of the planks when they had constructed the roof vault, and the mortar had dried around them, holding them in place. No similar nails were seen in the southern section of the culvert, and it is conceivable that the planks in the short northern section of the culvert may have been left in place and eventually rotted. A series of evenly spaced opposing pairs of holes for small (40mm x 40mm) horizontal timber batons were found at the foot of the roof vault throughout the culvert. These batons formed part of the base frame of the temporary form-work, and their ends were broken off and left in situ when the form-work was dismantled.

The base of the culvert was formed by a narrow offset tile drain, which had a partial plank base and passed beneath the central wall of Building 2. The depth of the cross-wall effectively closed off the top end of the culvert and its access

Fig 14 *Interior of culvert (S3), looking south from the access shaft; plank impressions of the vault former are just visible*

Fig 15 *View looking south along culvert (S3), with the lower vault level visible in the background*

shaft from the remainder of the structure, and meant that the southern part of the culvert could only have been serviced by entering it from an access point to the south. The drain channel was surprisingly narrow, being on average only 200mm wide and 400mm deep (Fig 15; Fig 16). It incorporated two small box silt traps made of oak planks in the southern section of the culvert (Fig 17; Fig 18).

The internal silt traps were shallow wooden boxes located at points where the course of the culvert changed and silt would have been likely to collect. The planks of the northern silt trap retained their sapwood but no bark edge, preventing a precise dendrochronological date being assigned to the felling of the timber, but suggesting that it dates to the later 2nd or early 3rd century, with an estimated felling date range of AD 176–221. There was no evidence of a plank base to the central drain beyond the southern silt trap. The base of the drain lay between 5.15m OD in the north and 4.96m OD in the south, a fall of 190mm over a distance of 13m, or a gradient of approximately 1:68.

The construction backfill over the culvert contained an assemblage of pottery dated to *c* AD 250–300 by the presence of jars, a round-rimmed bowl (Marsh and Tyers 1978, fig 242, nos IVH1–7) and a flanged bowl in Alice Holt/Farnham ware (AHFA). Also present were a Moselkeramik (MOSL) beaker with rouletted decoration, two Camulodunum form 306 bowls in unsourced sand-tempered ware (SAND) and an unusual

Fig 16 *Culvert (S3), looking south from the central silt trap*

Fig 17 Central silt trap in culvert (S3) (0.2m scale)

Fig 18 Southern silt trap in culvert (S3) (0.2m scale)

mortarium rim form in an unsourced oxidised ware (OXID) from A[416]. The same fill contained an enamelled belt plate <S1> (Fig 19), an enamelled copper-alloy disc brooch <S2> (Fig 19), a plain copper-alloy finger ring A<294> and a composite mount A<295>, possibly used on a box or furniture. The vessel glass included fragments of a cup and a bowl in colourless glass, <S3> and <S4> (Fig 19). The cup is an Isings type 85, an 'Airlie' type with a fire-rounded, slightly in-turned rim, dating to the late 2nd to mid 3rd century AD (Price and Cottam 1998, 99–100).

Belt plate <S1> is decorated with an enamel design of heart-shaped ivy leaves, now corroded, on a blue enamelled background. The form of the leaves is reminiscent of those found on seal boxes of the 2nd to 3rd century AD (Cool and Philo 1998, 100, fig 37, no. 493; Crummy 1983, 103, fig 106, nos 2523 and 2525) and also on mosaics (for example, Neal 1981, figs 63 and 73; Toynbee 1962, figs 209 and 214). Enamelled belt plates are known from a number of military sites, mainly in the north and south-west of Britain (Bateson 1981, 55). This type of belt plate probably dates to the 2nd

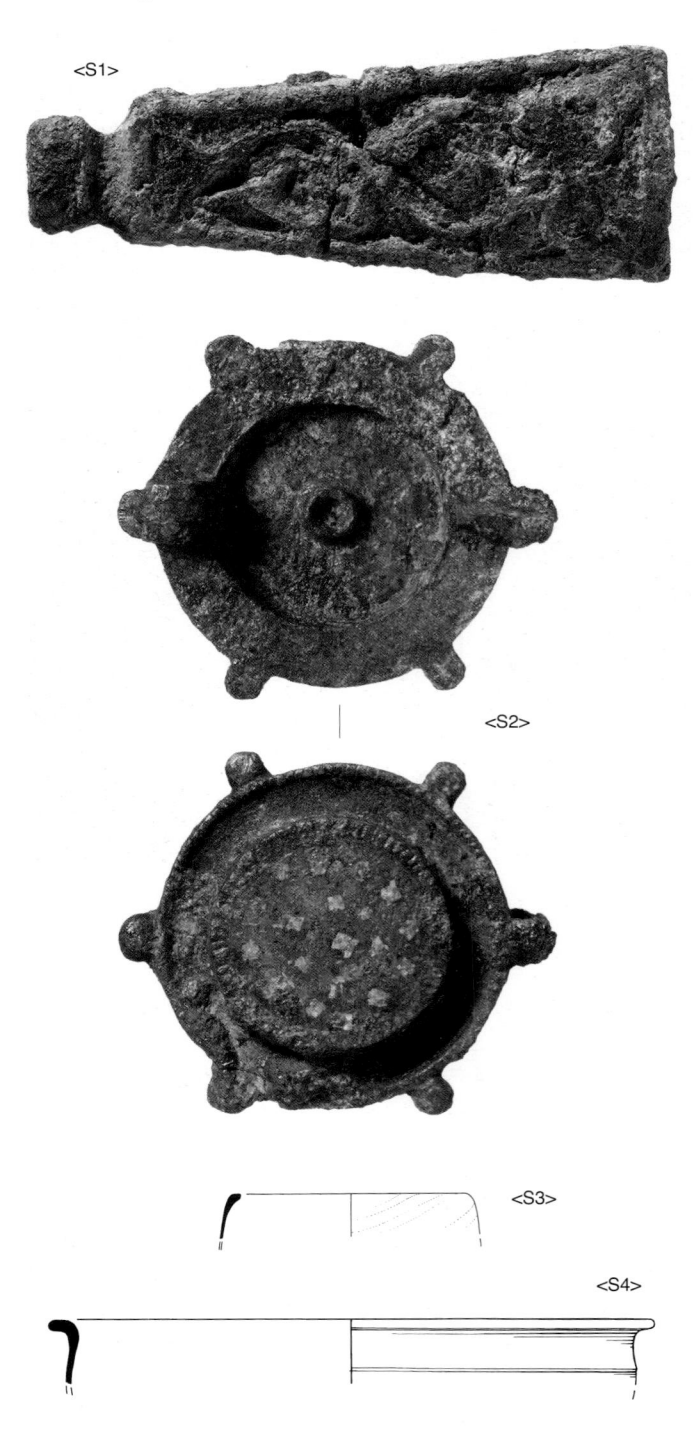

<S1>

<S2>

<S3>

<S4>

Fig 19 Finds associated with culvert (S3) construction backfills: enamelled belt plate <S1> and enamelled disc brooch <S2>, obverse and reverse (scale 2:1); rim fragment from an 'Airlie' cup <S3> and a colourless glass bowl <S4> (scale 1:2)

century AD. Brooch <S2> is also of 2nd-century date and is an unusual form, paralleled by an example found nearby at Billingsgate (Hattatt 1985, 148, no. 543). The raised central circular area is decorated with a *millefiori* chequer-board comprising small white squares or quatrefoils on a ?red ground.

USAGE OF THE CULVERT

The silt traps in the base of the access shaft and the culvert

indicate that both structures were designed to be serviced and maintained. Consequently the water-deposited fills in the silt traps and the tile drain at the base of the culvert probably represent deposits that had accumulated prior to final abandonment (Chapter 4.1, Sedimentation in the Roman culvert).

The pottery from the final usage fills is dated to after AD 270, based on the presence of Oxfordshire red/brown colour-coated ware (OXRC) bowls/dishes with rouletted decoration and a Young form WC5 mortarium in Oxfordshire white-slipped red ware (OXWS), as well as various forms in Alice Holt/Farnham ware (AHFA), a sherd of Moselkeramik (MOSL) and a Camulodunum form 306 bowl in unsourced sand-tempered ware (SAND). The fills also produced a near-complete bone pin with a flattened head A<301> and fragments from a Hofheim cup, part of which was also found in Structure 2. A large quantity of building material was made up principally of roofing tile and brick, with lesser quantities of ceramic tesserae, combed box flue, daub and fragments of painted wall plaster.

Charred cereal grains were recovered from two environmental samples from the culvert drain. Most of these grains were glume wheats, spelt (*Triticum spelta* L) grains and emmer (*Triticum dicoccum* L). Breadwheat (*Triticum aestivum* L), barley (*Hordeum sativum* L) and oat (*Avena* sp) were also observed, as was a small amount of wheat chaff. Occasional waterlogged seeds of damp ground plants were observed, including seeds of celery-leaved crowfoot (*Ranunculus sceleratus* L) and lesser spearwort (*Ranunculus flammula* L) and sedge (*Carex* spp). Waste ground plants were also observed as seeds of flax (*Linum usitatissimum* L), stinging nettle (*Urtica dioica* L), elder (*Sambucus nigra* L), knotgrass (*Polygonum aviculare* L) and henbane (*Hyoscyamus niger* L).

THE TERRACED BUILDING (B2)

Building 2 floor surfaces only survived in a narrow area on the east half of the site. Defined within this area were the truncated mortar floor surfaces and parallel robber cuts for two of the east–west walls. Parts of three east–west and two north–south robber cuts were recorded and suggest that the average width of the robbed walls was c 0.65–0.75m (Fig 10; Fig 20).

The only Building 2 masonry to survive was the deeply founded central wall where it crossed through the body of the culvert, and a section of the parallel south wall where it bridged the culvert above the step in the culvert roof. The exposed faces of the northern cross-wall, viewed from within the culvert, were fair-faced with the upper section composed of courses of split flint nodules and the lower coursing composed of Kentish ragstone. The continuation of this wall outside the culvert to the east was founded at a higher level and all of its masonry had been robbed, as was the case with all the other walls of the building in the excavated area.

In contrast to the central wall, the south wall was carried across the culvert on piers, with the span across the roof filled with tile (Fig 21). Robbing indicated that the wall had originally continued west on a stepped foundation. Timber piles in the base of the robbing cut had completely decayed,

Fig 20 Robber cut for the central wall of Building 2 at Monument House, centre foreground, with mortar floors of the building to the right, looking west

but post voids further west were clearly part of the same structure.

The difference in construction of the Building 2 cross-walls is intriguing, given that it would have been simpler for both to utilise a foundation arch to carry the load of the wall over the culvert. The foundation of the central wall must have been extended through the body of the culvert for other reasons. The wall may have been intended to slow the flow of water before it entered the southern section of culvert, and in doing so lessen the damaging scouring effect that fast-flowing water would have on the internal fabric of the structure. The wall would also have prevented anyone entering the culvert from the south from walking 'upstream' and gaining access to the shaft and the overlying building, although it seems unlikely that security was the major reason for the design.

At least four 'bays' or rooms can be conjectured in Building 2 and formed the south-eastern part of the building (Fig 10). The two northern room areas or 'bays' A and B were aligned east–west. The culvert access shaft lay within room area B, which was 3.4m wide, though it is possible that this was an internal courtyard. Two smaller rooms C and D were partially

Fig 21 The western tile pier for the south wall of Building 2 at Monument House, with robbing of the piled foundation visible in the foreground, looking east (0.2m scale)

defined in the south. The extent of the building to the west and north is unknown. Insufficient remains survived to determine whether 'bays' A and B had been divided into smaller rooms. It is tempting to suggest that the access shaft occupied a central position at the heart of the building, though this is unproven.

The robber cut for the northernmost extant wall of Building 2 shows that the footing was originally constructed in a shallow cut dug into the natural gravel at a level of c 8.48m OD. The parallel central wall, which crossed the culvert, was on average more than 1m deeper and was cut into the terrace make-ups at 7.27–7.42m OD. This wall served both as a load-bearing foundation and as a terrace retaining wall.

There was a difference of c 200mm between the floor surfaces in the northern and central rooms. In the central room the primary mortar surface was at c 8.41–8.55m OD and was sealed by a second worn mortar floor at c 8.60–8.70m OD. Bedding deposit A[214] for the secondary floor contained the remains of a child who had died around the time of birth, perhaps a deliberately laid foundation deposit. Truncation of the child burial prevented the application of all the ageing criteria, but the remains of a neonate or possibly stillborn child buried beneath a sealed mortar floor adds to the corpus of means of treatment of perinatal death in Roman Britain, though not necessarily 'foundation deposits' (Gowland and Chamberlain 2002; Scott 1999).

The floors and their make-ups contained a small assemblage of pottery dated to after AD 250 by the presence of a later everted-rimmed jar in black-burnished ware 1 (BB1) with obtuse lattice decoration, a jar, a bowl/dish and a plain-rimmed dish in Alice Holt/Farnham ware (AHFA), a Moselkeramik (MOSL) beaker with rouletted decoration, and a Camulodunum form 306 bowl in unsourced sand-tempered ware (SAND). The animal bone assemblage was very small and consisted of fragments of ox and sheep/goat rib, upper and lower limb, representing deposition of post-consumption refuse.

The make-up deposits for the secondary mortar floor contained a number of fragments of wall plaster, possibly derived from various rooms in the first phase of Building 2. Four different wall plaster groups were identified and details can be found in the research archive. Several ceramic tesserae were also present together with ceramic roofing tile and fragments of phylite.

SECONDARY STRUCTURAL ACTIVITY IN BUILDING 2

The mortar floors in the central and northern bays of Building 2 were sealed beneath layers of mixed sandy silt whose surface lay at c 8.90m OD to the north and c 8.7m OD to the south. Fragmented building material in these deposits suggests that they represent internal levelling make-ups associated with structural modifications or robbing. Two copper-alloy coins were recovered: A<286> dating to c AD 270–93 and A<307> dating to c AD 250–320.

A north–south slot c 4.50m long, 0.60m wide and 0.50m deep cut through these dumps, with its base sloping from 8.28m OD in the north to 7.97m OD in the south. The cut was butt-ended at its south end, which respected the north edge of the robber cut for the central wall of the building. The depth and irregularity of the cut would be unusual for a beam slot and it may be a robbed rubble footing. If the slot represents a structural division, it would have effectively created a corridor along the east side of the building and across the line of the north wall, which must have been at least partially dismantled. There were no associated floor surfaces.

The fills of the slot contained pottery dated to post-AD 350 and three 3rd-century copper-alloy coins, A<330>, A<331> and A<332>. The dating for the pottery is derived from a single sherd of a hook-rimmed jar of Portchester D ware (PORD). Other pieces of pottery likely to be contemporary with the hook-rimmed jar are an unusual sherd of Nene Valley colour-coated ware (NVCC) with ring and dot stamped decoration and rouletting <P5> from A[200] (Fig 22), a sherd of Much Hadham oxidised ware (MHAD), a storage jar in Alice Holt/Farnham ware (AHFA), a later everted-rimmed jar in black-burnished ware 1 (BB1) with obtuse lattice decoration, and an unsourced imported colour-coated ware (CC) beaker with white painted decoration. Wall plaster recovered from the make-up deposits and the fill of the beam slot was derived from three separate designs.

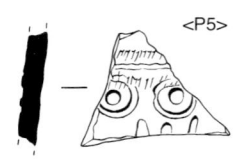

Fig 22 *Unusual sherd of Nene Valley colour-coated ware <P5> with ring and dot stamped decoration and rouletting (scale 1:2)*

Late Roman abandonment (period 3 phase 2)

Disuse and abandonment of culvert Structure 3

The culvert and access shaft had fallen out of use by the mid to late 4th century. The presence of medieval pottery in the fill of the shaft indicates that it was probably only significantly infilled when parts of the culvert capping were accidentally or intentionally breached long after the Roman period.

The pottery assemblage from the disuse fills of the culvert is mainly late Roman in date and includes Camulodunum form 306 bowls which may have been deliberately broken and thrown away as part of a ritual act (discussion in Chapter 4.1). The fills also contained two 3rd- to 4th-century AD copper-alloy coins A<288> and A<335>, and a variety of other finds which included Roman tile, tesserae and painted wall plaster.

The culvert produced one of the larger animal bone assemblages from the site, with material associated with its use and disuse, some of which was probably introduced after the Roman period. The assemblage as a whole was dominated by ox, with only comparatively minor contributions of chicken, sheep/goat and pig, and a single goose (*Anser* sp). The major domesticate waste derived mainly from carcase areas of good meat-bearing quality, with only minor components of head and foot elements, suggesting primary butchery in the immediate area. Most of the material derived from adult animals. Cat and dog were represented by several bones, some probably from the same animal.

There was considerable evidence of local fauna with recovery of frog/toad, probably common toad (*Bufo bufo*) and common frog (*Rana temporaria*), small passerine birds, rat (*Rattus* sp) and common shrew (*Sorex araneus*). There was also minor but definite evidence for the consumption of wild 'game' species, including bittern (*Botaurus stellaris*) and some fish. Occasional waterlogged seeds of blackberry (*Rubus fruticosus* sens lat) and elder (*Sambucus nigra* L) were observed.

Disuse and abandonment of Building 2 (OA3)

Building 2 appears to have fallen into disrepair at the same time as the culvert, and part of the building was robbed. Truncated accumulations of 'dark earth' sealed demolition debris in parts of the building. Some of the robber cuts were seen to cut through these layers, indicating that the walls were still extant when the 'dark earth' accumulated.

Finds within the 'dark earth' were mostly residual, but included a small copper-alloy spoon <S5> from a cosmetic set (Fig 23). Only a few fragments of ox horncore, tooth, lower limb and foot, with fragments of ox-sized rib and longbone, were found, suggesting disposal of primary processing as well as post-consumption waste.

Tegulae found in Open Area 3 may have been derived from the abandoned building. Evidence for the internal decoration of the walls comes from the 118 fragments of wall plaster recovered from context A[574]. These are predominantly red and black on a white background, but were very fragmentary, and not enough survives to reconstruct the overall decorative layout. The plaster has a cream backing layer around 30–38mm thick, with a 1mm thick white intonaco. In the base of many fragments are clear impressions of interwoven wooden laths, indicating that they came from internal wall partitions of timber construction.

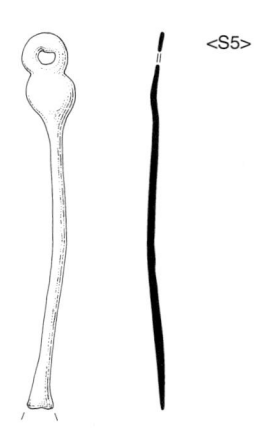

<S5>

Fig 23 *Copper-alloy spoon <S5> from a cosmetic set (scale 1:1)*

Late Roman occupation south of Building 2 (S4)

To the south of Building 2 truncated patches of brickearth surfaces and burnt occupation debris were cut by a cluster of stakeholes and an east–west line of more substantial stakes. The majority of these features may have been contemporary with Building 2 or some other late Roman occupation or external activity. Most of the finds recovered from the deposits were residual. The stakehole fills produced a fragment of a ceramic crucible A<375>, a copper-alloy coin of Theodosian A<281>, dating to AD 378–402, and a 3rd- to 4th-century decorated bone handle A<476> paralleled by one from Colchester (Essex) (Crummy 1983, 109, fig 110, no. 2930).

2.3   The early medieval and medieval sequence up to *c* 1500 (periods 4 and 5)

Documentary evidence

Tony Dyson

The Saxon period (*c* AD 400–1066)

Botolph Lane is one of a series of lanes, including Love (or Lovat) Lane, St Mary at Hill and perhaps St Dunstan's Hill, that extend north from the Thames frontage immediately downstream of London Bridge to Eastcheap, and continue from there to Fenchurch Street as Philpot, Rood and Mincing Lanes. In this they constitute a recognisable street grid comparable with the one centred on Bread Street and Bow Lane/Garlick Hill that extends from Queenhithe northwards to Cheapside in the western half of the City. Queenhithe and the streets accompanying it were established soon after King Alfred's reoccupation of London in 886 (Dyson 1990, 102–7), though the repopulation of the city at large did not occur until the second half of the following century. It was in the wake of this second and more general phase of settlement that the development of the waterfront in the eastern half of the city between the bridge and Billingsgate occurred at the end of the 10th century, creating a local street plan on the existing Queenhithe model (Dyson 1992, 123–4). The site lay not far north of Thames Street, itself most probably established during the 11th century to link together the separate centres of early commercial development on the Thames frontage at Queenhithe, Dowgate and Billingsgate (ibid, 130–1).

The medieval period (1066–1500)

With the increasing volume of trade in the Billingsgate area, especially from the late 13th century, these properties must have been particularly and increasingly sought after, fishmongers and (nearer Billingsgate) a number of ropemakers being conspicuous initially. There is little general evidence of size, the only available measurement of a Botolph Lane frontage relating to Tenement 3 (later St Botolph's churchyard), which in 1305 measured 33ft (10.06m) from north to south (CLRO, HR 33/71). This is broadly consistent with the average city tenement frontage of some 20 to 30ft (6.09–9.14m). Tenements 1 and 2, which by the mid 15th century were combined as a single property referred to as a 'great tenement', could therefore have measured at least 60ft (18.29m) along the lane. In 1305 Tenement 3 extended back from the lane for 84ft 9in (25.88m). Though the total distance between Botolph and Love Lanes was not great, room could still be found in some cases for a garden at the rear. This was so at Tenement 1, with the arbour (*herber*) that backed on to the tenement to the north and was part of a property fronting on to Love Lane (CLRO, HR 87/122), while the 'garden sometime of Richard Gosselyn' east of the churchyard of St Botolph Billingsgate (Tenement 3) must similarly have formed part of premises fronting on to Love Lane.

Some of these properties extended the whole way between Botolph and Love Lanes, as did Tenement 1 by 1349 (and the combined Tenements 1 and 2 by 1473), and another tenement three doors up from Tenement 1 by 1329 (CLRO, HR 57/33). Such an arrangement may help to explain the fleeting existence of Cat Lane, which ran along the line of the parish boundary between St George Eastcheap and St Botolph Billingsgate, which was also the property boundary between Tenements 2 and 3. Cat Lane was clearly located during the excavations, running immediately north of the St Botolph churchyard and (in documentary terms at least) within Tenement 2. First recorded in 1273–4 as the 'lane which is called Cat Lane' (*venella que vocatur Catelane*) (CLRO, HR 6/6; GL, MS 25121/box 10 no. 989), it recurs in relation to properties on its south side in both St George's and St Mary's parishes in June 1300 as *Catteslane* (CLRO, HR 29/59), in July 1305 as *Catenelane* (CLRO, HR 33/71), and in January 1310 as *Cattenelane* (CLRO, HR 38/47). A final mention comes in a deed of January 1313 specifying the 'tenement of Gilbert Cros once called *Kattelane*' as its northern abutments (CLRO, HR 41/48); this is an odd formulation but one strongly suggesting that the lane was by now defunct. It cannot have served much general public use, in contrast with Botolph Alley between Botolph and Love Lanes further north, and its eastern and western extensions Church Lane (between Love Lane and St Mary at Hill) and St George's Lane (between Botolph and Pudding Lanes). Almost certainly Cat Lane originated as a private alley, established within the boundaries of two tenements backing on to each other and in common ownership, a conclusion supported by the fact that the earliest deed to mention it reveals that Geoffrey Batecok held shops on both sides (CLRO, HR 6/6).

Up to the turn of the 14th and 15th centuries the predominant trade of the occupants of these tenements – on the infrequent occasions when it was specified at all – was fishmongering, with the exceptions of a linen draper (Tenement 3 before 1305), a vintner (Tenement 3 in 1313), a baker (Tenement 1 in 1349) and another vintner (Tenement 2

by 1392). Thereafter, however, other and more diverse trades took over, including a skinner (1406) and a grocer and an ironmonger (1413) at Tenement 1. In the 16th and 17th centuries drapers and merchants (Lombards up to the 1530s) were in the ascendant, at the expense of the fishmongers: John Bedham, who bequeathed Tenements 1 and 2 to St Mary at Hill in 1473, appears to have been one of the last fishmongers to survive. Just such a pattern is reflected, in far greater detail, in the changing occupations of property holders on the waterfront tenements along this sector of the river downstream of the bridge, where from the later 14th century the ubiquitous fishmongers came increasingly to be supplanted by merchants and entrepreneurs whose businesses depended on large-scale overseas trading (Schofield and Dyson in prep).

By the Reformation most of this property had come into the hands of the Church, in one or other of its manifestations. Tenements 1 and 2 came to the church of St Mary at Hill in 1473 for the provision of a chantry; the property north of Tenement 1 similarly went to the parish church of St George Eastcheap in 1375, supplementing some initial provision made in 1349, while the one north of that was bequeathed to the New Hospital of St Mary without Bishopsgate in 1432 (CLRO, HR 162/20; Sharpe 1890, 467).

A rare and valuable feature of the combined Tenement 1/2 is the survival of two detailed, room-by-room surveys, one dating from shortly before 1473 and the other from 1646. The two surveys have little in common and plainly describe quite different room plans and arrangements, following the extensive rebuilding of the 1510s and 1520s.

The present site corresponded with two early tenements (Tenements 1 and 2), amalgamated at some date between 1415 and 1448, and the north-western portion of a third (Tenement 3), which in 1393 became the cemetery of the church of St Botolph Billingsgate. Tenements 1 and 2 lay in the parish of St George Eastcheap, Tenement 3 in the parish of St Botolph. To the east of all three was a line of properties fronting on to Love Lane and lying within the parish of St Mary at Hill. Deeds previously collected for St Mary's parish, which extended past St George's as far north as St Andrew Hubbard parish, were used to throw additional light on their western neighbours, whose correct sequence (like their own) was not easy to establish.

TENEMENT 1 IN THE 14TH AND FIRST HALF OF THE 15TH CENTURY
A deed of January 1336, concerning a piece of ground called the arbour (*le herbier*) to the east of Tenement 1 in the parish of St Mary at Hill, names John Youn as neighbour to the west (CLRO HR 63/209). In his will dated 11 April 1349 and proved in May, Youn left to Richard Youn and Margery a mansion in the parish of St George for life and thereafter to their son John (CLRO, HR 76/155; Sharpe 1889, 540). On 8 October 1349 Robert White, executor of the elder John Youn's widow Joan, sold to John Halys, baker of Southwark, a tenement with shops, solars and rents between *Seint Botulpheslane* to the west and *Ropereslane* (Lovat Lane) to the east, and extending from the tenement formerly of John Crosse to the

north as far as the tenement formerly of Paulinus Turk (Tenement 2) to the south (CLRO, HR 78/173). White, a fishmonger, soon married Joan, and on 27 April 1350 they granted to Edmund de Lenham, fishmonger, and his wife Avice the tenement described as in the previous year but including a garden at the rear (CLRO, HR 82/62). In his will of 10 September 1361, proved in October, Edmund left to his present wife Joan all his property in the city charged with the maintenance of a chantry in the parish church of St George (CLRO, HR 89/202; Sharpe 1890, 54–5).

Following his mother's death, Edmund Lenham junior evidently sold the property, for on 7 May 1381 it was granted by John fitz Nichol to his brother Richard, who on 19 March 1382 granted it in turn to John Doget, vintner, and John Weston, and, on 8 February 1406, to John Bungeye and Hugh Lancastre. On 12 March 1406 Bungeye, describing himself as late rector of the church of Westgrenestede (?Sussex) and now of Hokewolde, Norfolk, granted the property to William Venour, John Selman and John Brikelys, skinners (CLRO, HR 134/97). From them it appears to have passed to John Stapelford, grocer, and by 1 November 1413 from him to William Sevenoke, grocer, and Nicholas Grafton, chaplain (CLRO, HR 142/26). On 27 November, Sevenoke and Grafton, at the wish of Stapelford and with the consent of his executors, sold to William Cauntbrigg, ironmonger, the tenement in St Botolph Lane, between the tenement belonging to the church of St George on the north and the tenement lately of Andrew Preston on the south in width, and extending in length from Botolph Lane to the west as far as Love Lane to the east (CLRO, HR 142/31). Cauntbrigg sold it on 18 January 1415 to Thomas Fawconer, then mayor, John Prophete, clerk, Sir John Philip, Thomas Chaucer, Thomas Knolles senior, Richard Merlowe, William Walderne, alderman, William Cheyne, William Babyngton, William Kyngwolmerssh and others (CLRO, HR 142/74, 143/8).

In his will proved in June 1473 John Bedham, fishmonger, left both the former Tenements 1 and 2 to the south to the church of St Mary at Hill for the upkeep of a chantry (see Tenements 1 and 2 combined, below), the property belonging to the church of St George (north of Tenement 1) forming its northern boundary, and the churchyard of St Botolph (Tenement 3) the southern. As Cauntbrigg at Tenement 1 is mentioned, but none of the occupants of Tenement 2, it looks as though the latter property had been acquired by the holders of the former. Some light is thrown on this by the text of Bedham's will and related documents preserved in the early churchwardens' accounts of St Mary at Hill. The will notes that Edmund de Lenham was one of the souls to be commemorated in the chantry, and explains that the former Cauntbrygg tenement (Tenement 1 and apparently Tenement 2 also) had been granted by Robert Mildenhale and Thomas Mayster on 20 May 1448 to Bedham, along with Henry Somers, Henry Langley, Walter Moyle, serjeant at law, Lawrence Cheyny and John Ansty, who had subsequently quitclaimed to Bedham and the now deceased John Dunham (GL, MS 1239/2, fo 16).

Thus the next known owners of Tenement 1 after William Cauntbrigg seem to have been Mildenhale and Mayster (perhaps his executors), from whom Somers, Bedham and others acquired it (presumably with Tenement 2) in 1448. Two further memoranda betray a fundamental lack of confidence in St Mary at Hill's title to the property, being compiled expressly as a defence against possible rival claims – not least one from the church of St George Eastcheap, to which Edmund de Lenham had first bequeathed the 10-mark (£6 13s 4d) chantry rent that Bedham was now diverting to St Mary's (GL, MS 1239/2, fos 22v–23r).

TENEMENT 2 IN THE 14TH AND FIRST HALF OF THE 15TH CENTURY

In a deed drawn up sometime before 22 January 1274 Elias le Bacheler and his wife Margery, one of the daughters of Geoffrey Batecok, granted to Ralph Pykeman and his wife Alice, the other daughter, their half share of a 28s per annum quitrent received from four small houses which Geoffrey gave in free marriage with Margery, two of them in the parish of St George in the lane called Cat Lane (*in venella que vocatur Catelane*) and two in the parish of St Mary at Hill, which came to Margery and Alice as Geoffrey's heirs (CLRO, HR 6/6).

Deeds of May 1334 and April 1350 relating to adjoining properties note the tenement formerly of Paul Turk as their western neighbour (CLRO, HR 62/81, 82/62). The earliest document found specifically relating to Tenement 2 is William de Kent's will of 3 March 1349, proved in May 1350, which left to his wife Joan for life his tenement in the parish of St George, to be sold after her death for pious and charitable purposes (CLRO, HR 78/114; Sharpe 1889, 634); a later deed of Joan's states that he had acquired it from one William Flambard (CLRO, HR 103/15). On 13 November 1374 Joan, as executrix of her husband's will, granted to John Wroth, alderman, Robert Virly, girdler, Thomas Morden, Andrew Pykeman, John Coggeshale, John Pountfreyt, Robert Pountfreyt, Gilbert Maufeld (and several others) for her life, and passing to them and their heirs after her death, the tenement in Botolph Lane in the parish of St George beween the tenement of Goscelin Osbarn and his wife Margaret (Tenement 3) on the south, the tenement once of Edmund Lenham on the north (Tenement 1), the street on the west and the tenement once of Andrew Pykeman to the east, paying her 20s per annum; William Mohaut, merchant, was to hold it during her life (CLRO, HR 103/15). Deeds of January and August 1375 relating to Tenement 3 name Joan widow of William de Kent and William Mohaut, respectively, as northern neighbours (GL, MS 59, fo iii/52; fo ii/4v–iii/5r; CLRO, HR 103/83). According to a deed of September 1392 relating to Tenement 3 to the south, Andrew Preston had replaced William Mohaut as occupant (CLRO, HR 121/32), having been granted the tenement jointly with John Pygot by Maufeld, Pountfreyt, John Claveryng and Henry Derby (CLRO, HR 126/110). Deeds of March 1406 and November 1413 relating to Tenement 1 name Andrew Preston as lately the neighbour to the south (CLRO, HR 134/97, 142/26).

No more is heard of Tenement 2 until 1472–3 when John

Bedham bequeathed it and Tenement 1 as a single property to the church of St Mary at Hill. His will and associated documents give less than complete details of the descent of Tenement 1 after 1415, and say nothing at all about the descent of Tenement 2 or Bedham's title to it; both properties had presumably been acquired by Robert Mildenhale and Thomas Mayster before 1448, and it was the combined tenement that was conveyed in that year to Somers, Langley and Bedham himself (see Tenement 1).

TENEMENTS 1 AND 2 COMBINED, IN THE SECOND HALF OF THE 15TH CENTURY

In his will dated 2 November 1472 and proved in June 1473 John Bedham, fishmonger, left to the church of St Mary at Hill a 'great tenement' in Botolph and Love Lanes in the parishes of St George and St Mary, charged with the maintenance of a chantry in the same church and various charitable payments (CLRO, HR 203/11; Sharpe 1890, 570; see also Littlehales 1904–5, 16–17). The combined property was described as formerly of William Cauntebrigge, ironmonger, and afterwards Henry Somers, and situated in width between the tenement belonging to the chantry of William Kyngston in the church of St George (ie north of Tenement 1) and the tenement in Love Lane belonging to the church of St Dunstan in the East on the north, and the parsonage and churchyard of St Botolph Billingsgate church (Tenement 3) on the south.

The earliest recorded tenant seems to have been Marin Conterys (ie Contarini), merchant of Venice, who occupied it before Bedham's death in 1473 (Littlehales 1904–5, 28; GL, MS 1239/2, fo 24r). In 1477–9 it was Lewis Lumbarde (Littlehales 1904–5, 76), and from 1483 until 1496 Gabriel de Urs (ibid, 114, 121, 123, 140–1, 167, 179, 211; GL, MS 1239/1, fo 128r), although Peter Contarini was noted as living there in 1485 (see below). The tenant in 1497 was Benet Tople or Cople (ibid, fo 138v).

An inventory of the contents as delivered by Bedham to Conterys 'when he entered into the place in Botolf lane' is dated 1485 (presumably the date at which it was transcribed into the St Mary's accounts) when Peter Contarini was stated to be living there (Littlehales 1904–5, 28–9; GL, MS 1239/2, fo 24r). The room-by-room survey comprised (fixtures omitted here): the chief chamber; the chamber over the parlour; a chamber within the same chamber; the inner chamber; another chamber; the parlour; the buttery; the chamber over the gate; the chamber over the kitchen; 'Antonye's chamber'; the chamber by the summer parlour; the chamber next St Botolph's churchyard; the next chamber; the kitchen; the larder house; the house next the garden; the stable; and the well; as well as some miscellaneous counters (in 'the chamber over the well,' 'antonyes chamber' and 'the highest chamber over the street'). There was also a listing of keys and locks for various doors including the postern gate.

The St Mary's churchwardens' accounts record the annual (sometimes biennial) rent payments in respect of the property from 1477, only four years after Bedham's death. It is variously referred to as 'the great Lambardes place in Botolph Lane'

(Littlehales 1904–5, 114) or as 'the great tenement of Bedaham' (ibid, 140–1) or the 'great place' (GL, MS 1239/1, fo 128). The annual rent for the property was £13 6s 8d per annum, but from at least 1483–5 tenants were annually rebated 53s 4d as an allowance for repairs, which they were presumably responsible for taking in hand themselves (Littlehales 1904–5, 121, 140–1, 167, etc). As a result, details of repairs are only incidental at this period; those in 1477–9 involved 'paving tile' and 'small paving tile', the mending of a siege (lavatory), iron and nails for the gate, a board for the kitchen, and the mending of a chimney (ibid, 104–5).

TENEMENT 3 (ST BOTOLPH BILLINGSGATE CEMETERY FROM 1393)

On 19 July 1305 was read a charter in which Richard de Parco and his wife Margery, once wife of Adam Box, granted to Richard Wolmar a 40s per annum quitrent from the tenement which they held in the parish of St Botolph Billingsgate by grant of Alexander le lingedrapier, son and heir of Benedict le lingedrapier, and which measured in width 11 ells (33ft, or approx 10m) between *Catenelane* to the north and the grantors' tenement to the south, and in length 28¼ ells (84ft 9ins, or 25.9m) from the street to the west as far as the tenement once of Roger de Mertone, roper (*cordarius*) to the east (CLRO, HR 33/71).

On 26 January 1313 Adam Box's son Robert granted to Elias Petri, vintner, and his wife Joan land with a house and stone walls, once of Alexander le lyndraper, which he held in the same parish between the tenement once of Martin de Garschurche to the south and the tenement of Gilbert Cros 'once called *Kattelane*' to the north, and extending from the street to the west as far as the tenement of Roger de Merton to the east (CLRO, HR 41/48). Most of the subsequent documentation derives from the register of the church of St Botolph Billingsgate, into whose possession the property was to come in the 1390s. On 28 February 1340 John Piers, son of Elyas Petri, granted to William Box all his tenements with buildings and rents in Botolph Lane between the tenement of William Haunsard to the south and the tenement once of Paulinus Turk to the north (GL, MS 59, fo ii/4v).

A deed of November 1374 relating to Tenement 2 names its neighbours to the south as Goscelin Osbarn and his wife Margaret (CLRO, HR 103/15), who had evidently acquired the property from William Box. On 15 August 1375 Gosselin and Margaret granted to Robert Gurdeler, Andrew Pykeman, John Coggeshale, Thomas Morden, Robert Pountfreyt, Gilbert Maufeld, John Claveryng and Thomas atte Blakelofte all their tenement in *Botulfeslane* in width between the tenement of William Warde, pepperer (ie grocer) and his wife Joan to the south and the tenement of William Mohaut to the north, and extending in length from the lane as far as the tenement of John, son of Nicholas Horn, and his wife Alice to the east (GL, MS 59, fo ii/4v–iii/5r; CLRO, HR 103/83).

Eighteen years later, on 7 August 1392, two of the grantees, Gilbert Maufeld and John Claveryng, purchased for 5 marks a royal licence to grant to the parson of the church of St Botolph a toft in London, to be held by the parson and his successors in perpetuity for a cemetery for the burial of parishioners of the church wishing to be buried there (*Cal Pat R Richard II, 1391–6*, 141; GL, MS 59, fo iii/5v). Armed with this licence, Maufeld and Claveryng on 20 September 1392 granted the toft in *Botulpheslane* to John Wolde, parson of the church of St Botolph Billingsgate, and his successors as a cemetery for the burial (*pro cimiterio ad sepulturam*) of parishioners and others (CLRO, HR 121/32). On 13 March 1393 John, bishop of Derry, with the permission of Robert, bishop of London, dedicated and consecrated the toft in London in *Botulpheslane* in the parish of St Botolph, which Maufeld and Claveryng had granted to John Wolde and his successors as an additional burial ground (*in augmentum sepultur*) (GL, MS 59, fo iv/6v).

TENEMENTS 1 AND 2, *c* 1500 TO THE GREAT FIRE OF 1666

Between 1498 and 1521 the rent for Tenement 1/2 was paid by Antony Baveron, except for an interval in 1500–5 when it was paid by Julian Serystory (GL, MS 1239/1, fos 187, 199, 211v, 222v, 234v). Baveron was followed by Rayner de Barde in 1521 to 1523 (ibid, fos 469–80v passim), and by Francis de Bard from 1523 to 1530 (ibid, fos 495v–582v passim). Only two of these foreign merchants occur in contemporary letters patent and close. One was Antonio Bavaryn, who on 24 March 1507 was included in a general pardon of 'subjects of Venice' for offences committed before 1 March and was licensed to trade in wool and other goods in any of the king's dominions for ten years therefrom, and with other foreign merchants including those 'commonly called "Lumbardys"' (*Cal Pat R Henry VII, 1494–1509*, 505), and on 25 November 1507 acknowledged his debts to the Crown (*Cal Close R Henry VII, 1500–9*, no. 830 (vi)). Giuliano Serristory appears in similar recognizances of 18 October and 8 November, as a merchant of Florence on the first occasion and of Lucca on the second (ibid, no. 830 (i, iii)). Thereafter the tenants were less exotic: Edward Burlace in 1530–5 (GL, MS 1239/1, fos 596v–637v passim), a Mr Capel in 1535–8 (ibid, fos 649–88), and a John Baptist Morrison in 1538–40 (ibid, fo 716). After this the next properly drawn-up accounts date from 1548–9, by which time the property had been confiscated by the Crown under the Chantries Act.

From 1506–7 the rebate paid to Baveron in respect of repairs was discontinued, but in 1510–11 there commenced a long series of extensive reparations and rebuilding which lasted, with only occasional breaks, until the confiscation of the property in 1547, and was at its height throughout the 1510s and 1520s. Perhaps because of the scale of the work the churchwardens, rather than the tenant, took charge of the operations and itemised them in the accounts. It seems clear that the whole tenement must have been virtually rebuilt, albeit in a piecemeal fashion, and in some cases (notably the tiling of the kitchen floor) appears to have been undertaken several times over. There are repeated references throughout these years to the payment of carpenters, masons, daubers, plasterers, tilers, plumbers, chandlers and labourers, and to the purchase of stone, brick, tiles, glass, lime, sand, lead, board of various descriptions, nails and a wide variety of iron fittings. Specific

parts of the building mentioned are the pentice (GL, MS 1239/1, fos 318, 495v), 'planks for the garden' (ibid, fo 333v), the kitchen (ibid, fos 348, 412, 443, 469, 518v), the 'middle gate', the kitchen and parlour chimneys (ibid, fo 364), the parlour (ibid, fos 409v), Antony Baveron's warehouse (ibid, fo 420v and also fo 665v), the hall (ibid, fos 469, 553v, 596v), the counting house (ibid, fo 469), and the great gate (ibid, fo 541). One notable entry, for 1530–1, concerns payments for work including 'cleansing of four draughts and making a pit to bury them in the ground' (ibid, fo 597r).

On 13 August 1550 Edward VI sold to Henry earl of Arundel for £186 13s 4d the recently confiscated St Mary at Hill chantry property, described as a great messuage in the tenure of John Swygo and formerly leased to John Baptist Morison in Botolph Lane in the parish of St George and Love Lane in the parish of St Mary at Hill, given by John Redman (sic) to priests, lamps and anniversaries in St Mary's, with all buildings, shops, cellars, solars, courts, vaults, entries, curtilages and gardens; its early value being £13 6s 8d (*Cal Pat R Edward VI*, iv.16). On 18 November 1556 Earl Henry sold it to Francis Barneham, draper, as the great capital messuage and tenement now or late in the tenure and occupation of John Swigo and previously leased to John Baptiste Morison, for £333 6s 8d (CLRO, HR 248/95). Thereafter the descent of the property is lost for almost ninety years.

On 4 July 1642 John Alden of Stafford (Staffordshire) and his wife Mary leased to John Becke of London the tenement or messuage in his occupation and lately that of Richard Hudson, carpenter, called the 'Peter and Paul' in Botolph Lane in the parish of St George and comprising several rooms, at the coming in on the street side, a cellar and a shop over the same; a buttery beneath the ground paved with Kentish ragstone; a kitchen half boarded and half paved with tiles with a little buttery paved with brick adjoining the kitchen under the stairs; and over the stairs at the going up into the house a little lodging room for servants; two chambers over the aforementioned buttery and kitchen; one chamber over part of the said two chambers; and the old gallery over part of the house already in Becke's occupation towards Buttolphes churchyard, which gallery was now divided into two chambers with a garret over the same two chambers, to be held from Lady Day 1646 for 27 years, paying £8 pa (CLRO, HR 319/14). This and the lease of September 1646 are the only documents to give the property the name 'Peter and Paul', and they do so at a strangely late date which makes it difficult to explain: neither Peter nor Paul had been among the saints to whom chapels were dedicated at St Mary at Hill (cf Jeffery 1996, 6). This deed (and the name) evidently related exclusively to the Botolph Lane frontage, and only part of that (Becke being already in possession of its southern end, next to the churchyard), and on the same day, 4 July 1642, Alden leased to Becke what can only have been the rest of the property, comprising the messuage and tenement, yard and garden with all shops, cellars, solars, courts, ways, vaults, watercourses, halls, parlours, warehouses, rooms, backsides (etc) in Botolph Lane in the parishes of St George and St Mary at Hill 'or one of them', late in the occupation of Abraham Beck, merchant deceased and father of

John Becke, and now in the latter's occupation, to be held from same date for same term at £60 pa (CLRO, HR 319/15).

On 25 September 1646 John Arden of Curborough Hall, Staffordshire, and his wife Mary leased to Arnold Beake (sic) of London, merchant, the entire property, including the 'Peter and Paul' in the parish of St George (as described four years earlier), as a single entity to be held from Lady Day last past for 31 years, paying £16 pa for the first year and £64 for the rest of the term (CLRO, HR 319/23). A schedule contains a detailed room-by-room survey of the premises and comprises the following features (here omitting fixtures and contents but including the numbers of 'easements' per window, which give some general idea of the relative size of individual rooms): the Hall (43); the kitchen next the garden (3 and mentioning a door under the stairs going up to the Hall); the great parlour next the kitchen (24 and mentioning one door to the kitchen and two others going into the Gallery); the Gallery (including a door at the 'coming in' next to the yard and one going up the stairs); the lesser parlour next the Gallery (14); the buttery over against the said lesser parlour (4); the stairs foot next to the said Buttery (4); a little room at the top of the said stairs (4); an entry next to the said room (a chamber with a bay window and 14 easements, and two other windows of 4 and 1 easements); an entry next to the said chamber (one window positioned 'over against the Compting House' and another window of 6 easements); the Compting House (22); the Great Chamber next the Compting House on the one side (a bay

window of 16 easements with two windows either side); the Chamber last mentioned (opening off the Great Chamber; 16 glazed easements); an entry next the said Chamber (5); the Chamber next to the said Entry (glazed almost its whole length); the room called the White Chamber up a pair of stairs from the Hall (26); the chamber at the end of the Entry (12); the chamber last mentioned (7); the uppermost chamber over the hall up a short flight of stairs (a great bay window towards the garden with 34 easements besides other windows); and the cellar next the kitchen. It seems quite clear from this that the house of 1646, as might be expected on the evidence of the extensive repairs and rebuilding of the 1510s and 1520s, was very different from that of the 1470s (Fig 24).

Late Saxon and early medieval occupation to the late 13th century (period 4)

External activity up to the late 11th century (OA3 retained)

The early medieval deposits had been heavily truncated by later cellars, with only small islands of stratification surviving. External activity included robbing of the Roman masonry walls and foundations associated with Building 2, undertaken in a piecemeal fashion at either the end of the Roman occupation or long afterwards (not illustrated). The robbing trench backfills contained three sherds of late Saxon shell-tempered ware (LSS), early medieval sand- and shell-tempered ware (EMSS) and early

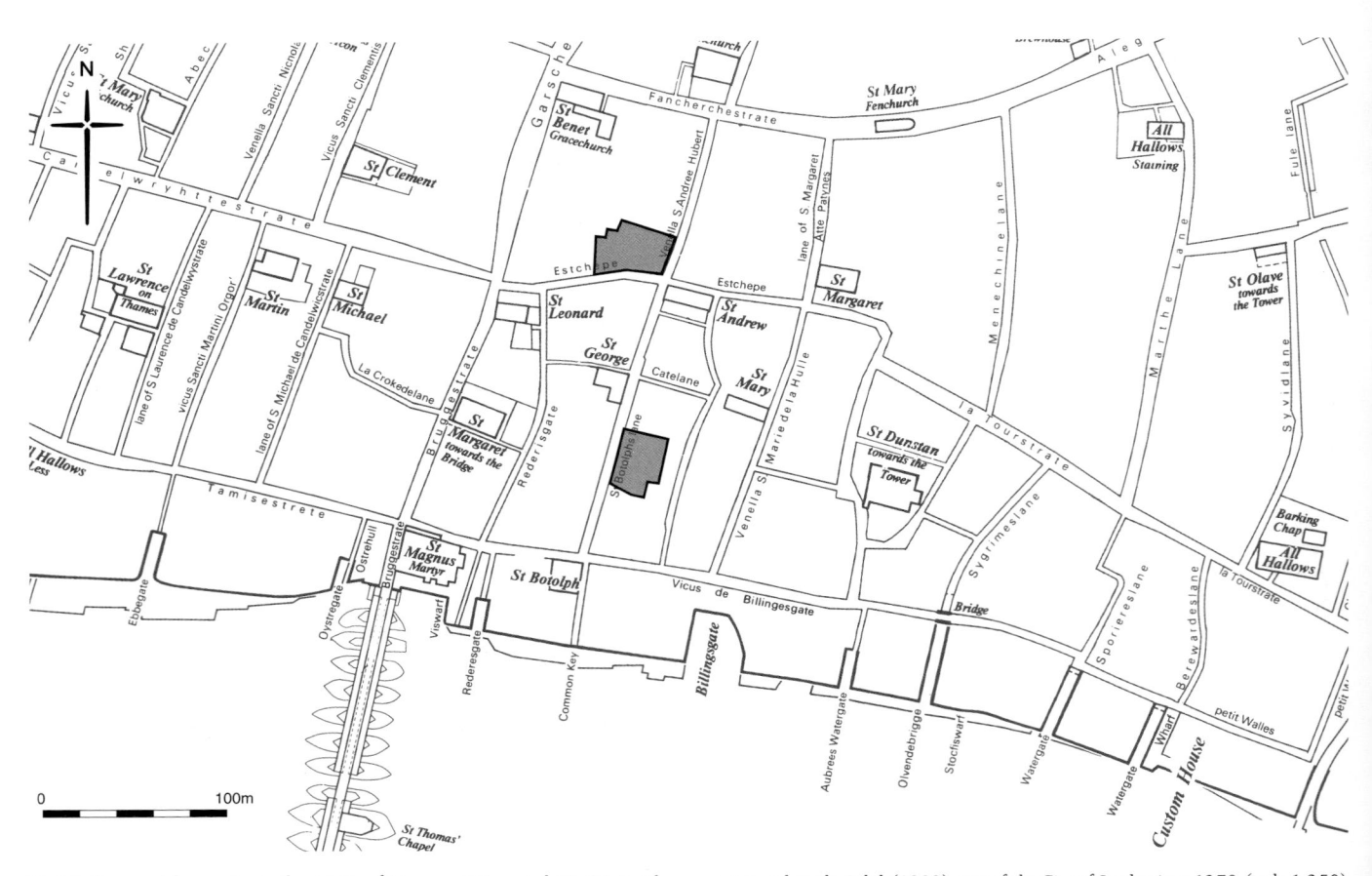

Fig 24 *Documented properties in the vicinity of Monument House and 13–21 Eastcheap, superimposed on the Lobel (1989) map of the City of London in c 1270 (scale 1:250) (by permission of Oxford University Press)*

Surrey ware (ESUR), and can be dated to c 1050–1100. A pit produced a small but diverse group of marine/estuarine fish, chicken and domestic mammals mainly representative of post-consumption waste, and a fragment of bone from the forefoot of a young roe deer (*Capreolus capreolus*).

Cellared building (B3) (phases 1 and 2)

Two phases of an early medieval cellared building were located in the south-east corner of the site (Fig 25; Fig 26). Only the north-west corner of the buildings and internal floor surfaces survived. There was no evidence to suggest that the east–west-aligned Cat Lane (see period 5) had yet been established.

The primary phase of Building 3 comprised a cellar at least 1.70m deep and had decayed post and stave walls. The base of the construction cut for the cellar lay at 5.78m OD. The floors were composed of brickearth clay, with the uppermost heavily scorched surface indicating the position of an internal hearth. Occupation deposits contained seven sherds of Late Saxon shell-tempered ware (LSS) and two sherds of early medieval shell-tempered ware (EMSH), suggesting a date of c 1050–60. A small group of animal bone fragments included adult

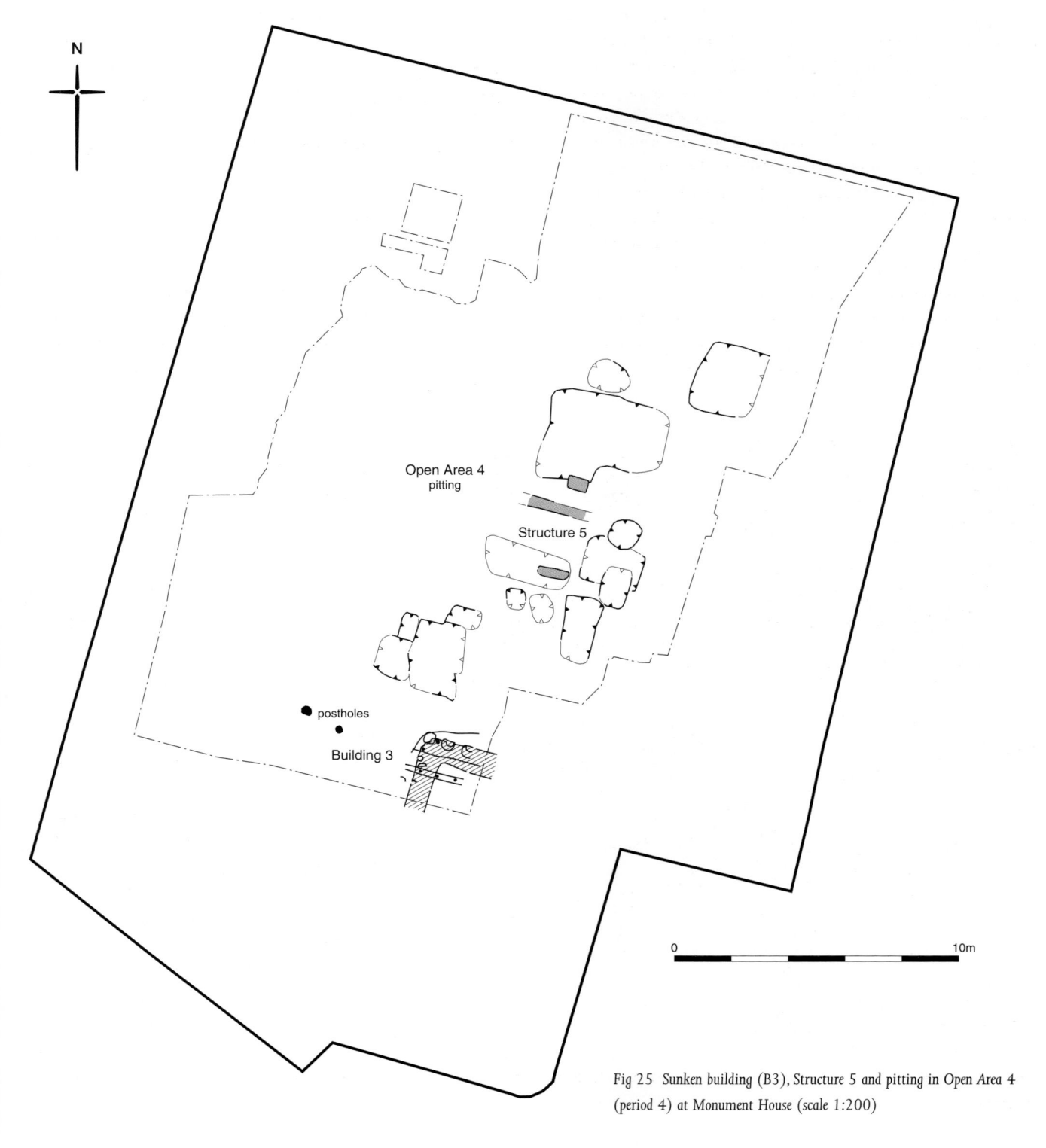

N

Open Area 4
pitting

Structure 5

● postholes
●

Building 3

0   10m

Fig 25 Sunken building (B3), Structure 5 and pitting in Open Area 4 (period 4) at Monument House (scale 1:200)

Fig 26 North–south section through cellared building (B3), looking east (0.5m scale)

sheep/goat tooth, vertebrae, upper limb and lower limb, with small numbers of plaice/flounder vertebrae, frog/toad vertebrae, ox and sheep-sized rib, and pig scapula and mandible.

Seventy-nine sherds of pottery were found in the disuse and consolidation deposits that filled the lower levels of the building, with LSS accounting for 72 sherds from 44 pots. The remaining sherds comprise early medieval sandy ware (EMS), shelly coarse London-type ware (LOND) and three sherds of Rhenish origin, including the rim of a greyware (RHGR) globular jar <P6> from A[577] (Fig 27), suggesting a date of c 1080–1100 for the dismantling of the building.

Several holed, circular ceramic loom weights A<362>, A<405> and A<426>–A<429> were also found in deposit A[577]. Weights of this form were used on the vertical, warp-weighted loom of the pre-Norman era (Walton Rogers 1997, 1753).

Following the partial consolidation of the primary phase building, a second cellar was set within its footprint. The new building phase also had post and stave walls that were originally jointed into a surface-laid timber base plate. The carbonised remains of the north wall showed that it was originally built of close-set vertical wooden staves varying in width from 200 to 300mm. The floor surface lay some 0.60m above the primary floor of the earlier cellar, with the base of the construction cut recorded at 6.40m OD. The absence of stone or ceramic roofing tile suggests that the building had a roof of thatch or wooden shingles. Twelve sherds of residual LSS were associated with the use of the second cellar.

The secondary phase of the building was destroyed in a fire. Destruction debris covering the floor included half of a burnt header piece from a barrel. The building was not rebuilt and the cellar appears to have been rapidly filled in. The disuse fill

contained 21 sherds derived from four pots. Two sherds are of LSS while the others are from a jar and a bowl in early medieval sand- and shell-tempered ware (EMSS) distorted from exposure to heat.

A sample from the deposit contained a rich charred assemblage dominated by oats (*Avena* spp) and barley (*Hordeum vulgare* L), typical of Late Saxon cereal assemblages (Rackham 1994, 134). Some arable weed seeds, including stinking mayweed (*Anthemis cotula*), brome grass (*Bromus* sp) and vetch (*Vicia/Lathyrus* sp), were present, but in smaller numbers than the grains, and it is likely that this deposit comes from a semi-cleaned cereal crop. The grain may have been destined for animal fodder, human food or brewing, before being accidentally burnt.

Fragmentary structural remains north of Building 3 (S5)

The fragmentary remains of two parallel east–west slots and a posthole to the north of Building 3 could represent the remains of contemporary structural features, although no associated surfaces were found. Two sherds of pottery were recovered from the features, including one from a slightly everted rim of a shelly-sandy ware (SSW) jar, which probably dates to between 1140 and 1220.

Quarrying and rubbish pits (OA4)

Evidence for 12th- and 13th-century gravel quarrying was represented by a series of large and generally discrete pit cuts. The quarrying must have been contemporary with, or later than, the final robbing of Roman remains. Extraction of gravel and robbing of Roman stonework may also have been associated with preparations for the construction of medieval stone buildings. Cat Lane was probably established on an east–west alignment across the southern part of the site in the 13th century, but surviving evidence of road gravels was not stratigraphically related to the pitting.

A total of 271 sherds from 126 vessels were recovered from the pits, most relating to the use of the quarries for the disposal of rubbish and cess, and dating to before *c* 1150. Two sherds are later: a rod handle from a London baluster jug dating to after 1180 and a large sherd of Mill Green ware (MG) dated to after 1270. An incomplete bone skate A<364> was made from an ox or horse longbone (cf Egan 1998, 294–5).

Notable assemblages of pottery include 58 sherds from rubbish pit fill A[419] which are typical of the period *c* 1150–80/1200. The 88 sherds from cesspit fills A[464], A[469] and A[473] mainly comprise London-type ware (LOND), including substantial parts of two jugs. One of these is of early rounded form with applied pellets; the other is an unusual waisted baluster jug <P7> (Fig 27). Also present are shelly-sandy ware (SSW), south Hertfordshire-type greyware (SHER) and the greater part of a cooking pot/cauldron in Kingston-type ware (KING). Taken together these suggest a date of *c* 1230–50 for the group, although some pieces may have been quite old when discarded.

Pit fill A[483] was also dated to the mid 13th century by Kingston-type ware and a highly decorated Earlswood-type ware (EARL) jug. Also present were part of a LOND baluster jug and a green-glazed ware from northern France (NFM). External surface A[422] contained eight sherds of Mill Green ware (MG) and three of Saintonge ware (SAIN), which date to after 1270/80. Other pottery included sherds of LOND, one of Scarborough ware (SCAR) and part of a KING frying pan <P8> with grouped thumbing around the base (Fig 27).

A large percentage of the building material from the medieval quarry pits is Roman, though two medieval peg roofing tiles were present. The other pits in Open Area 4 contained mainly medieval peg and shouldered peg roofing tile. The quarry fills also produced a small assemblage of marine/estuarine fish, ox, sheep/goat including sheep, and pig. The major domesticate material derived mainly from adults and areas of good and moderate meat-bearing quality, although there was some recovery of elements of the head and feet.

Later medieval development in the 14th and 15th centuries (period 5)

Cat Lane (R1)

A narrow, east–west-aligned lane or alleyway (Road 1) was located along the north side of the boundary wall of Tenement 3 and the St Botolph burial ground (Fig 28). The lane had a gravel surface at 7.78m OD. Documentary evidence identifies it as Cat Lane, first recorded in 1273–4, which ran along the line of the parish boundary between Tenements 2 and 3. Cat Lane appears to have been relatively short lived, with the last documentary reference to it dating from 1313 and indicating

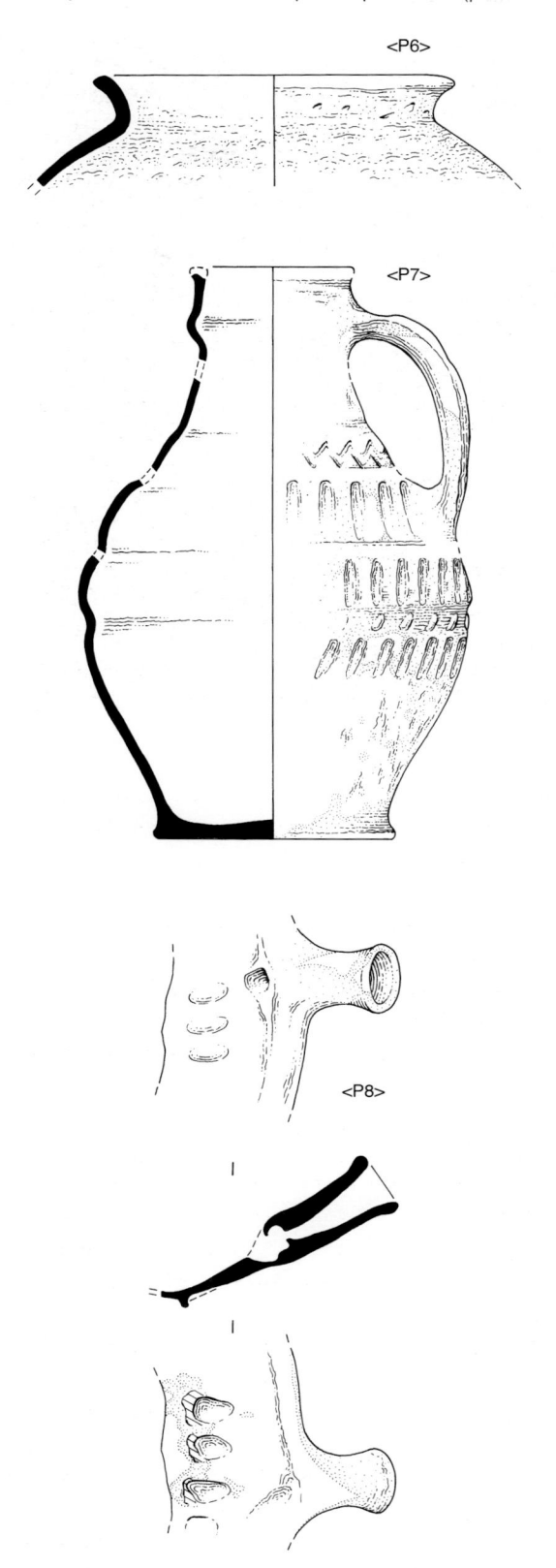

Fig 27 *Rhenish greyware globular jar <P6>, London-type ware waisted baluster jug <P7> and Kingston-type ware frying pan <P8> (scale 1:4)*

that it may have fallen out of use by that time, although the archaeological evidence suggests that it survived longer. No dating evidence was recovered from Road 1, other than two residual sherds of Late Saxon shell-tempered ware.

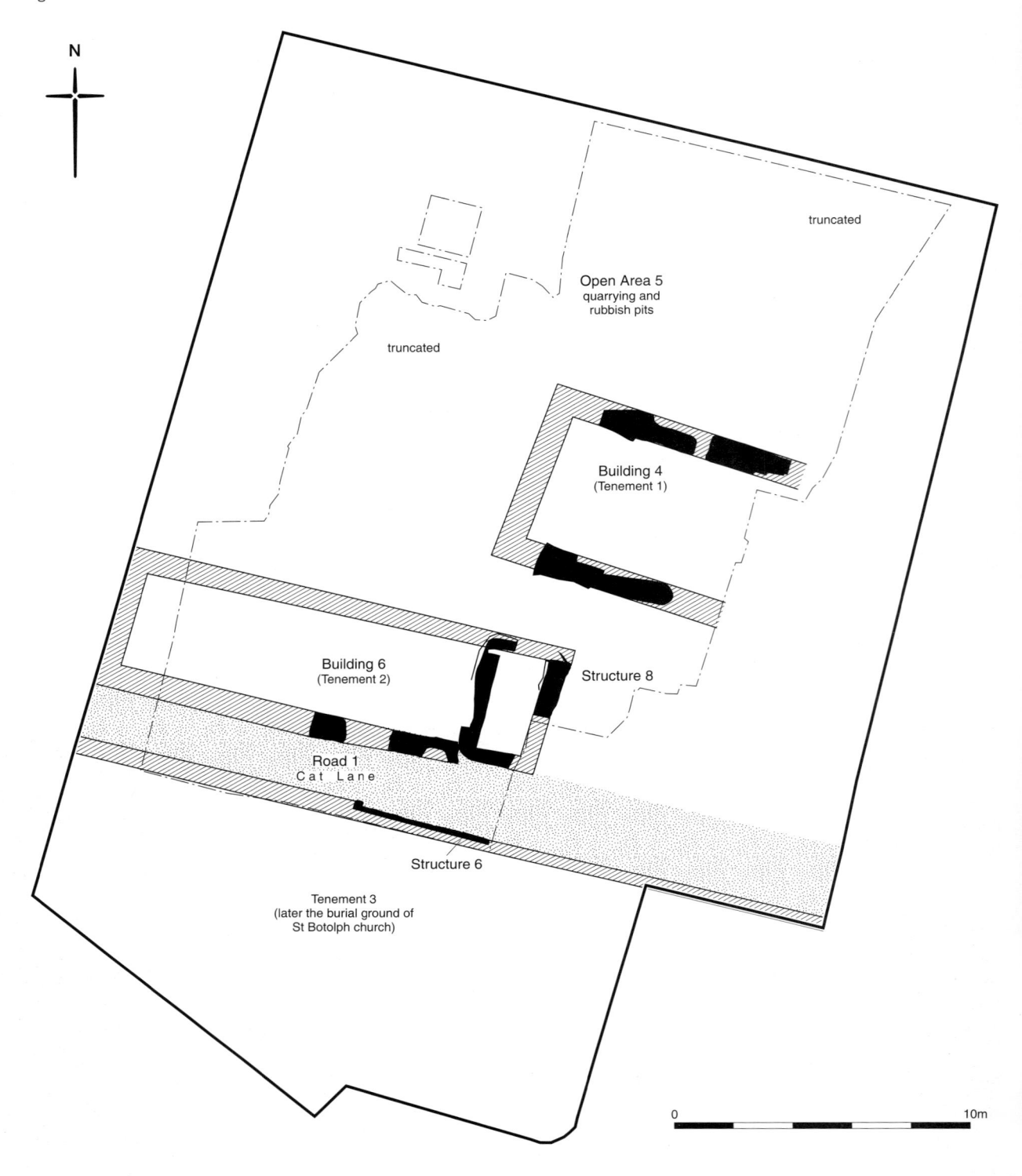

Fig 28 *Cat Lane (R1) and properties to the south and north (period 5) at Monument House (scale 1:200)*

Northern boundary wall of Tenement 3 and St Botolph burial ground (S6)

The northern boundary of Tenement 3 became the north wall of the upper burial ground of St Botolph Billingsgate when a cemetery was established on the plot formerly occupied by Tenement 3 in 1392. The east–west-aligned boundary wall (Structure 6) was built of chalk and Kentish ragstone bonded with mortar, with a foundation base at 7.64m OD. Where the wall crossed the line of the Roman culvert, it neatly arched over the roof of the earlier structure. Cat Lane lay to the north of the wall.

Pottery from the construction backfill includes sherds from a large dish in early medieval sand- and shell-tempered ware (EMSS) and other fabrics dated to the 11th or early 12th century. One sherd, from the base of a London-type ware baluster (LOND BAL) jug, could date to the 13th or early 14th century. The latest find is a sherd of Dutch redware (DUTR) dating to after 1350.

The Tenement 2 property north of Cat Lane (B6) and associated cesspit (S8)

Tenement 2 was aligned east–west along the north side of Cat Lane and represented by Building 6. The only parts of the Building 6 primary phase to survive were its deeply founded south wall and a chalk-lined cesspit (S8) at the east end of the building. The wall foundation was built of Kentish ragstone bonded with mortar and incorporated two basal courses of Flemish-type bricks, which plugged a narrow breach in the roof of the underlying Roman culvert. Flemish-type bricks (fabric 3031) were used in the London area from the 14th century, and are dated to *c* 1295–1305 at Eltham Palace (Turner 1999, 27). There was no indication that the Building 6 examples had been reused, suggesting that construction took place in the 14th century.

Two cuts within the area of Building 6 and sealed by later floors may be associated with the robbing or modification of primary structural features. Fills within the cuts contained 11th- to 12th-century pottery. Fill A[578] contained a small group of bone, mainly derived from marine/estuarine fish including herring, plaice/flounder and cod.

Attached to the east end of Building 6 was a north–south-aligned rectangular, chalk-lined cesspit Structure 8 (Fig 29). The lining of the cesspit incorporated broken peg roofing tiles used to level the courses, along with Flemish-type brick. The base of the cesspit lay at 6.20m OD and was cut into the natural gravel to facilitate drainage. It is assumed that an associated 'privy-chamber' would have been set over it at first-floor level. A total of 43 sherds of pottery were recovered from the construction fill behind the lining of the cesspit, but nearly all of the pottery was residual 12th-century material, some of it joining with sherds from Open Area 4 (see period 4).

Stone building (B4)

Building 4 was the earliest of the extant buildings to the north of Tenement 2 Building 6, in the area identified from documentary sources as the approximate location of Tenement 1. Two parallel east–west-aligned robber cuts marked the position of masonry walls constructed from a level of 9.60m OD and deliberately deepened where they crossed earlier pit fills (Fig 28). The robber cuts lay some 5m apart and extended for at least 7m. Building 4 may originally have extended westwards to the Botolph Lane frontage, but the area to the west was truncated by post-Great Fire basements (see period 7; below, 2.5). A 19th-century building had truncated all evidence of horizontal medieval deposits in the north-west quarter of the site (see period 8).

Fig 29 *Chalk-lined cesspit (S8), with Cat Lane (R1) to the left beneath the scale, looking west (1m scale)*

Cobbled courtyard (OA5)

The fragmentary remains of a cobbled surface, located between the Building 4 robber cuts, may have been part of a contemporary courtyard (not illustrated). The pottery from the surface amounts to 50 sherds, of which only two are residual. Surrey whitewares in Kingston-type ware (KING) and coarse Surrey-Hampshire border ware (CBW) dominate and, together with three sherds of late medieval Hertfordshire glazed ware (LMHG), date the group to c 1340–50. Of note is part of a CBW basket-handled bowl <P9> (Fig 30).

Robbing of Building 4 and other external activity (OA5 continued)

Deposits associated with the robbing of Building 4 contained 64 sherds, all of which may be residual. Stratigraphically associated pit fills yielded 33 sherds from 16 pots. Of the possibly contemporary material, Kingston-type wares (KING) dominate and include parts of two highly decorated baluster jugs and another with lattice and ring-and-dot stamps. Also of note are two cauldron legs in south Hertfordshire-type greyware (SHER), one stabbed, and an unusual jug decorated with applied strips in a calcareous fabric that could be from London or Hertfordshire <P10> (Fig 30). One pit or robbing-cut fill A[458] contained a sheep skull showing removal of the horncores. Chopping at the base had allowed later removal of the horn sheath for use as a raw material and this was the only instance of working waste from the assemblage.

Several other pits may have been contemporary with the robbing. The latest pit fill A[383] contained pottery dated to c 1340–1400, but many pit fills were dated c 1140–1200 and may have been in use during period 4 or have contained only residual pottery. A total of 592 sherds of pottery were recovered from the various pits and quarries, of which fewer than 20 could date to the 14th century. These comprise Kingston-type

ware, London-type ware (LOND) baluster jugs, and single sherds of Mill Green ware (MG), Saintonge ware (SAIN) and late medieval Hertfordshire glazed ware (LMHG), the latter the only fabric that is definitely later than 1340.

Two woolcombs <S6> from pit fill A[313] are an unusual find (Fig 31). They were used, usually in pairs, to align fibres in one of the first processes of textile manufacture.

Deposits associated with a group of these pits produced the largest and most diverse assemblage of animal bone from the site. The bone derived mainly from ox, with smaller components of sheep/goat, including sheep, and pig and occasional fragments of chicken and goose. There was a small but diverse group of marine/estuarine fish comprising herring, eel, cod, haddock and gurnard (*Triglidae*). Much of the material represented carcase areas of at least moderate meat-bearing quality, although the large ox group from fill A[385] contained a considerable component of head and, particularly, foot and toe elements, perhaps derived from primary processing. Most of the material derived from adults.

Plant remains from the pits included a small, mostly charred, assemblage dominated by grass seeds, poa (*Poa* spp), low numbers of grains of wheat (*Triticum* sp L), barley (*Hordeum sativum* L) and grains too poorly preserved to be identified. Individual charred seeds of fat hen (*Chenopodium album* L), elder (*Sambucus nigra* L), stinking mayweed (*Anthemis cotula* L) and spike rush (*Eleocharis palustris* L) were also present.

Stone building (B5)

The fragmentary remains of Building 5 were composed of two chalk and Kentish ragstone foundations bonded with mortar and set at right angles (not illustrated). The building did not have a cellar and no associated surfaces survived. The east–west-aligned south wall of the building was located directly over the robbed northern wall of Building 4, showing continued use of a significant property boundary. Building 5 may have extended west to the Botolph Lane frontage but the evidence was truncated by a post-Great Fire cellar. There was no dating evidence associated with Building 5, although it can be dated to the 14th century on stratigraphic grounds.

2.4 Post-medieval occupation up to and including the Great Fire (period 6)

Properties north of Cat Lane and the St Botolph burial ground

Rebuilding of Tenement 2 (B6) with an associated well (S7)

Tenement 2 was completely rebuilt before reaching its final form as the southern range of a larger property enclosing a courtyard in the early to mid 16th century, by which time documentary sources indicate that it had been merged with

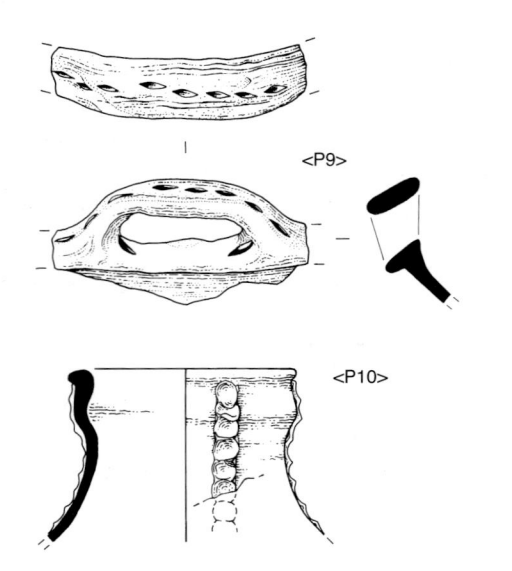

Fig 30 Basket-handled bowl <P9> with stabbed decoration (fabric CBW) and jug <P10> decorated with applied strips, from London or Hertfordshire (scale 1:4)

<S6>

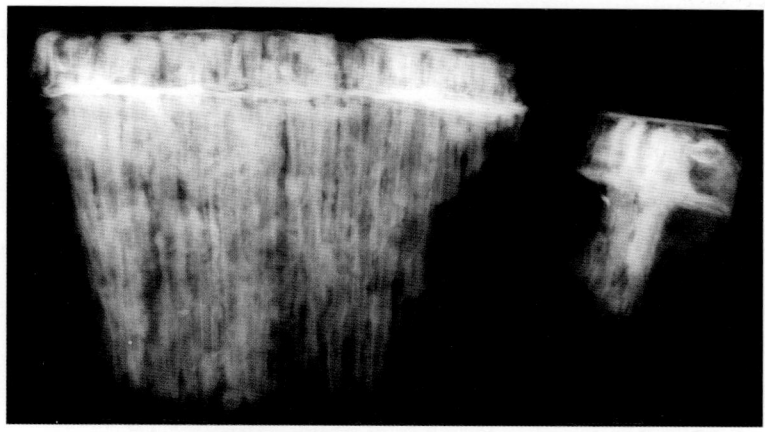

Fig 31 Corroded woolcombs <S6> from fragments A<450> and A<397> (scale 1:2); X-ray of A<397>

Tenement 1 to the north. Most of the surviving walls of Building 6 were associated with the rebuilding in the late 15th or early 16th century. Like its predecessor, the south range of the building occupied a narrow plot 4m wide but in excess of 8m long, fronting Botolph Lane in the west (Fig 32).

The north and south walls of the building were quite different in size and composition and were built of a variety of materials including chalk, Kentish ragstone, flint and brick. The south wall was built directly on the foundation of the building's primary phase (see period 5) and incorporated light-brown Flemish-type brick of similar type to that used in the underlying foundation, as well as occasional peg roofing tile. The north wall was much wider at 1.40m and had a chalk rubble core which was faced on its south side.

The east section of the north wall was unusual in that it incorporated a circular chalk-lined well (S7), which was probably only accessible from within the building. The lower levels of the well lining were composed of typical Tudor-type red bricks first used in London in the later 15th century. The lining also contained peg roofing tile with fine moulding sand and square and diamond-shaped nail holes, features which first appear about 1480.

The brickearth floor of Building 6 contained seven sherds of pottery, one of coarse Surrey-Hampshire border ware (CBW), the others from an early post-medieval redware (PMRE) bunghole jar with mortar adhering to it. Partly sealed beneath the brickearth floor was a small vaulted chalk soakaway or drain

which had been neatly constructed in a hole in the roof of the Roman culvert, probably added following the accidental discovery of the underlying feature.

The pottery from the sump's construction fill A[474] included approximately half of a Siegburg stoneware (SIEG) funnel-necked beaker (*Trichterhalsbecher*) dating to the mid 15th century. A small but interesting group of pottery was found in a water-worn hollow in the uppermost culvert fill A[584], beneath the soakaway. This comprises 38 sherds from a rounded jug with stabbed handle in CBW (cf Pearce and Vince 1988, no. 430), 16 sherds from a second CBW jug and 28 sherds from a Cheam whiteware (CHEA) cooking pot (cf ibid, no. 567). Also present was one sherd of early post-medieval calcareous redware (PMREC), suggesting a date of c 1480–1500 for the group.

Robbing and external activity overlying Building 5 (OA6)

A physically isolated, severely truncated area of stratification overlying Building 5 included evidence for a robber trench and a pit (not illustrated). The features may have been associated with the clearance of Building 5 and preparatory to the construction of Building 7 (below). The only dating evidence was residual.

The eastern range of the new building (B7)

The construction of Building 7 on the east side of the site at the

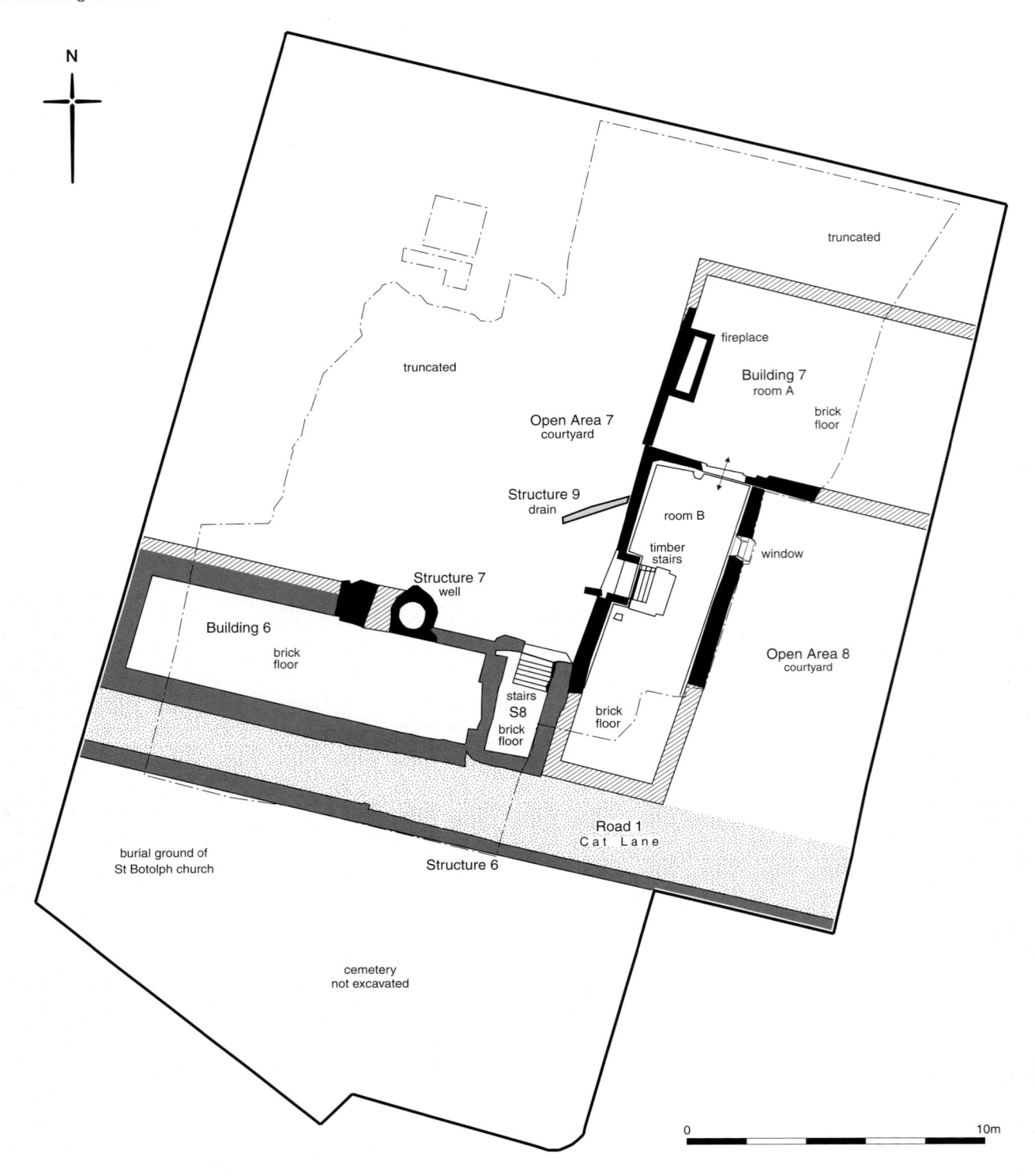

Fig 32 Building complex Building 6 and Building 7 enclosing courtyard Open Area 7 (period 6) at Monument House (scale 1:200)

end of the 15th century was part of a larger development carried out in conjunction with the rebuilding of Building 6 to the south. There is little doubt that this ambitious programme of rebuilding was undertaken to unify the disparate elements of Tenements 1 and 2, which are known to have been combined by the mid 15th century. Building 7 had two connecting cellars which together formed an inverted L-shape in plan and shared a common frontage along a courtyard to the west (Fig 33).

The narrower south cellar (room B) was rectangular and

aligned north–south, with its west wall abutting the back of the chalk cesspit (S8). The cellar to the north (room A) was aligned east–west. The rooms were terraced at different levels, reflecting the prevailing hillside slope across the site, and consequently the level of the floor in room A was c 0.50m higher then the floor in room B. The cellar walls were made of dressed chalk blocks interspersed with flint and peg roofing tile bonded with mortar. In room B the cellar walls survived up to the base of the springers for the roof vault, a height of 1.56m. The only external opening defined in the cellars was a small, recessed window set into the east wall of room B. An internal doorway allowed access between the two cellars, although it is possible that it was inserted at a later date. The original floors of the cellars had been truncated and associated finds were residual.

A courtyard (OA7) and associated chalk-lined drain (S9)

A large courtyard (OA7), located to the north of Building 6 and west of Building 7, was severely truncated by a post-Great Fire basement. Near the east side of the courtyard, adjacent to the west wall of Building 7, the base of a narrow chalk-lined drain (S9) ran north-east to south-west. The floor of the drain was at c 9.68m OD, and although there was no apparent fall, it probably served to drain surface water away from the building.

A possible courtyard to the east of Building 7 (OA8)

A second courtyard may have lain in an external area to the east of Building 7 room B and south of room A (OA8).

A note on Lombards Place

A large merchant's house known as 'Lombards Place' was established to the east of Botolph Lane at some time in the 15th century. At least part of the property bordered St Botolph's churchyard, which lay to the south. It is possible that Lombards Place occupied part of the Monument House excavation area, and an association with Building 7 seems the most likely.

Modifications to Building 6

The chalk-lined cesspit (S8) at the east end of Building 6 was substantially remodelled during the late 15th century, when it was backfilled to the level of the adjacent brickearth floor (Fig 34). The upper section of the west wall of the cesspit was then demolished, enabling the floor of the building to be extended 2m to the east. A staircase was also inserted in what was now the north-east corner of the enlarged building. The base of the staircase was set on to a mixed stone footing incorporating a stone threshold. This stair gave access to the courtyard (OA7) to the north.

Fig 33 Building 7 rooms A and B (foreground), Building 6 and well (S7) (upper left) and courtyard (OA7) (upper centre) at Monument House, looking west

Fig 34 Chalk-lined cesspit (S8) incorporated into Building 6 with new brick floor and staircase access, looking east (0.5m scale); note pot <P11> set into the floor

The consolidation fills of Structure 8 contained residual medieval pottery derived from late 14th- or 15th-century rubbish, and a large number of floor tiles, mostly fragmentary plain green-glazed and yellow tiles of Low Countries type and probably from a floor in Building 6 or 7. The tiles show little if any wear and are of a smaller 'medieval' type which was superseded by larger Low Countries tiles around the 1480s (Betts in prep), suggesting that at least one of the buildings had been constructed as early as the mid 15th century.

The Structure 8 make-up fill A[389] also contained a Penn tile A<363>, dated to the 1330s or 1340s and of an unpublished design type. The tile may be from the nearby church of St Botolph Billingsgate, which is known to have been paved with Penn tiles (Betts 1994, 136). The pottery associated with the installation of the new Building 6 floor (A[243] and A[532]) comprises four sherds of Dutch redware (DUTR), Saintonge ware (SAIN) and an early Valencian lustreware (VALE) jug, while a sherd of early post-medieval redware (PMRE) was found in make-up layer A[351]. Together they suggest that the modifications to Building 6 took place c 1480–1550. During the early 17th century a red brick and tile floor A[148] was laid throughout Building 6.

The new floor raised the Building 6 cellar level by c 250mm: the staircase in the north-east corner of the building had to be modified and the threshold raised. A window may have been inserted at the side of the staircase, but only the sill survived. The new floor included a near-complete pot set into and flush with the surface and located at the foot of the staircase. This was a deep two-handled jar <P11> of possible bunghole form in post-medieval fine redware (PMFR) and probably of 17th-century date (see Fig 36). The pot is unlikely to have served as a drainage device, as it was not associated with channels or slopes in the floors, and it would not have acted as a natural sump. A more intriguing interpretation is that, if baited, the pot and others like it set in the floor near doorways in Building 7 could have been used as mousetraps (Chapter 5.2).

Modifications to Building 7

Internal modifications and repairs to Building 7 took place during the late 16th or early 17th century, most of them similar to those executed in Building 6 to the south. Several of the wall faces of the Building 7 cellars were repaired and partly underpinned with brick. In the north cellar (room A) a substantial, hollow rectangular brick structure, measuring 2.20m x 0.45m, was added against the west wall to support an internal chimney stack and fireplaces on the upper floors (Fig 32; Fig 33). The broken remains of a large section of a fine late 16th-century fireplace mantelpiece in Reigate stone, carved with decorative foliage work, was found in the destruction debris in the cellar, close to its original position (Fig 35).

A<36>

Fig 35 Ornate fireplace mantelpiece in Reigate stone A<36> recovered from Great Fire debris in the cellar of Building 7 room A at Monument House (scale 1:10)

The fireplace mantelpiece, although in excellent condition, had no evidence for paintwork. In terms of the materials used and execution, the fireplace is entirely late medieval, but the decorative scheme employs Elizabethan and Jacobean elements such as cardwork flanking a central shield. The moulding continues this mixed theme and is essentially the same as the moulding employed in fireplaces in Sutton House, Hackney dated to *c* 1540 (Mark Samuel pers comm) and undated fireplaces from the site of the nunnery of St Mary Clerkenwell (Samuel in prep). The chief difference is the substitution of an ovolo for the double ogee of the minor order directly surrounding the opening, and the implication is that the Monument House fireplace is later than *c* 1540.

The angular arch opening is a variant on more common semi-elliptical forms and resembles a dated fireplace arch at Knole, Kent dated to *c* 1520. An example of the angular type has been excavated in London (Samuel 1997, 193). The Monument House fireplace is significantly later, and further underlines the conservative form of these fireplaces. The fragments would permit a complete reconstruction of the fireplace, with the exception of the bases of the jamb, although this has not been attempted here.

Red brick floors were laid throughout the cellars and incorporate Low Countries floor tiles, one dating to around 1480–1550. Each of the cellar floors incorporated at least one complete pot, set into and flush with the surface of the floor. The pot from room B floor A[147] is a squat, rounded two-handled jar in a slipped and green-glazed post-medieval redware (PMSRG), with thumbed neck. A virtually identical jar <P12> (Fig 36) was found set into the top of a well-made circular brick sump A[149] in room A (Fig 37). The sump housing the pot was 0.55m deep and had a brick base. The feature would clearly have been watertight and the majority of the sump below the pot was filled with fragmented mortar. This

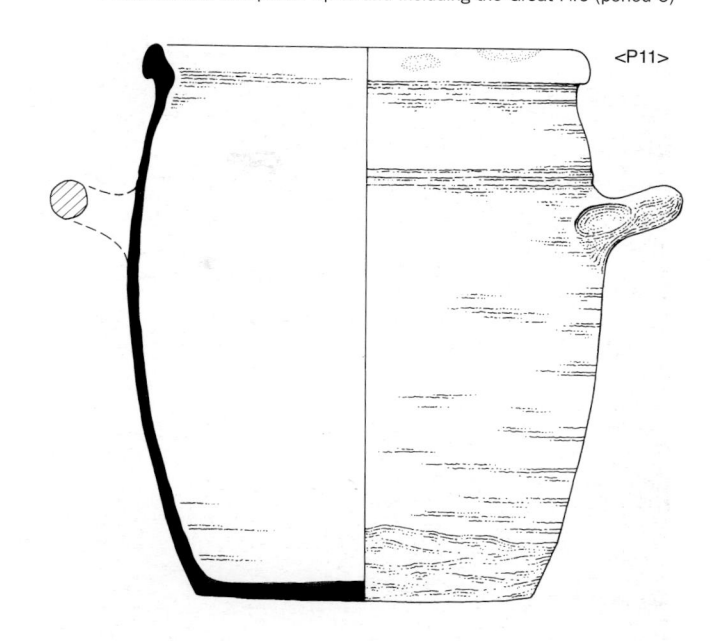

<P11>

<P12>

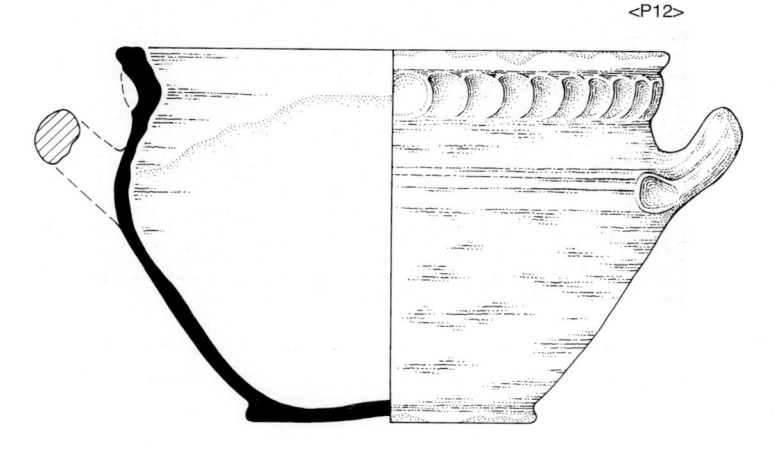

Fig 36 *Deep two-handled jar <P11> (fabric PMFR) and squat, rounded two-handled jar <P12> (fabric PMSRG) (scale 1:4)*

Fig 37 *Removing sunken pot <P12> from the sump in Building 7 room A; the fireplace surround lies to the left*

fill produced a small but distinctive group of animal bone derived from juvenile ox and sheep/goat, with fragments of smelt, eel and cod, together with the game species grey partridge, rabbit and snipe (*Gallinago gallinago*).

An internal staircase was inserted through the west wall of the south cellar (room B) to provide access to the external courtyard (OA7). The new staircase was immediately to the north of the stair leading into the rear of Building 6. Although only carbonised traces of the wooden stairs survived, the profile of the steps could be made out at the base of the brick stairwell wall, which was

constructed over it (Fig 38). The walls of the stairwell were of red brick but also incorporated plain unglazed Low Countries floor tiles dating to the late 16th century or the first half of the 17th century. The floor at the base of the staircase was composed of well-worn, squared limestone slabs, laid as a hardwearing surface in the area most vulnerable to damage from barrels and other heavy goods being loaded into the cellar. The window in the east wall of room B was bricked up at about this time (Fig 39) and may indicate that Building 7 was extended eastwards across the courtyard (OA8) and subsumed into the 'great tenement'.

Fig 38 *The remains of the staircase walls and limestone floor slabs in Building 7 room B at Monument House, looking south-west (0.5m scale); the wooden stairs were destroyed in the Great Fire*

Fig 39 *The blocked window in the east wall of Building 7 room B, looking east (0.2m scale)*

The Great Fire horizon

Destruction of the 'great tenement' in the fire; collapsed and redeposited debris (OA9)

The 'great tenement', incorporating Buildings 6 and 7, was destroyed in the Great Fire of 1666 and not rebuilt. The destruction debris (OA9) filling the interconnecting cellars of Building 7 produced a very large and diverse assemblage of finds. This includes the largest group of ironwork yet to be recovered from a Great Fire deposit. Most of the finds would probably have come from the collapsed upper floors of the building, and they provide a wealth of information regarding the decorative scheme and function of the overlying rooms.

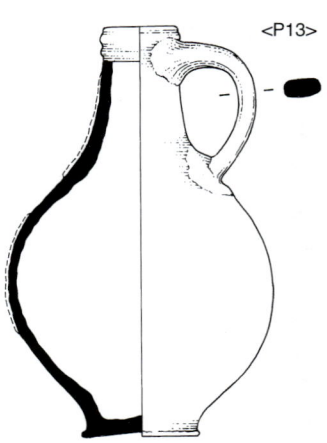

Fig 40 Frechen stoneware bottle with applied medallion dated 1645 <P13> (scale 1:4)

The pottery from the destruction debris A[104] in the north-eastern cellar (room A) comprises 18 sherds, most dated to c 1630–80 and including two sherds of Frechen stoneware (FREC), one sherd from the base of a bird pot, and burnt fragments of three tin-glazed dishes and a small ointment pot (TGW). The pottery from debris A[119] in the south-western cellar (room B) is very similar, but has a higher proportion of imports, with two Frechen stoneware Bartmann jugs and part of a tin-glazed fluted dish from Portugal. The local tin-glazed wares comprise two small ointment pots, and sherds from a drug jar, a chamber pot, a jar and three dishes. Also present are sherds from jars/pipkins and chamber pots in Surrey-Hampshire border whiteware (BORD), a slipped post-medieval redware dish (PMSR) and a post-medieval redware (PMR) pipkin handle. Of particular interest is a Frechen stoneware bottle with applied medallion showing a vase (probably of metal) containing flowers, which bears the date 1645 <P13> (Fig 40). The tin-glazed wares are all fire-damaged, providing clear evidence that they were in use at the time of the Great Fire.

The destruction debris filling the cellars also contained a large quantity of floor and wall tiles, as well as smaller quantities of peg roofing tile, brick and plaster mouldings. The earliest floor tiles are of lead-glazed medieval type and some of these may have originally paved the floor of St Botolph church. The later lead-glazed and plain floor tiles and those imported from Spain, Antwerp and the Netherlands are more likely to have formed internal decoration in Buildings 6 and 7 or other high-status buildings nearby. The same is true of the large numbers of early Dutch tin-glazed wall tiles present.

Finds recovered from the Great Fire debris

TILES

Ian M Betts

Tile fabric numbers referred to below follow a standard Museum of London fabric reference system; expanded descriptions are available from the archive.

Medieval

Penn (c 1350–90); fabrics 1810 and 2894
Four decorated tiles from the tilery at Penn in Buckinghamshire carried Eames (1980) designs 1803, 2037, 2118. In addition to the decorated examples there are nine tiles which have had their top surface removed through wear but were probably originally decorated.

Dieppe, France (late 14th–early 15th century); fabric 3241
Late 14th-century decorated floor tiles from northern France are known from fewer than a dozen sites in London. Work by Norton (1993, 85) has shown that these tiles were probably manufactured in the Dieppe area in the last quarter of the 14th century, although production may have extended into the early years of the 15th century. Of the six tiles from the site, four are

decorated while the remaining two are too worn to identify the design. The identified decorated tiles are Norton design numbers 32 and 53.

Glazed Low Countries floor tile (1300–c 1480); fabrics 1678 and 2504
Nine plain yellow, brown, green and greenish-brown glazed medieval Low Countries floor tiles were found. These have either four round nail holes, one in each corner, or five round nail holes, again one in each corner with an additional hole in the middle.

Post-medieval

Seville, Spain (c 1500–38); fabric 2292
Fourteen polychrome tin-glazed floor tiles of Spanish origin were recovered from the site. Such tiles are very rare in London, with the only other large group being recovered from the All Hallows church, Lombard Street. The Monument House examples are all of *arista* type, made by impressing a clay stamp to produce a series of shallow recesses separated by very narrow ridges (*arista*) in the tile blanks. These recesses could then be filled with coloured lead glazes and white tin glaze. The tiles were fired horizontally, separated by three small clay lumps which leave indentations marring the tile surface (Ray 2000, 309). Such marks are present on some fragments, which are decorated in blue, white, green, purple and yellowish-brown coloured glazes. Many are blackened as a result of intense heating in the Great Fire of 1666.

Design <T1> shows a stylised flower-head set within a decorative lozenge border, dated to c 1500–38 (Fig 41). This was one of the designs invented by Niculoso Francisco, an Italian potter who arrived in Seville shortly before 1500 (Ray 2000, 357). There are at least two different stamps with this design, one illustrated in Ray (2000, 369, no. 917), which is also known from All Hallows church (MoL 15646), and the other on the tiles from Monument House. The end shape of the smaller petals is different on the stamp used to make the Monument House tiles.

Design <T2> has an angular interlace of Moorish design (Fig 41). It is not in Ray's recent publication on Spanish tiles and pottery (2000), but he does illustrate a border tile with a similar pattern from Seville, dated c 1520–50.

Antwerp, Belgium (mid 16th century); fabrics: variants of 1819 and 3067
Two early tin-glazed tiles came from the debris. The first, <T3>, painted in blue, yellow and brown on white, has a cherub head in a repeating circular pattern (Fig 42), while the other seems to have a blue-on-white geometrical pattern, although it is badly worn. The latter has a manufacturing mark, either a number or letter, in blue on the base. Neither design has been found on any other London tile. Their size and thickness suggest an Antwerp origin, as would the decoration. The cherub-head tile shows marked similarity to a mid 16th-century tile from Antwerp (Fries Museum 1971, 79, cat. 128).

Fig 41 Early 16th-century Spanish floor tiles <T1> (A[+] A<361> and A[119] A<63>) and <T2> (A[107] A<57>) (scale 1:2)

Fig 42 Mid 16th-century Antwerp floor tile <T3> (A[104] A<119>) (scale 1:2)

London (early to mid 17th century); fabrics 1819, 2196, 2197, 3064, 3067 and 3079

Five different designs are present on 35 tin-glazed floor tiles, including one in both blue on white and polychrome, <T4>–<T12> (Fig 43). The tiles are a curious mixture: some are very worn, some totally unworn; and others are blackened as a result of the Great Fire, suggesting that they came from different floors or different areas of the same floor. The tiles were clearly laid in groups of four to produce an intricate repeating pattern of flowers, fruit and various geometric shapes.

Design 1: Quadrant tile with one quarter of 'Tudor rose' surrounded by strapwork pattern in blue on white <T4> and polychrome (similar to Noël Hume 1977, 57, fig II, nos 1–2; Britton 1987, 175, no.196). Two polychrome versions are present, one with the flower petals and other areas in orange and yellow (six tiles) <T5> and one with the same areas in brown and yellow (one tile) <T6>. Many tiles show little or no wear.

Design 2: Quadrant tile with the so-called 'star and tulip' design in blue on white <T7>. Many tiles have been blackened in the Great Fire (similar to Noël Hume 1977, 57, fig II, no. 3).

Design 3: So-called 'star' design in blue on white <T8> (for polychrome version see Noël Hume 1977, 57, fig II, no. 5).

Design 4: Floral design with fruit, flowers and leaves in polychrome <T9>.

Design 5: Quadrant tile with one quarter of a star pattern with grapes, fruit and cone shape. Two versions are present, <T10> and <T11>, one of which is very similar to that published by Horne (1989, 14, no. 4). All four tiles with this design show marked wear. Tiles of this design from other London sites, including Billingsgate (BIG82), differ in certain details from the Monument House examples.

Most common is the so-called 'Tudor rose' design which was

<T4>
<T5>
<T6>
<T7>
<T8>

Fig 43 Early to mid 17th-century London floor tiles: <T4> (A[104] A<37>), <T5> (A[104] A<128>), <T6> (A[104] A<53>), <T7> (A[104] A<39>), <T8> (A[119] A<75>), <T9> (A[104] A<52>), <T10> (A[104] A<43>), <T11> (A[104] A<122>) and <T12> (A[104] A<55>) (scale 1:2)

<T9>

<T10>

<T11>

<T12>

Fig 43 (cont)

one of the most popular tile patterns used in London buildings during the late 15th and the first half of the 16th century. Tiles of this type were made at the delftware factories situated at Aldgate, Pickleherring and at Platform Wharf, Rotherhithe. The 'star and tulip' and 'star' designs are also known from both Pickleherring and Platform Wharf, while the 'fruit and flower' design was painted on tiles made at Pickleherring. The most likely source of the Monument House tiles is the delftware factory at Pickleherring established around 1618, although tiles with the same designs were also made in the Netherlands and a Dutch origin cannot entirely be discounted.

Particularly notable is a fragment of polychrome tile with a blurred and partially blackened 'Tudor rose' design <T12>. This blackening is a defect caused during firing and, remarkably, orange paint was applied after the tile had been fired, either because the colour was accidentally omitted by the tile painter or it was thought necessary to improve the appearance of a poorly made product. The paint shows no sign of wear, so it seems unlikely that the tile was ever actually set into a floor. The

addition of paint to the upper surface of a delftware tile after firing is unknown on any other delftware tiles from London.

Dutch (c 1630–66); fabrics 3064, 3078 and 3254
Forty-two Dutch tin-glazed wall tiles are present in the Great Fire debris, all but one of which are painted in blue on white, <T13>–<T18> (Fig 44). A number of tiles have been badly blackened, the result of the Great Fire.

There are four main groupings of Dutch wall tiles, although a variety of individual designs are present within each group:

Soldiers on horseback and barred ox-head corners: 26 tiles. Similar to Pluis 1997, 356, A.02.07.03 dated c 1635–60; <T13>, <T14>.

Warships and barred ox-head corners: 5 tiles. Similar to van Dam 1991, 80, no. 89 dated c 1645–75; <T15>.

Water nymph riding a fish with barred ox-head corners: 2 tiles.

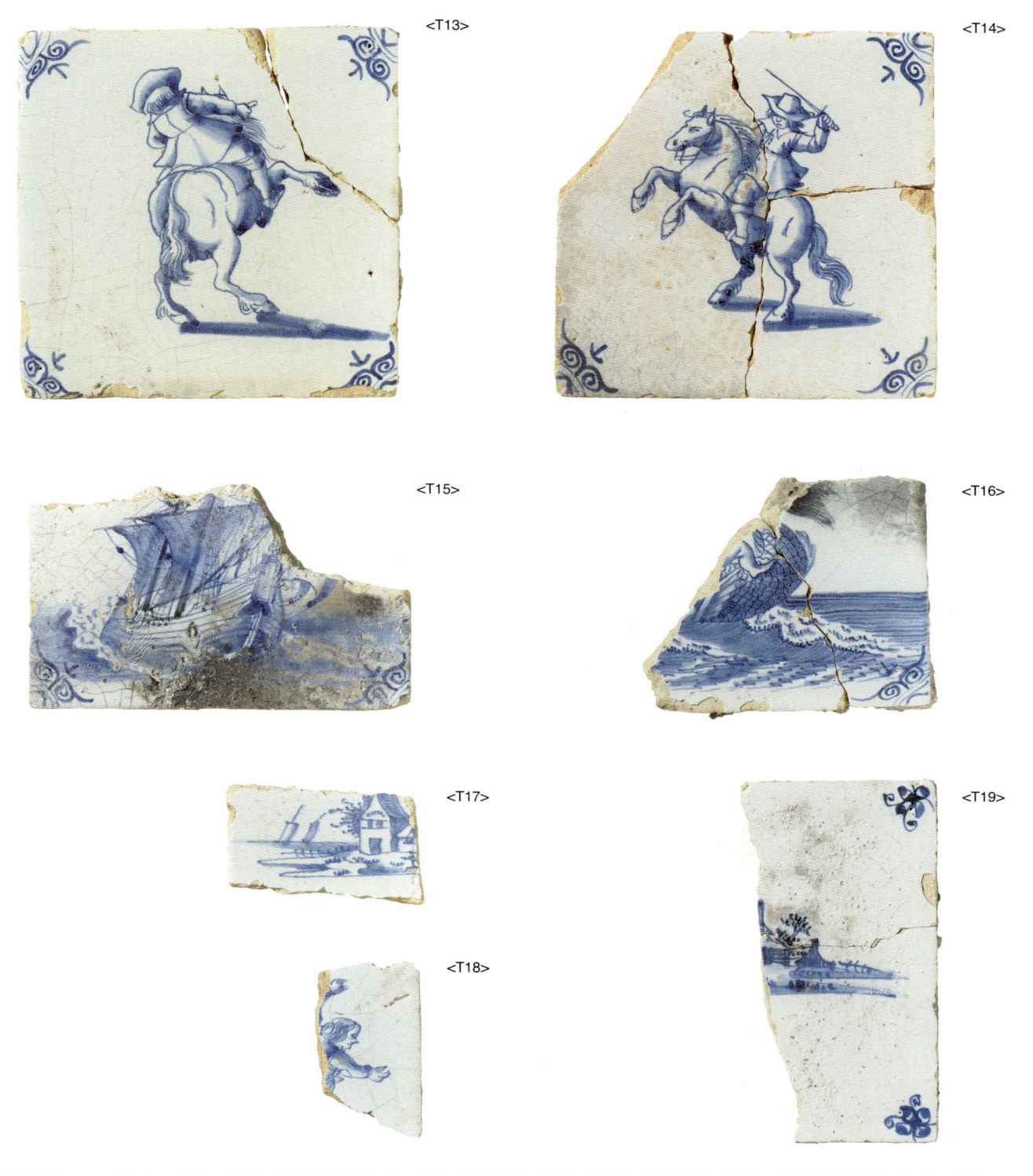

<T13>

<T14>

<T15>

<T16>

<T17>

<T19>

<T18>

Fig 44 Mid 16th-century Dutch wall tiles <T13> (A[104] A<85>), <T14> (A[104] A<86>), <T15> (A[104] A<80>), <T16> A[119] A<68>), <T17> (A[119] A<71>), <T18> (A[2] A<15>) and <T19> (A[123] A<106>) (scale 1:2)

Similar to van Dam 1991, 81, no. 93 dated c 1650–80; <T16>. Landscape scenes and spider-head corners: 2 tiles. Similar to van Dam 1991, 79, no. 88 dated c 1660–1700. These are slightly thinner (8–9mm) than the other tiles present (9–11mm), suggesting they arrived in London slightly later. The date given by van Dam implies they arrived just prior to the Great Fire. <T17>.

Only two other tiles can be identified: part of a figure with

outstretched arms <T18> and a badly blackened tile in purple and blue on white. Purple was not used on Dutch wall tiles until around 1650 (Pluis 1997, 103).

Other pre-Great Fire, Dutch tin-glazed wall tiles were residual finds in period 7 Building 8 and included another landscape tile <T19>.

The Dutch wall tiles from the Great Fire debris are highly

significant as very few from London can be securely dated to before 1666. The earliest documentary reference to the import of Dutch tiles is the account of Sir William Brereton, who in 1634/5 bought matching pairs of soldiers and horsemen (perhaps similar to those at Monument House) and other tiles from a pottery dealer in Amsterdam to decorate his house in England (Ray 1973, 59). The only other major group of pre-Great Fire wall tiles was found at the adjacent site of Billingsgate (Betts 1991) and these were also decorated with mounted soldiers, suggesting that they came from the same building.

Low Countries (c 1580–1666); fabric 3092
One complete, unglazed Low Countries tile was recovered from the debris, with nail holes in two diagonally opposite corners.

Intrusive tiles (18th century)
Eight fragments of 18th-century landscape and biblical tiles in blue on white and purple on white were recovered from contexts A[6] and A[119] but were clearly intrusive. All are probably of London origin with the exception of one tile with a spider-head corner, which may be Dutch.

THE PLASTER MOULDINGS

Terence P Smith

Twenty plaster mouldings were recovered from the fire debris, some very fragmentary but the largest 150mm long (Fig 45). Where the full depth is preserved it is some 50mm, corresponding to an imperial measurement of 2in. The plaster is fairly coarse and off-white in colour, presumably the traditional mix of sand and lime. Organic impressions visible under magnification represent fibrous material added as a binder. The mouldings are consistent, comprising a frontal bead flanked on each side by a plain chamfer and a further bead. At least two (possibly three) pieces show a slight curve <WP1>;

another shows two slight curves (or possibly one curve and one straight run) meeting at an angle of 90° <WP2> and two further pieces show straight runs meeting at an obtuse angle of 135° <WP3>. Drag marks, caused by the template used to form the mouldings, are clearly visible and white paint is present, but no trace of other colours or of gilding. The paint is crazed and scorched from the fire.

The pieces derive from a moulded plaster ceiling which would have included curves (perhaps full circles), as well as straight-sided and curved-sided polygons. Most of the pieces show on their rear faces the impressions of the ceiling laths to which the plaster was applied, some preserving the grain of the wood. The laths were between 30 and 35mm wide, thus narrower than the minimum of 2in ($\approx$ 50mm) laid down by an assize of 1528 (Salzman 1967, 240) and less even than the $1^{1/2}$in ($\approx$ 38mm) mentioned by Richard Neve in the early 18th century (Neve 1726, 181; Neve notes, however, that 'they are commonly less, and are seldom exact'). The laths would have been of riven oak.

The creation of decorative plasterwork, external (pargeting) as well as internal, became an important craft during the Tudor period. Its application to ceilings remained an especially English craft and Neve's early 18th-century observation was no less true of the Tudor period: 'plaister'd Ceilings are much used in *England*, beyond all other Countreys' (Neve 1726, 101; cf Gotch 1914, 196). In the City of London the 'Guild or Fraternity of … Pargettors …, commonly called Plaisterers' was incorporated by a charter of 10 March 1501, and its first Hall was set up in 1556 in a house (subsequently destroyed in the Great Fire) in Addle Street given for the purpose by William Elder, himself a plasterer; the Guild (or Company) was granted corporate arms on 20 January 1546 (Melling 1995, 87; Bromley 1960, 201).

The mouldings are essentially Gothic in form and the ceiling dates from the later Tudor (Elizabethan) period. The mouldings have a superficial resemblance to stone vault ribs,

<WP1> <WP2> <WP3>

Fig 45 Late Tudor decorative ceiling plaster from Great Fire debris A[119] in Open Area 9: <WP1>–<WP3> (scale 1:2)

and some have seen in this a direct relationship between the two forms (Musson 2000, 14). But the mouldings, and the type of ceiling in which they were used, derive from prototypes in wood (Gotch 1914, 197; Lloyd 1949, 79, 422). With its combination of straight and curved runs, intersecting at various angles, the ceiling probably resembled that of 1580 in the Great Hall at Plas Mawr, Conway (Conwy), Wales (Musson 2000, 14). Such work indicates a degree of sophistication and status, although it falls short of the finest, and more classically inspired, plasterwork of the period, represented in London in, for example, the late 16th-century ceilings at Canonbury Tower, Islington (Godfrey 1962, 151 and pl 43a).

ACCESSIONED FINDS

Geoff Egan

Much of the mid 17th-century assemblage of more than 200 accessioned items, mainly from A[104] and A[119] and principally ironwork, has been damaged by exposure to great heat. This has resulted in many items becoming very brittle, rendering both cleaning and definition extremely difficult, as several of the objects most severely affected had fused together. Comments below are in many cases based on information derived from X-ray plates. At least one area seems not to have been seriously affected by heat, as evidenced by glass wine bottles completely lacking even surface signs of alteration and a lead token that at least retains its shape, all from A[119].

The ironware includes several identical or closely similar items, some in different sizes. Seriation is most evident in the locks, of which there are 22 or 23, and the round grids, of which there are 6. The wider group includes several large-scale items that have not previously been recognised among contemporary excavated material. As a whole, the assemblage is markedly different from any other published domestic group. A few items may not have been fully finished, most obviously some of the lengths of strapping, raising the possibility that some were in store for a smithy. These aside, the present finds are most readily explained as comprising the stock of an ironmonger or hardware retailer, along with a few objects from his household. Several of the fixtures retain nails for attachment, showing they had been used. Some could have come from the building that was consumed in the Fire. The knives, too, may well be domestic, like the glass wine bottles, while a rapier and armour fragment may also be household goods rather than commercial stock. It is notable that none of the objects listed seems to have a tin or similar coating – perhaps this was a fashion that had largely become outmoded by this date.

At first sight, perhaps the most readily comparable archaeological assemblage, in that it features extensive, large-scale ironwork and also came through a fire, is a domestic group from one of the properties burnt in the 1507 fire at Pottergate in Norwich (Norfolk) (Goodall 1993). At a detailed level, however, it soon becomes clear that there is little direct correspondence item-by-item between the equipment of the single kitchen there and the present retail stock, beyond the scale of the largest items recovered. The chronological gap of one and a half centuries is arguably less significant, since material culture of several relevant categories perhaps saw relatively few changes over this period. Despite the number of excavations of deposits from the 1666 London Fire, no similar finds group has been traced, and several of the items in this present assemblage appear to be unique survivals, in scale at least.

The following catalogue includes all the illustrated items and selected references to other finds from the assemblage.

Structural ironwork

<S7> Window catch (Fig 46)
A[104], A<155>
Moulded strut, L 141mm, with ornate trefoil terminal; doubled-bar spring latch and oval swivel (35mm x 43mm) attached; still in place on window-frame strip, surviving L 225mm, W 24mm and with four countersunk holes for attachment. Cf Alcock and Hall 1994, 33 for similar sprung catches in buildings dated between 1594 and 1699, and ibid, 28 for ?door latches in Surrey buildings dated 1616 and 1687.

Iron security equipment

There are ?4 mounted locks, at least 16 large padlocks (12 D-shaped, 2 heart-shaped, ?2 rectangular) and 1 small padlock, and 13 keys. Only those illustrated are described here. Where it is possible to say, all the padlocks have a rectangular, swivelling cover for the key aperture, a U-shaped hasp, and they were discarded unlocked. Two appear from X-ray plates to have had the keys still in place when they were burnt. In the case of keys measurements for the bit include the adjoining stem, for comparison with dimensions given for the length of padlock-key apertures.

<S8> Mounted lock (Fig 47)
A[119], A<164>
Plate, 100mm x 82mm, with key aperture (L 23mm) and two concentric key-ward arcs: bolt, retaining frame, etc. of mechanism survive, along with ? displaced holding device for setting in unlocked position (unless this is a separate item fortuitously adhering).

<S9> Mounted lock (Fig 47)
A[104], A<153>
Obscured by corrosion products: rectangular back sheet, 250mm x 150mm; smaller plate, 123mm x 90mm, with ornate ends, apparently secured by two sets of paired rivets; robust bolt (horizontal) apparently governed by a large spring (?incomplete) with a curved top and ? set against a vertical, fixed tab (perhaps allowing the bolt to be set unlocked by hand from the inside); key aperture, L 35mm, with provision for lateral flanges and two concentric-arc wards; (with fragments). ?For a door (? sprung for self-closure) – the decorative elements would presumably be visible (and to some extent the complexity of the mechanism appreciated) from the inside of the building or room.

<S10> D-shaped padlock case (Fig 48)
A[119], A<138>
Complete case 76mm x 72mm, Th 23mm; key aperture L 23mm and catering for lateral flange (though X-ray plate suggests bit of key L 19mm and lacking any lateral tab is inserted); hasp span 65mm, H of arc 35mm (Th of locking end 4mm).

<S11> Shield-shaped padlock case (Fig 48)
A[119], A<160A>
(Described from X-ray plate): complete, including mechanism (case angled at base): 75mm x 85xmm; aperture for key L

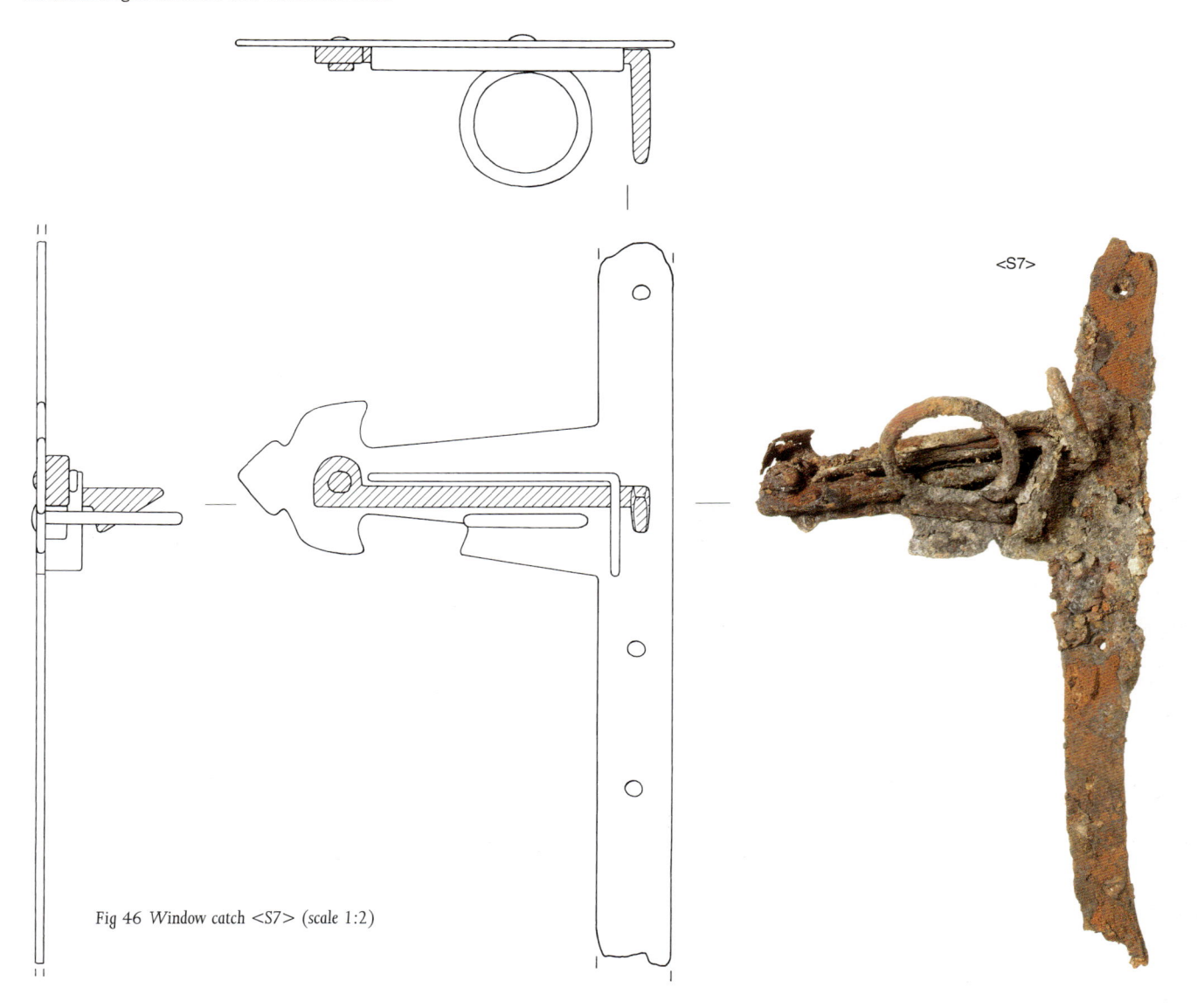

Fig 46 Window catch <S7> (scale 1:2)

Fig 47 Mounted locks <S8> and <S9> (scale 1:2)

<S10>

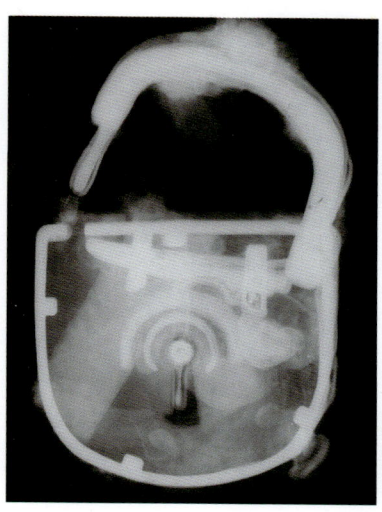

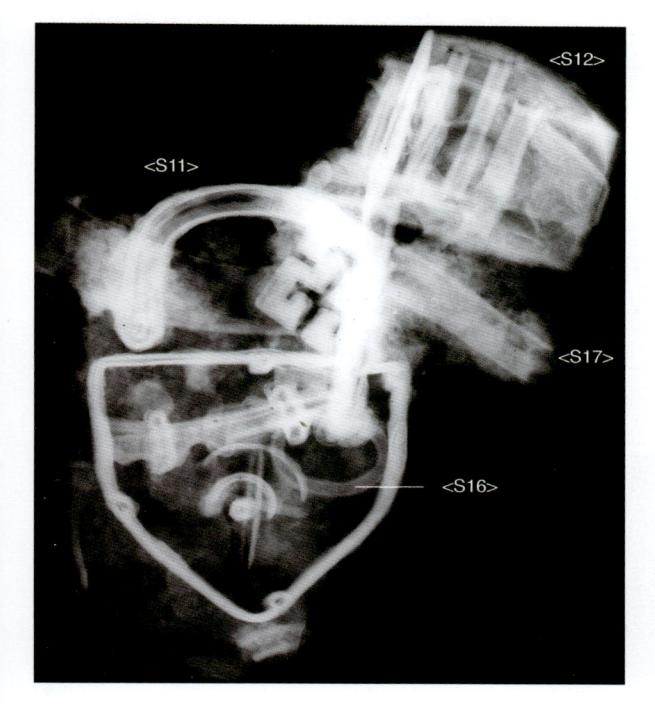
<S12>
<S11>
<S17>
<S16>

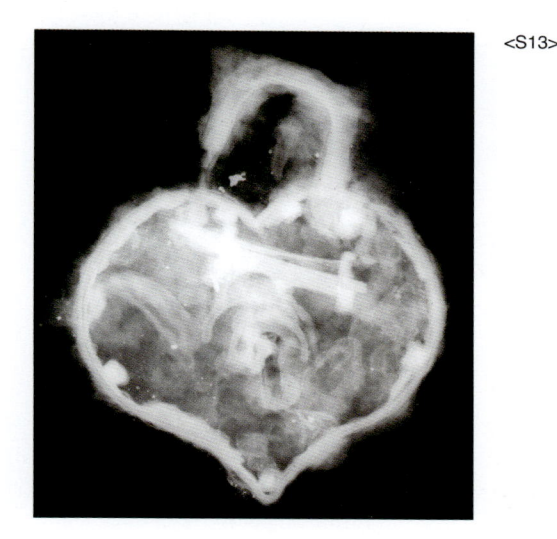
<S13>

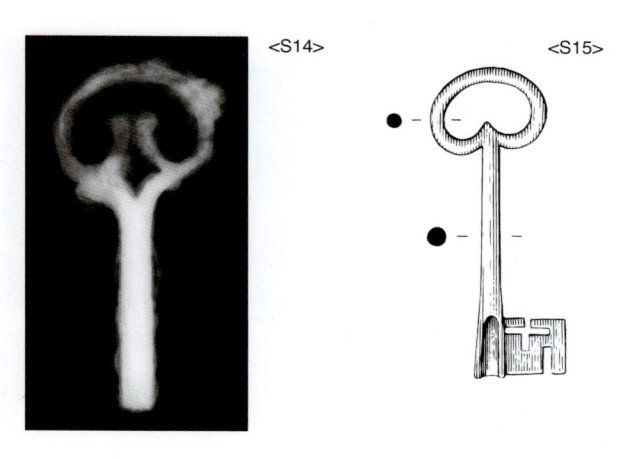
<S14>
<S15>

27mm, with lateral flanges; (surface details obscured).

<S12> Rectangular/square padlock case (Fig 48)
A[119], A<160C>
60mm x 45mm, with half-heart section, Th 33mm; X-ray plate shows ?strengthening bars horizontally and vertically (hasp broken off). This form was designed to be set closely against the edge of a chest (see Jenning 1974, 6 and pl 9 for six examples surviving on the lid of the late 17th-century 'million bank' (ie lottery) chest in the Public Record Office).

<S13> Heart-shaped padlock case (Fig 48)

A[119], A<144>
Complete case c 97mm x 85mm, Th 23mm; key aperture ?L c 20mm; ?mechanism and hasp complete, span c 70mm, H of arc 35mm.

<S14> Key (Fig 48)
A[119], A<186>
Ornate, oval bow, 37mm x 33 mm, with opposed, recurved internal terminals; surviving L of stem 50mm; (bit missing).

<S15> Key (Fig 48)
A[119], A<265>
Incomplete; ?oval bow; L of hollow stem 78mm; elaborate bit L 22mm.

<S16> Key (Fig 48)
A[119], A<160D>

Fig 48 Padlock cases and keys: case <S10>; cases <S11> and <S12> with associated keys <S16> and <S17>; case <S13>; keys <S14> and <S15> (scale 1:2)

Overall L 82mm; oval bow 31mm x 22mm; bit has cruciform cut-out.

<S17> Key (Fig 48)
A[119], A<160E>

Incomplete stem and symmetrical bit 35mm x 28mm from large key, surviving L 75mm – the only one recovered compatible in size with the larger padlocks in the assemblage.

<S18> Sliding bolt for lock
(Fig 49)
A[104], A<154>
Details obscured by corrosion:
round-section bolt, Diam 16mm,
with right angles, overall L
c 250mm and with lateral handle;
at least one of the original two
staples holds it to a rectangular
plate, 187mm x 65mm

<S19> Drop handle (Fig 49)
A[104], A<196>
Robust ? drop handle, with
angled profile, resembling the
form of a jew's harp, with a
central constriction; L 75mm, W
53mm. Cf Alcock and Hall 1994,
27 for several similar but not

identical versions from buildings
dated to the 17th century.

<S20> Ornate strapping (Fig 49)
A[104], A<195>
Robust bar, L 72mm, tapering from
23mm to 10mm, with thick end,
one plain and one ornate (fleur-de-
lis style); robust handle, L 43mm,
at right angle, with ball terminal; a
bent, looped staple through the
attachment hole in the fleur retains
part of a slightly domed, ornate
sheet quatrefoil, 45mm x ?45mm,
with a hole for attachment in each
leaf. The splayed ends of the staple
obscure part of the robust decorative
terminal, which is likely to have
been designed to be nailed in place.

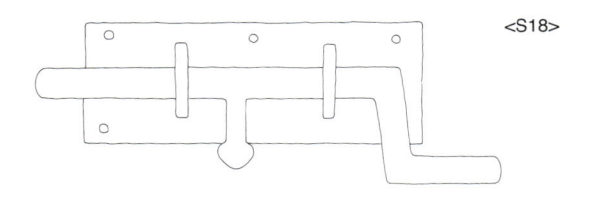

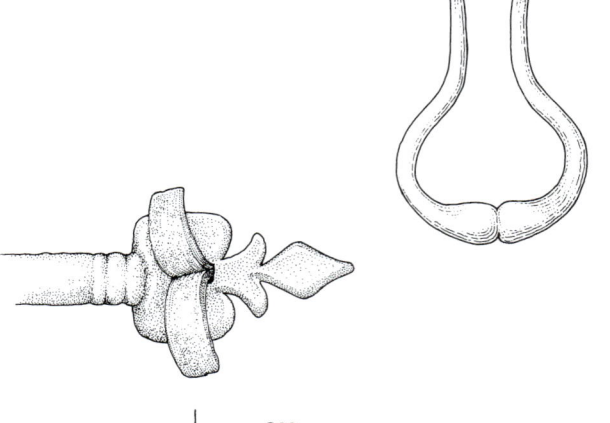

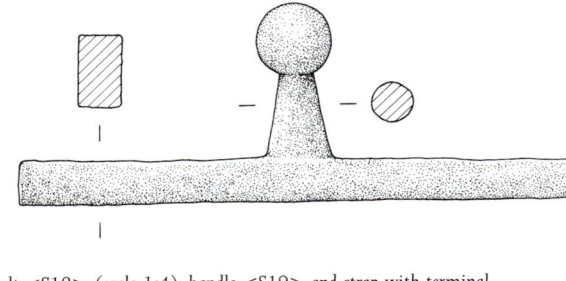

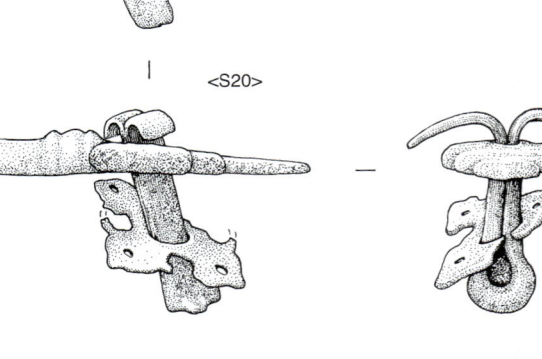

Fig 49 Sliding bolt <S18> (scale 1:4), handle <S19> and strap with terminal <S20> (scale 1:2)

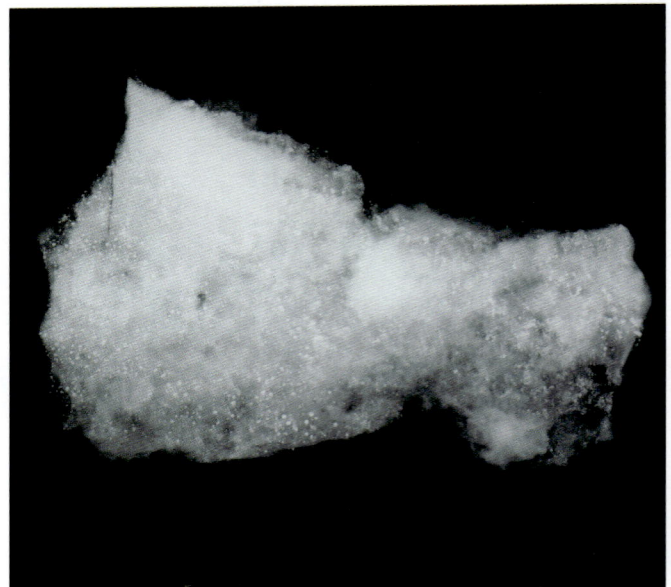

Fig 50 Cast-iron vessel <S21> (scale approx 1:2)

Iron vessel

<S21> ?Cooking vessel (Fig 50)
A[7], A<2>
?Cast, ?vertical walling fragment,
Diam c 250mm. A very rare
instance from excavated material
of a domestic object from before

c 1700 even provisionally
identified as cast iron. (Seymour
Lindsay includes three cast-iron
tripod vessels in Scotland,
which are claimed to be of
15th-century date, but the

basis for this is unclear; 1970,
nos 113–15. Aside from
occasional cannon barrels and
decorative firebacks, few other
excavated cast-iron objects
this early have been traced in
print: there are fragments of

tripod cooking vessels from
Norwich (Norfolk) (Goodall
1993, 94–5 nos 562–5) and
another fragment from
Newcastle (Northumberland)
(Whittingham 1983, 200–1
no. 115).)

Iron footwear

<S22> Patten (Fig 51)
A[119], A<170>, A<177> and
A<220>
For wearing as overshoes to keep
the feet up, out of mud:
fragments of wavy form,

?comprising original pair: the first
two constitute a single patten,
c 170mm x 100mm, and the last
about a half; the wooden
platforms are missing. Cf Grew
1984, 106–7 nos 57–8.

Iron domestic equipment

<S23> Round grate (Fig 52)
A[119], A<260>
With closely spaced, parallel bars
– ? for retaining fuel in a hearth.
Corroded: Diam 133mm; six bars
survive of seven, including central,
thicker one with hole in middle.

Several different sizes are
represented among the round
grates recovered, including:
A<238A> Diam 125mm;

A<171> Diam 140mm with four
of original five bars surviving;
A<163A> Dia 183mm with five
of original ?seven bars surviving;
and A<249> Diam estimated
c 250mm with seven bars, each
with two holes.

<S24> Waffle tongs (Fig 53)
A[119], A<269>
Pair of robust rectangular blocks,

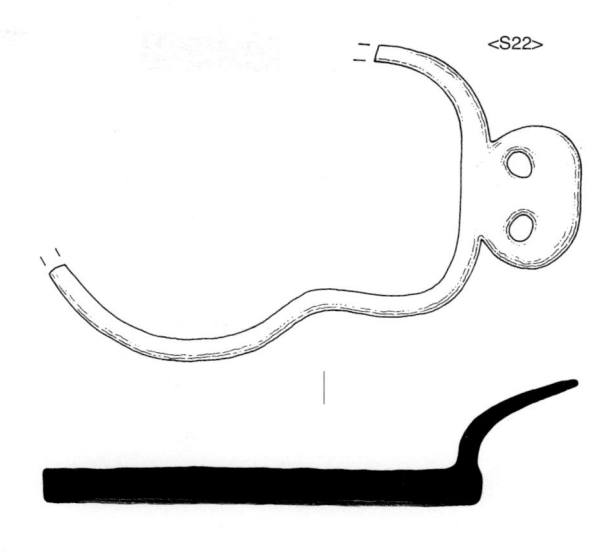

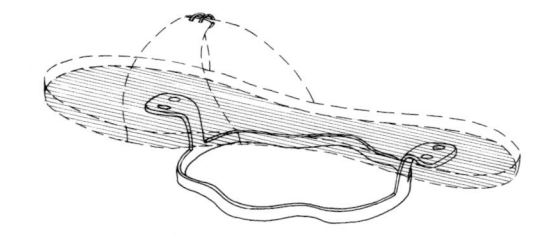

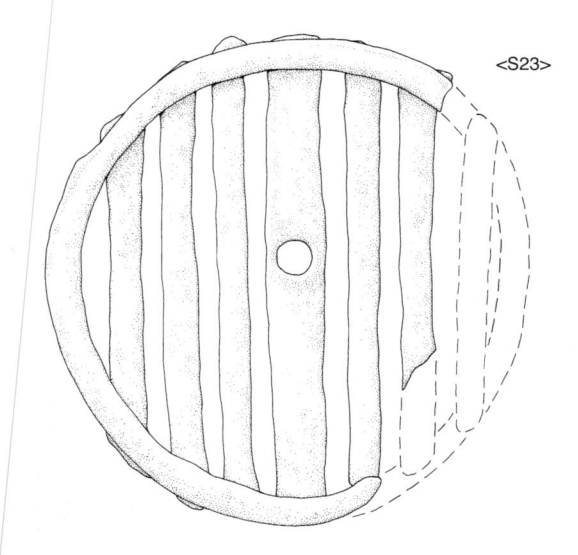

Fig 52 Round grate <S23> (scale 1:2)

Fig 51 Patten <S22> (scale 1:2) and reconstruction showing use

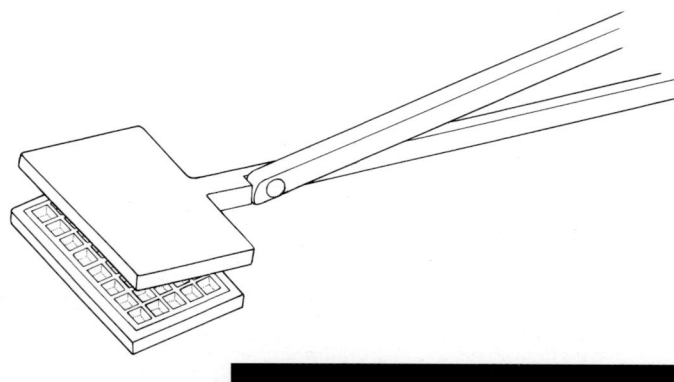

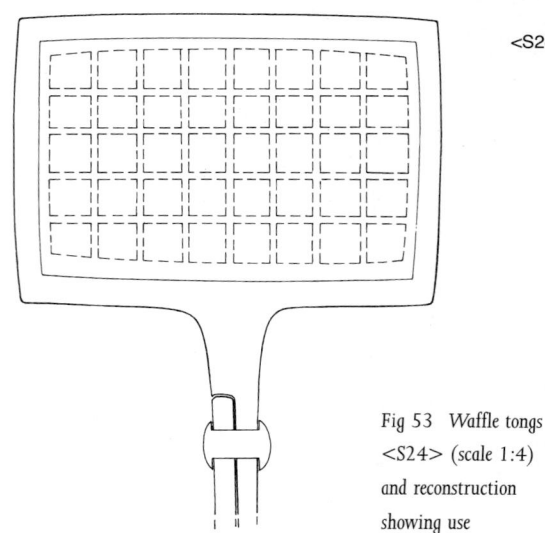

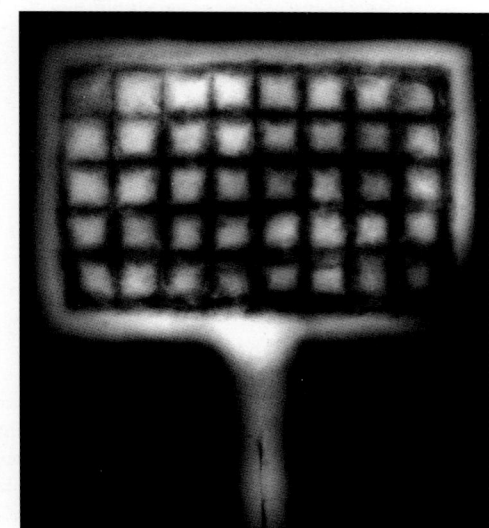

Fig 53 Waffle tongs
<S24> (scale 1:4)
and reconstruction
showing use

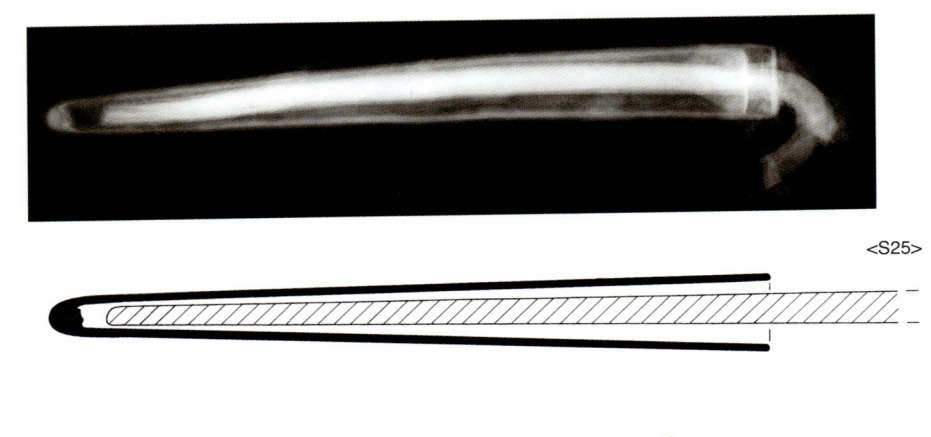

<S25>

Fig 54 *Goffering iron <S25> (scale 1:2) and reconstruction with straight handle*

230mm x 159mm, Th 48mm together, with 5 x 8 grid internally (shown in X-ray); incomplete, bipartite pivoting handle centrally at a right angle, surviving L *c* 130mm; Wt of surviving parts (including corrosion products) almost 8.5kg. A number of early tongs for making decorated wafers survive (eg Seymour Lindsay illustrates some round versions; 1970, nos 148–9), but these are far less robust than the present item for the familiar, much deeper, plain products. The heaviness of the excavated tongs is to be explained partly by the thickness of the product and perhaps by a need to retain heat in the greater mass for multiple production. It must, nevertheless, have been feasible only for a very strong operator to use this industrial-scale implement satisfactorily.

<S25> Goffering iron (Fig 54)
A[119], A<239B>
These (commonly used in pairs) were heated and applied to linen ruffs/collars to make rounded folds: sheath, L 190mm, tapers from 20mm to 10mm; incomplete heating iron within the former, L 189mm, W 9mm, and is broken off at ?U-shaped bend (if not distorted) to missing ?handle. Cf Seymour Lindsey 1970, 36 and see nos 192–5 and 198–201, for different forms.

<S26> Iron and bone rod for ?knife (Fig 55)
A[119], A<130>
Bone (heat-altered) and iron, the latter part incomplete: multifaceted bone rod, surviving L 87mm, Diam 6mm, with pointed end defined by collar with cable decoration; set in forked stub of iron. The used end may have been in the missing iron part (? a specialised knife).

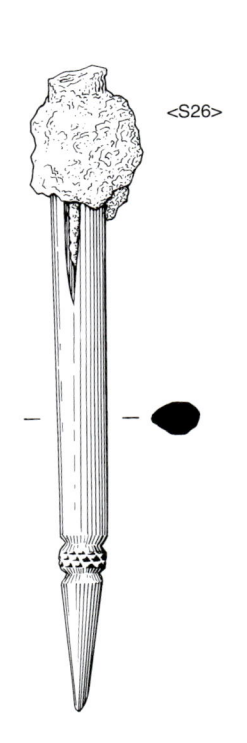

<S26>

Fig 55 Bone and iron
tool <S26> (scale 1:1)

Iron military equipment

<S27> Rapier (Fig 56)
A[119], A<161>
Double-edged blade, W tapering from 18mm to 16mm, is incomplete: surviving L 490mm; pommel, Diam 35mm; double-shell cup hand guard, *c* 110mm x 85mm; stubs of quillions survive (rest of quillions, knuckle guard, and grip missing). A second 125mm length of blade, W 18mm, would seem to be all that is recognisable from another

weapon (unless the distinct widths are a product of differential corrosion). Cf Valentine 1968, 46 no. 34 (German or possibly English, *c* 1640).

Sheet sexfoil (not illustrated)
A[119], A<166C>
Sheet sexfoil, apparently held to fragments of plate by a screw, is probably from armour (described from X-ray plate).

<S27>

Fig 56 *Rapier <S27> (scale 1:2)*

Other items

<S28> Iron ?lid (Fig 57)
A[119], A<268>
Robust, flat, ? oval lid, *c* 250mm x
465mm (none of original edge
survives; other details from X-ray
plate), incomplete handle, Diam
17mm, L *c* 80mm, W 12mm,
with two right angles and broken
off at collar; A<232> appears to
be other part of the handle, H
c 100mm.

<S29> Glass wine bottle (Fig 58)
A[119], A<146>
Neck fragment with seal: mitre,
.. P to sides. This seal is known
from several finds (more than
one mould), which show that

the missing initial was W. An
earlier suggestion that these were
seals of a bishop has been
abandoned in favour of
identification with William Pagett
or William Proctor, each of whom
was a mid 17th-century
proprietor of a Mitre Tavern, the
latter in Wood Street (Dumbrell
1992, 179 pl 80, and 296). A
further example has been found
at the site of a glasshouse in
Vauxhall, perhaps the place of
production of these particular
bottles (Tyler and Willmott
2005). Another bottle seal with
the initials HV A<145> was also
found in A[119].

<S29>

Fig 58 Glass wine bottle seal showing a
mitre and the initial 'P' <S29> (scale 1:1.5)

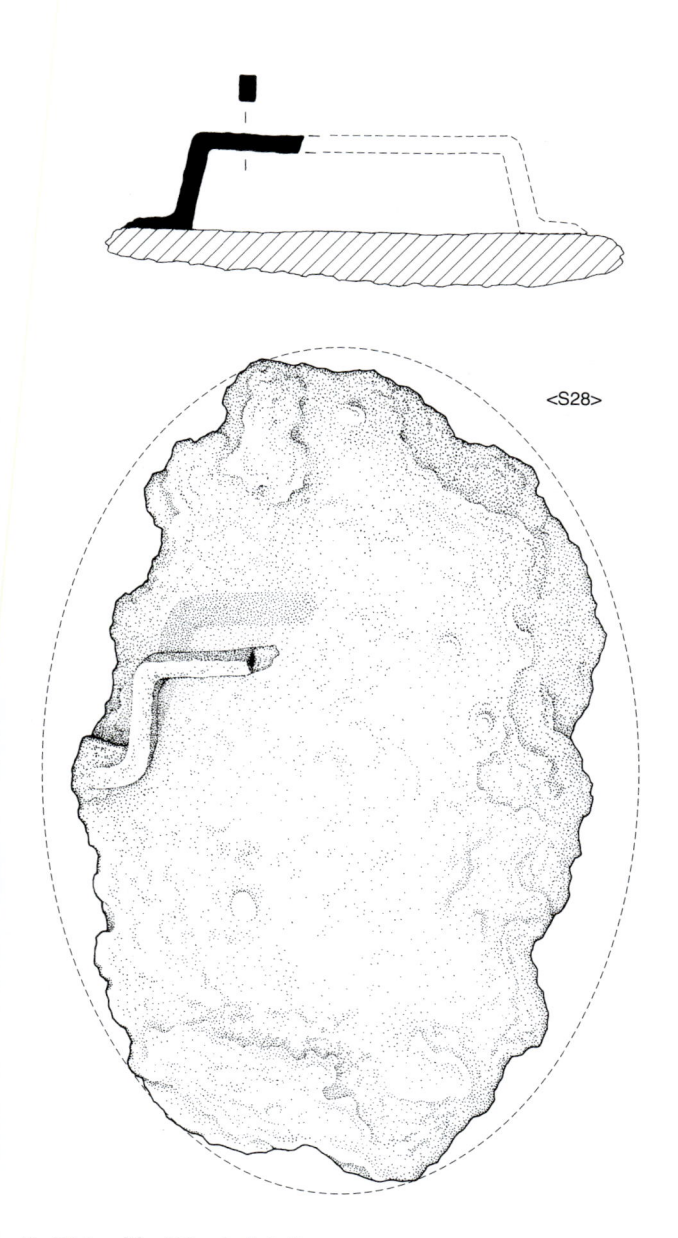

<S28>

Fig 57 Iron lid <S28> (scale 1:4)

CLAY TOBACCO PIPES

Jacqui Pearce

An important group of clay pipes was found in the Great Fire
debris A[104] and A[119]. The two contexts include 27 bowls
of type AO15 in Atkinson and Oswald's 1969 typology of
London clay pipes (here referred to as AO types), with three
pipes that can be reconstructed as complete from A[104]
<S30> (Fig 59). In addition, there is one type AO13 pipe and
one AO18 pipe bowl in context A[119]. All three types date to
the period *c* 1660–80. A total of 16 mouthpieces and 50 stem
fragments (apart from the reconstructed pipes) were also found
in the group. The pipes from A[119] do not cross-join with any
from A[104] and appear to be more abraded.

Of the 27 pipe bowls from context A[104], 7, including the
3 complete pipes, are encrusted with a powdery, whitish
material, which appears to be burnt clay. Of the 23 stem
fragments, 16 also have similar encrustation. All these pipes are
distinctly pink in section, although with the usual white
surfaces, and appear not to have been fired satisfactorily or
completely. It is possible that they were used as reinforcement
within the muffle of a clay pipe kiln, which often disintegrates
in the ground. If so, this would indicate that pipe manufacture
took place on the site.

Two of the three complete pipes in context A[104] come
from the same mould (called 'Mould A' here). As well as these
complete pipes, there are six more type AO15 pipes comprising
between two and four joining fragments, and two of these also
come from Mould A, as do a further three of the remaining
seven AO15 bowls (including two spur fragments). Four pipes
from context A[104] appear to have been made in a second,
different mould (Mould B).

There are 11 complete AO15 pipe bowls in context A[119]
and one spur, but none of these appears to have been made in
either of the moulds recognised on the site. One of these pipes
can be reconstructed from three fragments as almost complete.

A<438>

A<437>

A<436>

Fig 59 Complete clay pipes <S30> (from top to bottom: A<438>, A<437> and A<436>) dated to c 1660–80 (scale 1:2)

Only one of the other 20 type AO15 pipes from the site could be matched with either of the moulds. The large number of joining fragments and mouthpieces, 14 in A[104] and 2 in A[119], suggest that the pipes were broken *in situ* at or near the time of the Great Fire. Many have been burnt but very few were smoked, suggesting manufacture on site, although several of the AO15 pipes from other contexts had been used.

Complete pipes are very rare in excavated material and only about 20 examples dating to *c* 1660–80 are known, most of them from London (David Higgins pers comm). Their stem lengths, measured from the back of the heel or spur, nearest the smoker, to the mouthpiece, range from 250mm to 330mm. The stems of the Monument House pipes measure 311, 320 and 321mm. Broadly speaking, the longer the stem, the more expensive the pipe. Most of the pipes in this group are fully milled around the top of the bowl, or almost so, which indicates a good standard of finishing. Two pipes from A[104] made in Mould B are burnished, as well as one from context A[119], again indicating high manufacturing standards. One stem fragment has part of a band of roller-stamped decoration, made with a milling tool, running around the stem at least three times.

It is possible that pipemaking was taking place on the site between *c* 1660 and 1680, but without evidence from kiln structures or related features associated with manufacture this cannot be confirmed. Nevertheless, the large number of pipe bowls of the same type, especially those made in the same mould and all closely dated by association with the Great Fire, add to the significance of the assemblage.

2.5 The post-Great Fire and modern sequence (periods 7 and 8)

Documentary evidence

Tony Dyson

Fire Court hearing on the 'great tenement'

On 22 November 1667 a case was heard before the Fire Court, set up in the City after the Great Fire to adjudicate on disputes arising from the rebuilding of burnt properties, many of them – as in this instance – bearing on the respective obligations and rights of landlords and tenants in the matter. On the petitioners' side were John Alden's descendents, represented by Zachary Babington, and on the other was Arnold Beake, to whom Alden had leased the messuage in question, the 'great tenement' in Botolph Lane, in September 1646 (above, 2.3). The action was clearly collusive, intended to give legal force to an agreement that the parties had already reached, and the Court duly decreed that Beake, who had occupied the property until it was burnt in the Fire, should rebuild it at a cost of £1500, have 40 years added to his existing lease (making it run for 50 years from Lady Day 1667) and have the rent reduced to £30 pa payable from Lady Day 1669. It further ruled that, on coming of age, Alden Babington, the heir to the property, should execute a new lease adding a further 21½ years to the term in return for an additional rent of £10 pa (Jones 1970, 13–14, C 22v). Beake applied on 10 January 1668 for a foundation to be set out, and one Samuel Beake applied for another foundation on 8 December 1668 (Mills and Oliver 1966, 11), but no plan or further reference to a survey occurs there.

St Botolph Billingsgate churchyard

The churchyard appears to have survived the church, which was not rebuilt after the Fire of 1666 (Fig 60), and is noted in 1720 and 1755 and by Rocque's map of 1746. By 1903 its site was occupied by Billingsgate Ward School and Storay Steps Warehouse (Harben 1918, 94).

Rebuilding after the Great Fire (period 7)

A courtyard (OA10) and 'Wren's House' or Beake House at 32 Botolph Lane

In the rebuilding that followed the Great Fire much of the east side of the site was covered by a large enclosed courtyard measuring c 13m east–west by 15m north–south with a surface at c 10m OD (Fig 61). The courtyard, which was entered through a gateway on Botolph Lane, survived until the 1998 redevelopment.

The courtyard belonged to a fine house set along the east side of the site and commonly known as 'Wren's House', though there is no evidence of a connection with Sir

Christopher Wren (Fig 62). Arnold and Samuel Beake, who rebuilt the house in 1670, were members of a wealthy family of Dutch merchants who had leased the property before the Great Fire (Alcock and Galinou 2006). The house at 32 Botolph Lane was one of the finest post-Great Fire merchants' houses in the City and its ground floor contained a Painted Room of 33 exotically decorated panels by Robert Robinson (1651–1706). The building was converted into Billingsgate Ward School in 1852 and demolished in 1906 despite considerable protest (ibid). The panelled room was saved and rebuilt in the boardroom of Sir John Cass's school at Aldgate.

Building 8 south of the courtyard (OA10) and north of the cemetery

Within 10 years of the Great Fire the whole of the Botolph Lane frontage had been redeveloped. Building 8, to the south of the courtyard, was aligned east–west and constructed over the remains of Building 6 along the north side of St Botolph cemetery (Fig 61). The north wall of Building 8 was 0.70m wide and returned north at the south-west corner of the courtyard. The lower levels of the wall were composed almost entirely of reused stone and tile from buildings destroyed in the Great Fire, including pre-Great Fire, Dutch tin-glazed wall tile <T19> (Fig 44).

The make-up deposit for the brick floor in Building 8 produced 67 sherds of 17th-century pottery, mainly tablewares

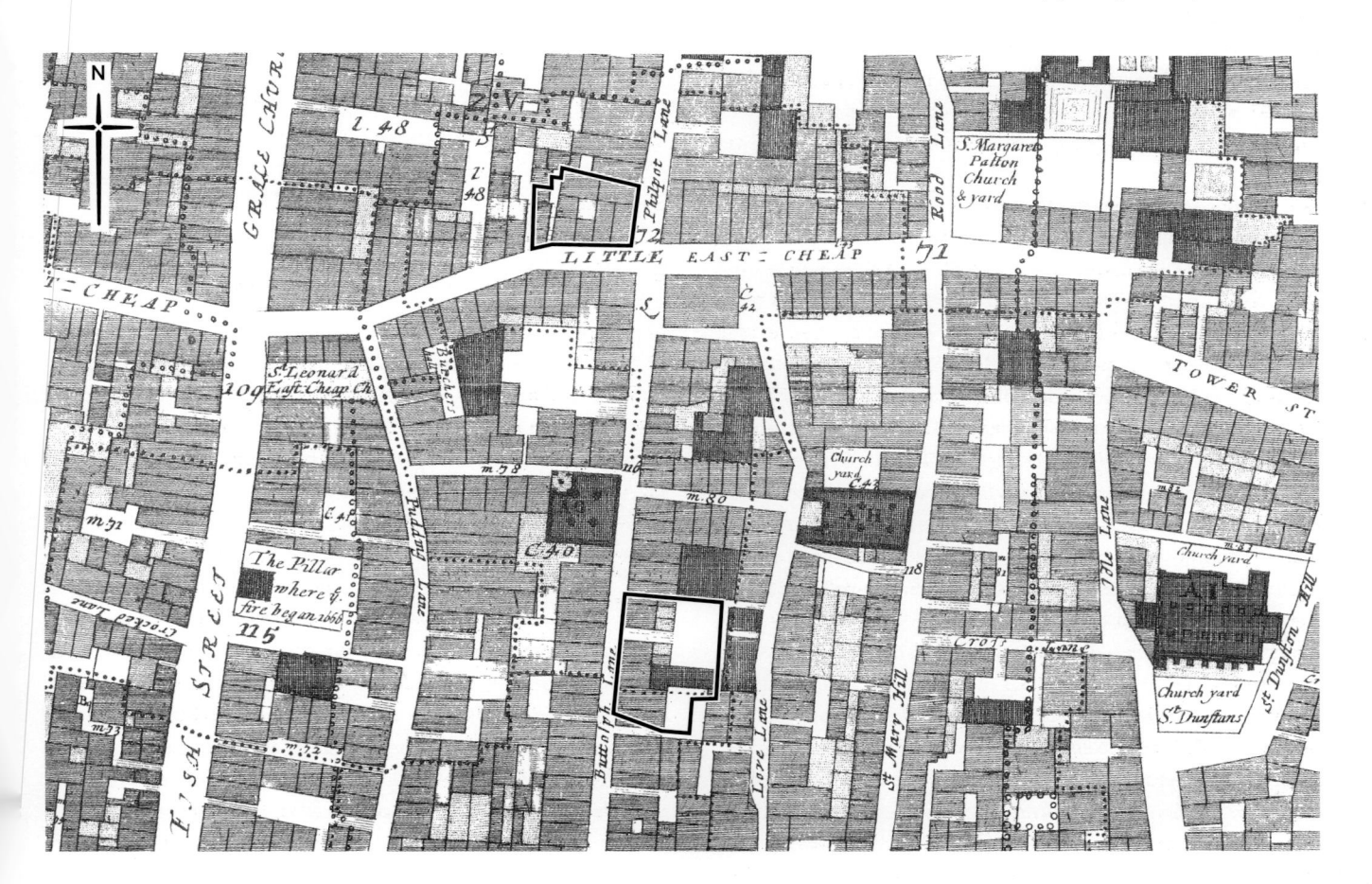

Fig 60 Ogilby and Morgan's map of 1676 with the Monument House and 13–21 Eastcheap sites highlighted

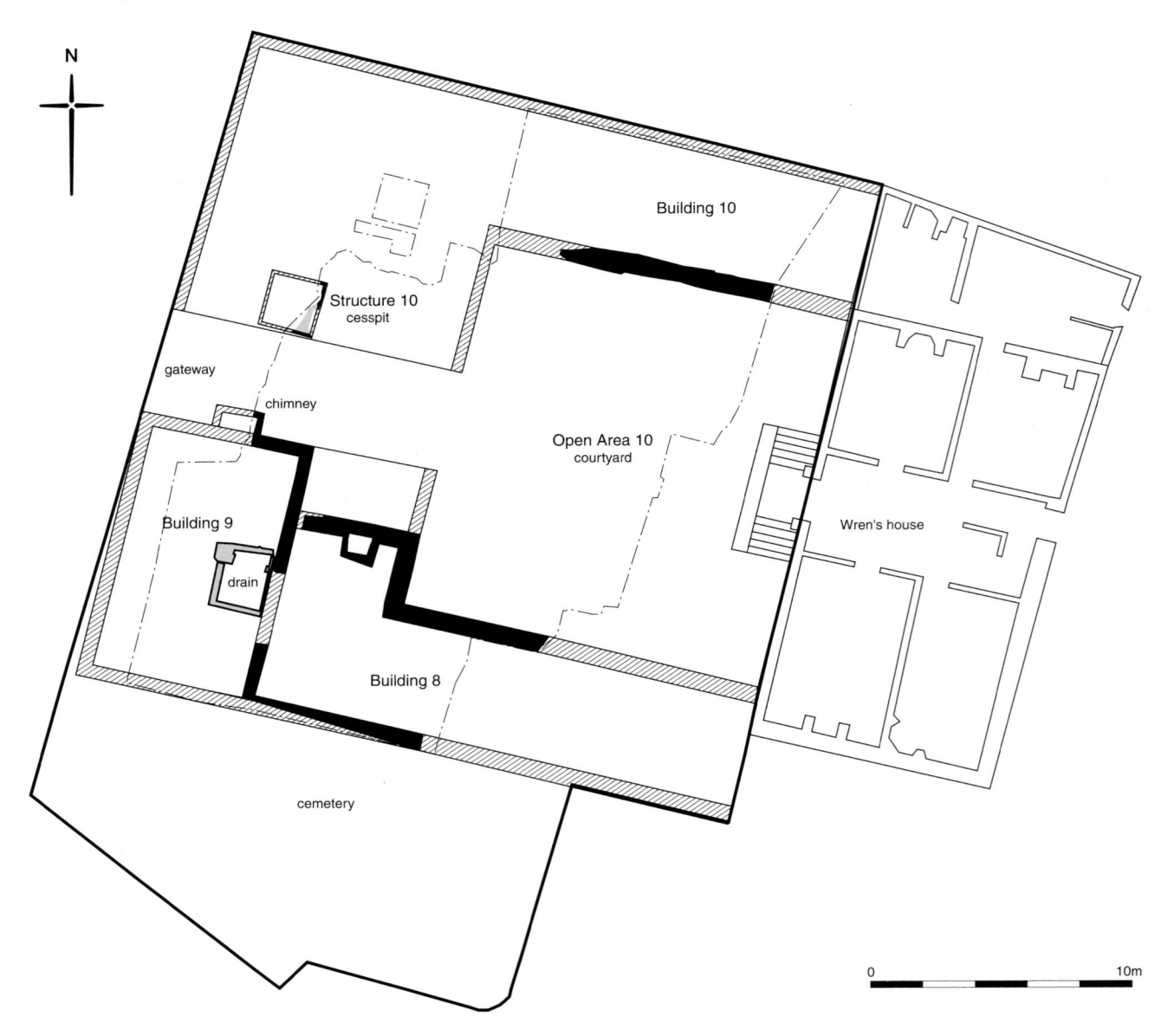

Fig 61 *Post-Great Fire development (period 7) at Monument House, with 'Wren's House' to the east (scale 1:250)*

and serving wares. Whitewares and redwares are more common than tin-glazed ware, with the latter including the base of a mug with manganese-speckled glaze. All datable pipes from the building belong to types AO15 and AO18, made between c 1660 and 1680. The pipe bowls found in the make-up for the floor are fully and clearly milled, and one bowl has three joining stem fragments. Most pipes appear to have been smoked and none are encrusted with deposits similar to those in the Great Fire destruction debris.

The north-western part of the north wall of Building 8 was founded on the earlier chalk well of Building 6. A square brick shaft against the south side of the wall allowed access to the well shaft below, which may have continued in use as a source of fresh water or a convenient soakaway. Two sherds of English stoneware (ENGS) and Staffordshire salt-glazed stoneware in the disuse fill of the well show that the structure finally went out of use in the 18th century.

During the 19th century the building underwent a number

of structural modifications, including the addition of several internal brick pier bases and a north–south cross-wall. A small brick-lined pit with a brick floor, located in the south-west corner of the courtyard against the outer wall of Building 8, may have been an external ash pit.

Building fronting Botolph Lane, south of the entrance into the courtyard (B9)

Adjoining the west end of Building 8 were the brick cellar walls of north–south-aligned Building 9, which fronted on to Botolph Lane (Fig 61). The cellar was 10m long x 6m wide and had been built against the north wall of the cemetery. Its partially robbed brick floor lay at 7.05m OD. Attached to the outer face of the north wall of the cellar was a narrow rectangular brick structure 0.80m deep, which may have been the base of a chimney stack or lightwell.

The pottery associated with the construction of the cellar

Fig 62 'Wren's House' at 32 Botolph Lane, viewed from the west in an 1888 watercolour by J Appleton (Guildhall Library, Corporation of London)

dates to the 17th century and mainly comprises post-medieval redware (PMR) and tin-glazed ware (TGW) dishes. One of the latter has part of a bird-on-the-rock design while another could be Portuguese; also present is one sherd of Frechen stoneware. The pipes from Building 9 consist of three type AO15 bowls and one type AO18 bowl, all dated to c 1660–80.

Set centrally along the east wall of the cellar was a vaulted brick sump or cesspit sunk 1.38m into the floor, with a base on natural gravel at c 5.55m OD. Part of a tin-glazed ware plate of Britton type I with brown-edged rim and simple floral decoration may be associated with the use of the structure and probably dates to the 1720s. The disuse fill contained a sherd of Chinese porcelain (CHPO) from a coffee or chocolate cup dating to the 1750s–1760s and two fragments of decorated tin-glazed wall tile. One tile, which is in purple and blue and has part of a vase design with carnation-head corners, is a London product which can be dated to c 1730–50 (for similar tiles see Horne 1989, 62–3). The latest pipe is an OS12 bowl (the prefix OS denotes Oswald's simplified general typology of 1975) which dates to c 1730–80. The heel is marked with the initials 'IH' in relief. This could stand for the makers John Howell, recorded at St Andrews, Holborn in 1730, John Hornbuckles Jr, apprentice to J Bayley in 1731, or John Harvey, recorded in the Bristol Polls in 1739 (Oswald 1975, 138).

Building to the north of the courtyard (B10)

The south wall of Building 10 bordered the north side of the courtyard (OA10). The wall was substantially rebuilt and deepened to create a cellar for the narrow east–west-aligned strip building (Fig 61). Many of the bricks used in Building 10 have sunken margins characteristic of pre-Great Fire brickwork, implying that bricks from demolished pre-Fire structures were salvaged for reuse.

A brick-lined cesspit near Botolph Lane and north of the entrance to the courtyard (S10)

Structure 10 represents the remains of a brick-lined cesspit situated to the north of Building 9 and defining the northern side of the entranceway into the courtyard (OA10) to the east (Fig 61). Later truncation had removed the upper levels of the cesspit and any associated building, but it is likely that the cesspit was originally situated within a cellar.

Pottery found in the disuse fill is dated to the early 18th century by a variant of a Britton type I dish (Britton 1987, 194). Other finds comprise post-medieval redware, Staffordshire mottle-glazed ware (STMO), a Staffordshire white dipped stoneware (SWSL) tankard and part of a large Chinese porcelain teabowl with floral decoration. Taken together the pottery dates to c 1710–60. Five type OS11 pipe bowls were also found, dated to c 1730–80. Three of these are marked in relief on the sides of the heel with the initials 'TD'.

External pitting in the north-west of the site (OA11)

Three quarry pits, located in the north-west corner of the site, may have post-dated the demolition of Building 10 and pre-dated construction of a new gateway into the courtyard (see period 8). The pits contained residual medieval pottery, one sherd of English stoneware dating to after 1700 and one type AO27 pipe bowl dated *c* 1780–1820 and marked 'DW' in relief on the side of the spur.

Reconstruction in the 19th century (period 8)

A new gateway into the courtyard (B11)

The Building 9 cellar was backfilled and new walls constructed as part of a new and wider gateway (B11), immediately south of the original entrance to the courtyard (OA10) (not illustrated). The new gateway gave access into the south-west corner of the courtyard (Fig 63).

Finds from the consolidation backfill of the Building 9 cellar included four pipes of type OS12, and one type AO26, dating to *c* 1740–1800. The OS12 pipes are of particular interest since they are good examples of a type with decorated stem made in Chester (Cheshire), which was highly regarded for its decorative pipes (David Higgins pers comm) and exported them over some distance, although they are rare in the capital. All come from the same mould, and one has a length of stem on which the start of a band of roller-stamped or rouletted decoration remains <S31> (Fig 64). The decoration starts 69mm from the back of the heel, which is very small, and consists of a band of stylised ?fleur-de-lis above a band of lozenges with central dots. This decoration is quite

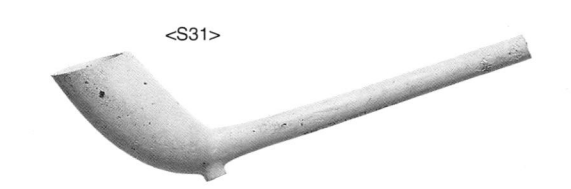

Fig 64 *Decorated type OS12 clay pipe, made in Chester <S31> (scale 1:2)*

late in the type-series developed for decorated Chester pipes (border type 105: Rutter and Davey 1980, 186–7, fig 62). The bowl is a typical Chester bowl form 90 and should date to *c* 1710–40 (ibid, 222, fig 83), earlier than the usual dating for type 12 in Oswald's general typology (*c* 1740–80). At the time the Chester typology was developed, no examples of decorated stems with bowls attached were known and type 105 border decoration was dated to *c* 1760–90. The London finds therefore suggest that this dating should be amended (Peter Davey pers comm).

A new warehouse on the north-west part of the site (B12)

During the 19th century a substantial new cellared building (B12) was erected on the north-west part of the site, along the west side of the courtyard and north of the new entranceway to it (not illustrated). The Building 12 cellar measured *c* 11m

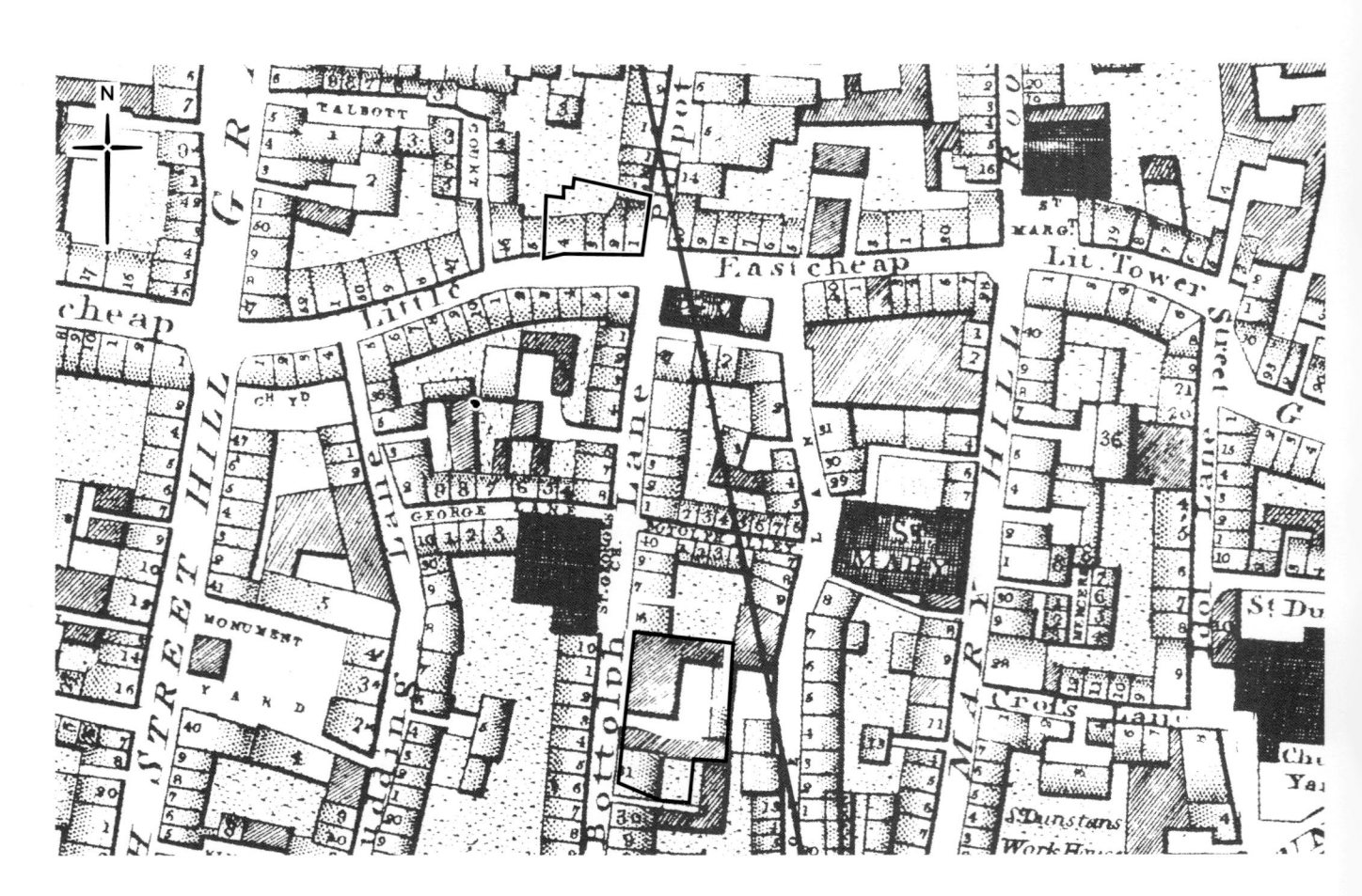

Fig 63 *Horwood's map of 1813 with the Monument House and 13–21 Eastcheap sites highlighted*

east–west by 16m north–south and incorporated a series of internal piers to support the ground floor. Part of a Purbeck marble headstone with a partly legible inscription was incorporated into one of the piers and may have come from the cemetery to the south. The brick floor of the cellar lay at c 7.85m OD and sealed a large vaulted brick drainage sump which collected rainwater from the roof or courtyard.

Eight pipe bowls were found in the lower fill A[285] of the structure, six of them of Atkinson and Oswald's (1969) type AO28 (c 1820–40), one of AO27 (c 1780–1820) and one of AO30 (c 1850–1910). Two of the AO28 bowls are stamped on the back with the maker's name and address 'BALME MILE END' inside a shield. The Balme family was working in Mile End from 1805 until at least 1876. The one type AO27 pipe in the same context is stamped on the back of the bowl with the City of London arms, and marked with the maker's initials 'MC' in relief on the side of the heel <CP5>. This may be the pipemaker Matthew Charlton, who is recorded in Cow Cross Street in 1799–1807 (Oswald 1975, 134). Use of the City arms starts in c 1680, and was appropriated by several makers (eg Atkinson and Oswald 1969, fig 8, nos 59–63). Another of the AO28 pipes in context A[285] has leaf-decorated seams on the back and front of the bowl and is marked with the initials 'ID' on the heel. This is possibly John Dearden, who is recorded in Bell Street, Edgware Road in 1823–40, or James Davis of Dutton Street, Cromer Road in 1826–32 (Oswald 1975, 135).

3

The archaeological evidence from 13–21 Eastcheap

3.1 Geology and prehistory (period 1)

Natural topography of the area

Natural deposits (OA1)

The site of 13–21 Eastcheap lies near the southern edge of the Second River Terrace gravels north of the Thames. To the south of Eastcheap the ground falls away steeply. Natural brickearth was recorded at 11.75m OD at the south-west corner of the site (not illustrated). The underlying gravels were observed between 10.93 and 11.38m OD. There was a moderate slope downwards towards the edge of the terrace to the south, but the natural surface appears to have been relatively level. Roman terracing had truncated much of the natural ground surface and may have destroyed both prehistoric and early Roman evidence.

3.2 The Roman sequence (periods 2–4)

Early Roman occupation, *c* AD 50–125 (period 2 phase 1)

Terracing and early occupation (B1)

The first extant activity was terracing of the natural ground slope for building. This may have initially taken place as a single event over an extensive area, followed by further piecemeal landscaping. The construction levels of a timber building survived on the south-west part of the site (Building 1), along with some associated occupation debris (Fig 65).

Contexts containing only pre-Flavian pottery are predominantly the lowest general levelling deposits or reworked brickearth, along with some early make-up dumps. The absence of Boudican fire debris, recorded nearby at 41 Eastcheap (Pitt in prep) and at the forum (Dunwoodie 2004), may be a result of later 1st-century truncation.

Finds within the construction layers included a copper-alloy coin B<20>, possibly of Nero (AD 60–5). The pottery is consistently early and contains a high proportion of pre-Flavian samian ware, represented by a la Graufesenque samian (SAMLG) Ritterling form 9 cup and Ritterling form 12 bowl, Dragendorff form 24/25 cup and Lyon colour-coated ware (LYON) dated *c* AD 50–70. Diagnostically early Romano-British fabrics are Eccles ware (ECCW), Sugar Loaf Court ware (SLOW) and early Roman micaceous sandy ware (ERMS), all dated *c* AD 50–70/80. The pottery and accessioned finds are domestic in character, lacking large amphorae or imported pottery.

Late 1st-century AD development (period 2 phase 2)

Building 2 and Open Areas 2 and 3

Building 2, located on the north-west part of the site, consisted

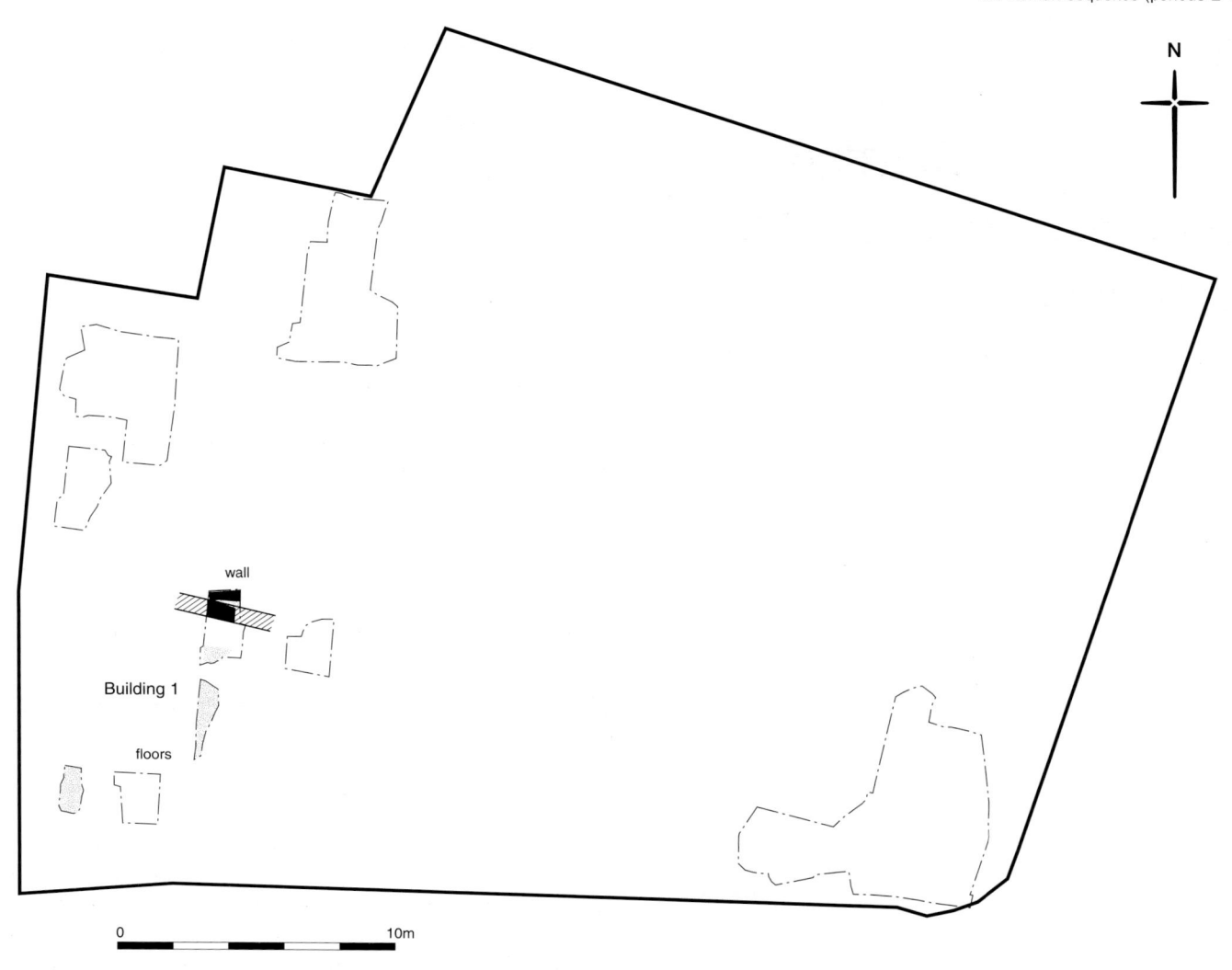

N

wall

Building 1

floors

0   10m

Fig 65 Building 1 (period 2 phase 1) at 13–21 Eastcheap (scale 1:250)

of levelling and make-up deposits (Fig 66) and was probably constructed in the aftermath of the Boudican revolt. Occupation debris contained an unusual form of Highgate Wood ware C (HWC) dish which has an internal slip and is influenced by Gallo-Belgic moulded dishes and Dragendorff form 15/17 dishes. Highgate Wood ware C is usually indicative of a post-AD 70 date (Davies et al 1994, 82), but it does occur in earlier assemblages and this may be a pre-Flavian form.

Adjacent to Building 2 to the north-east, Open Area 2 was represented by small-scale pitting and dumping. On the east side of the site Open Area 3 contained a north–south feature more than 6m long and 0.5m deep, with a vertical revetted west side and a flat base on the natural gravels. The cut contained no waterlain or windblown sediment or litter and had probably been backfilled soon after its excavation. It did not appear to be a ditch or drain and also seems unlikely to have been a terrace edge or quarry. Its location, date and north–south alignment suggest that it may be a feature associated with some unknown activity outside the conjectured western side of the post-Boudican military enclosure found at Plantation Place (Dunwoodie et al in prep). Part of a glass beaker with a flat pad base <S33> (Fig 67)

and a fragment of a glass bottle B<3> were recovered from its fills.

Open Areas 2 and 3 produced a small quantity of pottery which is broadly contemporary with the assemblage from Building 2. There is one sherd from a London oxidised ware (LOXI) lid, a fabric dated to c AD 85 (Groves 1993, 126–7).

Early 2nd-century AD occupation (period 2 phase 3)

Buildings 3–6; Open Areas 4 and 5

Building 1 was replaced by timber Building 3 on the same alignment (Fig 68). Further to the north, timber Building 4 had a complete votive pot incorporated into sill B[212], an unsourced grog-tempered ware bead-rimmed jar (GROG 2A) which contained the base of a south Gaulish samian ware cup (SAMLG 6) and several unidentified metal objects. A corroded copper-alloy coin, possibly of Nero or Hadrian, was recovered from the initial make-up for Building 4, possibly also a good-luck charm. The pottery from the construction deposits and floors was residual. Good-quality painted plaster found in the make-up for

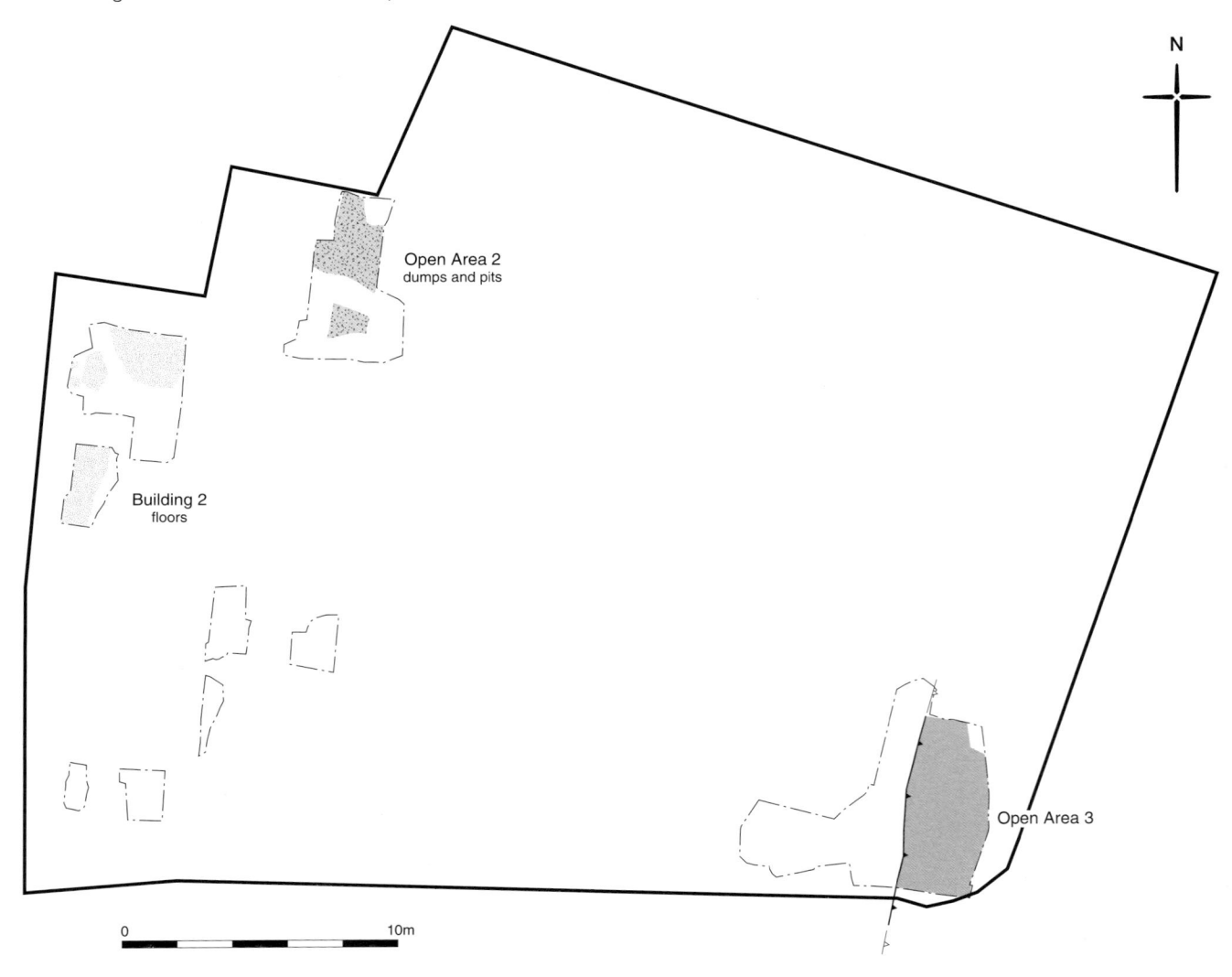

Fig 66 *Building 2 and external activity up to c AD 125 (period 2 phase 2) at 13–21 Eastcheap (scale 1:250)*

Building 4 included a panel design of white lines on red and grey backgrounds, with adjacent red and yellow fields.

Building 4 quickly fell out of use and became a rubbish dump, composed principally of oyster shells in deposits B[177] and B[179] in Open Area 4 (not illustrated). The oysters were probably dredged from wild beds in the Thames estuary and were presumably sold and consumed near the site. There was a well-documented trade in pearls from Britain from the 1st to the 4th century AD, but Jessica Winder (pers comm) believes these were derived from the freshwater pearl mussel (*Margaritifera margaritifera*) rather than common, or flat, oysters (*Ostrea edulis*).

Timber Building 5 (not illustrated) was constructed over the rolled and flattened oysters. A single sherd of a black-burnished-style ware (BBS) jar with acute lattice decoration

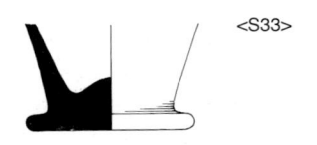

Fig 67 *Pad base from glass beaker <S33> (scale 1:2)*

from floor surface B[248] dates to after c AD 120. Associated finds included a fragment of shale tray B<110>, window glass and several fragments of vessel glass, one of which was burnt. Buildings 3 and 5 were covered by burnt demolition debris thought to be from the Hadrianic fire.

On the east side of the site the Open Area 3 cut feature was filled in and the ground level raised by make-up dumps. These formed the base for the fragmentary remains of the north-east corner of timber Building 6, which shared the same alignment as the buildings recorded to the west. Pottery from its foundation levels is dated to c AD 70–160.

Building 6 was followed by external activity in Open Area 5, represented by a large, shallow oblong cut feature aligned east–west and surrounded by stakeholes. The cut contained domestic rubbish, including fragments of glass vessels and copper-alloy coins of Domitian and Trajan. A large pottery assemblage is dated c AD 120–60 on the presence of black-burnished ware 1 (BB1), BBS jars with acute lattice decoration and a sherd of Verulamium region white ware (VRW) ring-necked flagon with a prominent rounded rim.

Despite the proximity of the forum, the surviving early 2nd-century AD remains do not appear particularly substantial

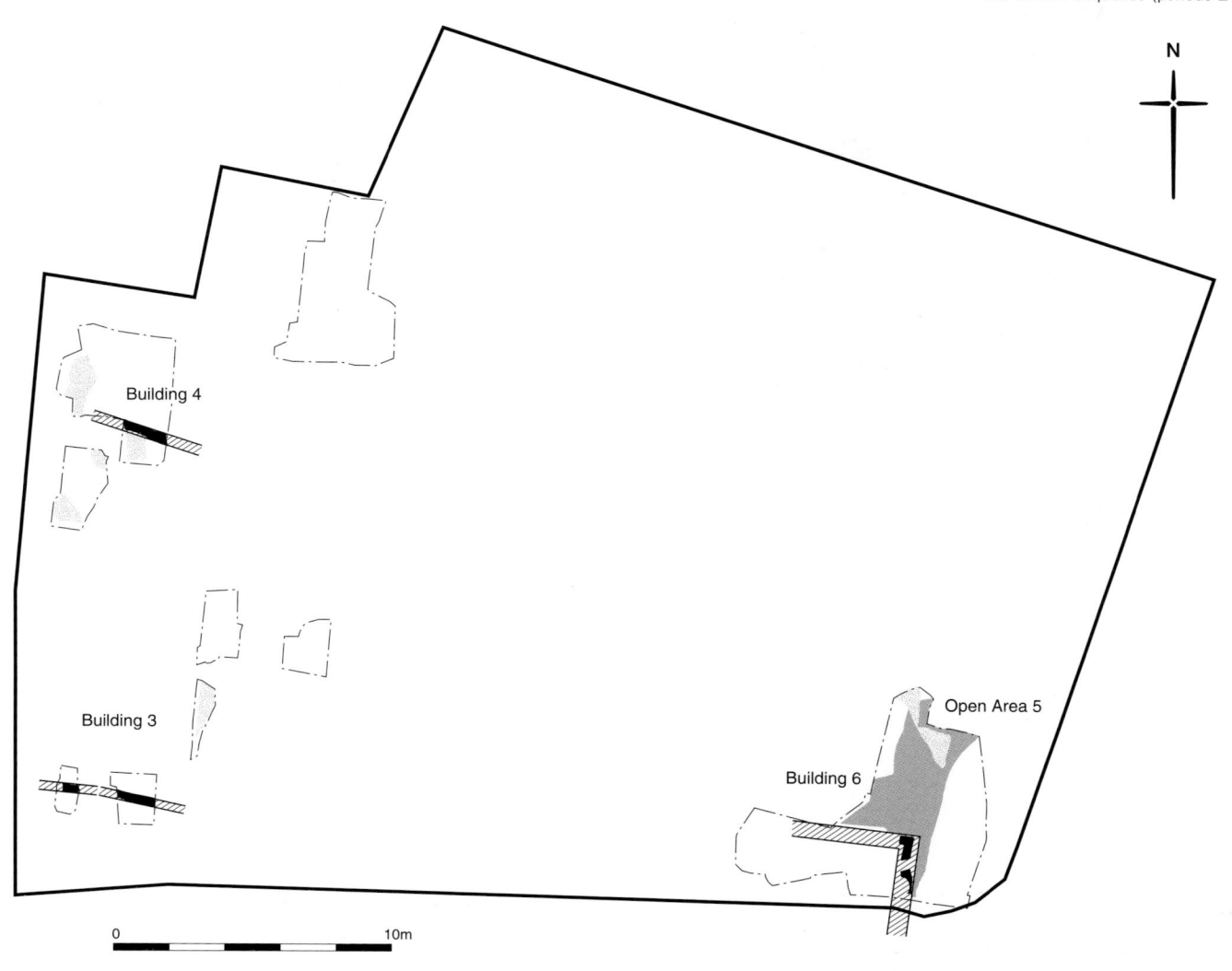

N

Building 4

Building 3

Open Area 5

Building 6

0   10m

Fig 68 Early 2nd-century AD buildings (period 2 phase 3) at 13–21 Eastcheap (scale 1:250)

or prestigious, perhaps because the site lay some distance from the nearest major road frontages.

A Hadrianic fire horizon of *c* AD 125 (period 3 phase 1)

Fire debris in Open Area 7

Open Area 7 (not illustrated) consisted of a 600mm thick deposit of burnt demolition debris found at 12.3m OD on the west side of the site and between 11.4 and 12.0m OD to the east. The debris consisted largely of burnt daub mixed with charcoal, roof tile and brick in local fabrics, as well as small chalk and shale tesserae from a mosaic floor and a fragment of daub with chevron keying on the surface. Evidence from nearby sites indicates that buildings across the area were destroyed in the Hadrianic fire of *c* AD 125 but that a second fire damaged the forum-basilica shortly afterwards (Davies 1992, 71).

The fire horizon contained household objects, although the low number of roof tiles present indicates that the debris may have been sorted for the salvage of building materials. Finds included a fragment of a stone palette B<113>, probably for

mixing cosmetics, a possible copper-alloy seal box <S36> (Fig 69) and part of a glass phial. Burnt debris from the collapsed walls of Building 5 contained a burnt and deformed but possibly complete unguent jar in colourless glass <S34> (Fig 69).

Post-Hadrianic rebuilding up to *c* AD 200 (period 3 phase 2)

Buildings 7–9; Open Areas 6, 8 and 9

The fragmentary remains of two timber buildings (B7 and B8) were recorded on the west side of the site (Fig 70). Contexts associated with these two buildings contained only five sherds of pottery and cannot be closely dated.

Open Area 8 (not illustrated) lay between the two buildings and consisted of ashy pit fills containing pottery dated to *c* AD 120–60, including two sherds of black-burnished wares. Metal finds included a copper-alloy mount <S37> and a copper-alloy fitting <S38> (Fig 71), which may be part of a strap tag or scabbard runner and has some similarities with a terminal from South Shields (Allason-Jones and Miket 1984, 197, no. 3.649). Open Area 8 deposits also contained fragments of painted

Fig 69 Copper-alloy seal box <S36> and unguent jar <S34> (scale 1:1)

plaster in a red, white and green colour scheme and characterised by crushed calcite crystals on the painted surface, used to increase its light-reflective properties.

The reworked external deposits in Open Area 8 were cut by two parallel, east–west-aligned box drains up to 1.7m deep and defining Open Area 6. The drains would originally have contained timber plank bases, sides and possibly covers, but traces of wood only survived as staining in the southern drain.

On the eastern part of the site, the north-eastern corner of Building 9 survived as a badly truncated but substantial Kentish ragstone foundation. The associated construction cut had been backfilled with London Clay and this may have been an intentional waterproofing, similar to that found along the walls of Roman cellared buildings at Lloyd's Register (Bluer and Brigham 2006). Associated occupation levels did not survive, but 2nd-century AD pottery was recovered from construction and make-up levels.

Just to the east of Building 9, the large north–south-aligned Open Area 3 cut feature was apparently redug further to the east in Open Area 9. The new cut was more than 6.5m long and at least 1m deep, cutting into natural gravels. It contained no identifiable waterlain or windblown sediments, suggesting that it must have been cleaned out regularly. The feature had a short life and is of unknown purpose. Associated pottery is dated c AD 120–60 but is predominantly Trajanic to early Hadrianic. One notable sherd was a stamped base from a fine micaceous reduced ware cup (FMIC 6) B<107>. The stamp on the internal base of the cup is set centrally within a single incised circle. The

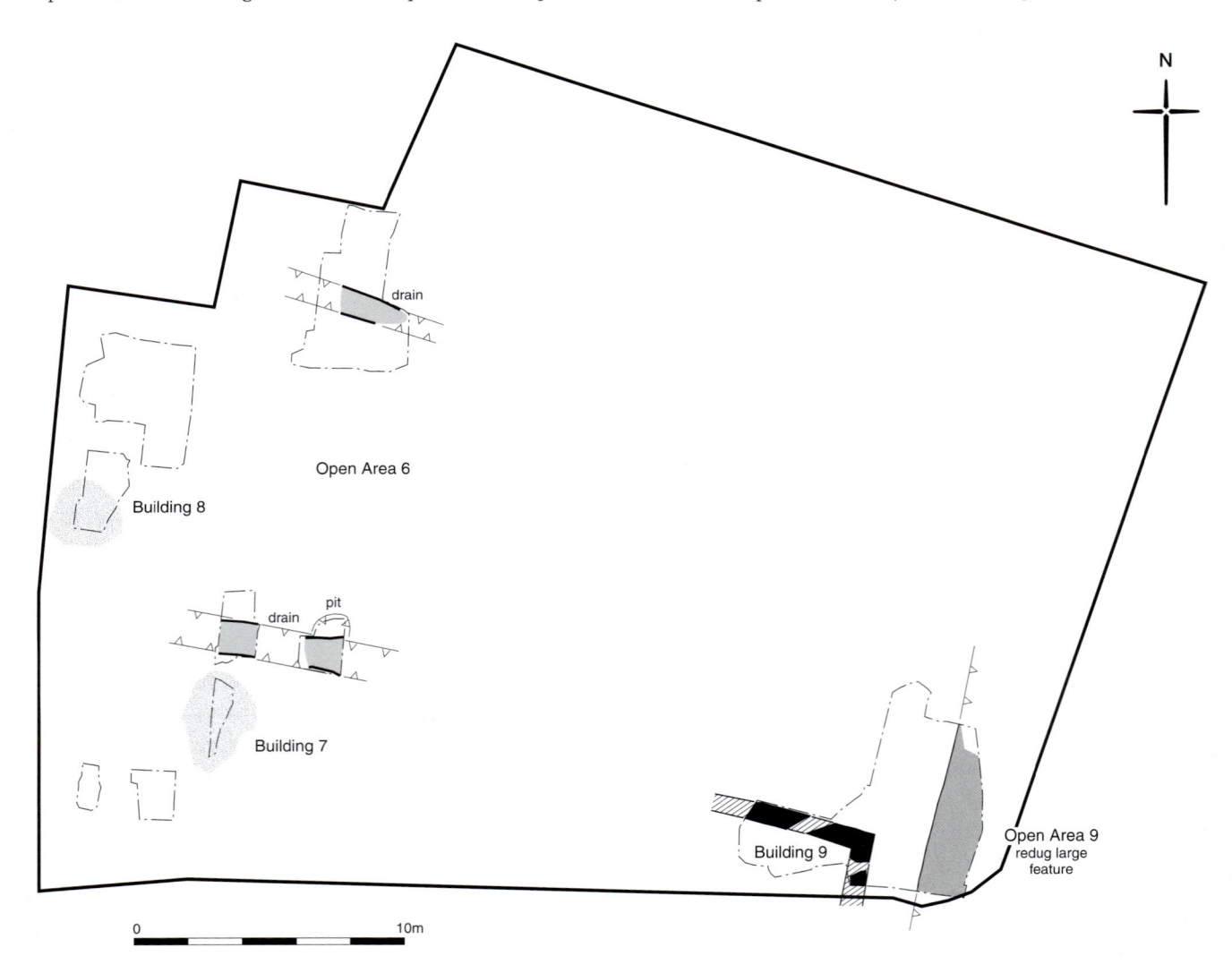

Fig 70 Post-Hadrianic activity (period 3 phase 2) at 13–21 Eastcheap (scale 1:250)

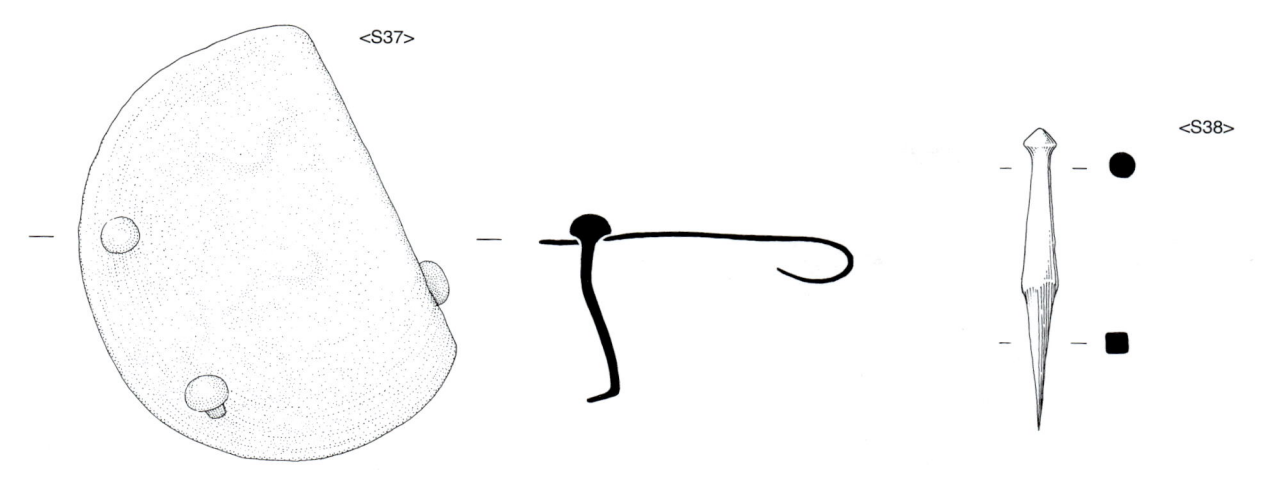

Fig 71   Copper-alloy circular plate mount with rivets <S37> and a possible scabbard runner or strap tag <S38> (scale 1:1)

die-style, with motifs of V and dots, is similar to a group of related dies from West Stow (Suffolk) and other sites north of the Thames and into East Anglia. No actual stamped vessels from West Stow have been identified in London, but other stamps in a comparable die-style have been recorded and dated to after *c* AD 80 (Davies et al 1994, 165 no. 477; Louise Rayner pers comm).

Other finds included an annular glass bead <S32> and several layers of window glass which had been burnt and melted together into a single lump <S39>, although possibly all originated from the same pane (Fig 72).

Fig 72   Annular glass bead <S32> (scale 2:1) and melted window glass <S39> (scale 1:1)

Late Roman change from *c* AD 200 until the 5th century AD (period 4)

External activity in Open Area 6 retained and Open Area 10

The parallel box drains defining Open Area 6 were intentionally backfilled in the early to mid 3rd century AD (Open Area 6 retained; not illustrated) but the contemporary ground surface did not survive later truncation. The 3rd century witnessed the disuse of many roadside drains, sometimes providing evidence for the abandonment of infrastructure associated with decline, although the rerouting of drains was sometimes associated with renewed investment and the construction of late Roman masonry buildings.

The southern drain's backfill B[113] contained a significant group of Roman pottery, amounting to 355 sherds or 9.7 EVEs and weighing 8523g. A small proportion of the pottery is residual, but most is in a fresh condition and clearly forms a homogeneous group datable to the early to mid 3rd century AD from its composition and comparison with other independently dated assemblages (Fig 73). Well over half the group by EVEs (75%) and weight (71%) is made up of reduced wares. Of these, 28% by EVEs and 22% by weight is black-burnished ware 1 (BB1), 13% by EVEs and 10% by weight is black-burnished ware 2 (BB2), 9% by EVEs and 11% by weight is black-burnished-style wares (BBS), 7% by EVEs and 9% by weight is Alice Holt/Farnham ware (AHFA), and 14% by EVEs and 18%

by weight unsourced sand-tempered ware (SAND).

The BB1 consists of shallow simple dishes and everted-rimmed jars. There are two bowl sherds, presumably from flanged bowls. The dishes have burnished intersecting arc decoration on the exterior and burnished curvilinear base decoration <P14> and <P15>. The jars have curved everted rims of similar diameter to the jars' girths, and burnished lattice decoration in obtuse and large irregular acute styles <P16>. The change from acute to obtuse lattice is thought to have taken place in *c* AD 220 (Holbrook and Bidwell 1991, 96; Tyers 1996, 185). The dishes and jars are very similar to those from the early to

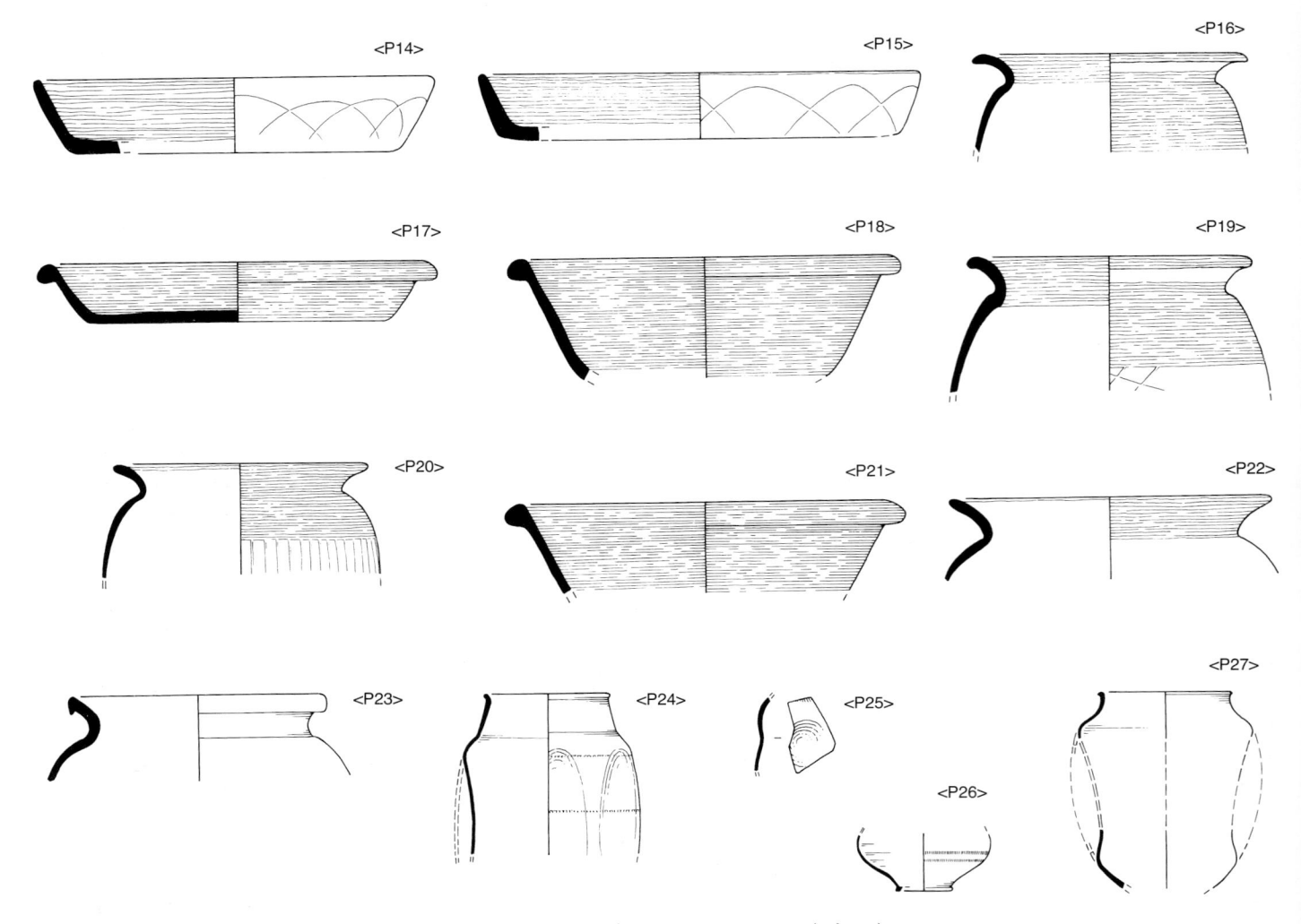

Fig 73 A 3rd-century AD pottery assemblage <P14>–<P27> from drain backfill B[113] in Open Area 6 (scale 1:4)

mid 3rd-century groups at New Fresh Wharf (NFW74) (Richardson 1986) and to jars from West Escape Shaft, Bridge Street (LBA95) (Rayner and Seeley 2002, 140, fig 100, nos <P203> and <P204>). The absence of any definite examples of flanged bowls may be significant, as these are common later 3rd-century AD BB1 forms.

The BB2 is mainly the later 2nd- and 3rd-century AD fine fabric (BB2F), a fine dark-grey ware thought to have been made in Essex or Kent <P17> and <P18>. Undecorated bowls and dishes with rounded rims predominate. Nearly all the jar sherds have been classified as BBS. They are similar in form to the BB1 jars, and have burnished grouped and spaced vertical line decorations <P20>, and in one case large widely spaced acute lattice <P19>.

The AHFA ware also consists of BBS forms. A round-rimmed bowl <P21> is very similar to BB2 4H5 and is dated c AD 150–220 (Lyne and Jefferies 1979, 45, fig 31, no. 5A.1). A later BBS everted-rimmed jar 2FX <P22> is a common 3rd- and 4th-century AD form. This example does not have the more exaggerated curve of the later 3rd and 4th centuries and is probably early 3rd century. There is also an everted-rimmed jar with a shoulder carination comparable to an example dated c AD 180–270 (ibid, 37, fig 22, no. I.31). The fabric is

unsourced but obviously local. Nearly all the sherds are from jars, and rims are slightly everted, reduced or hooked <P23>. A Verulamium region white ware (VRW) necked jar (2T) is also present.

Fine wares account for 16% of the group by EVEs and 3% by weight. Of these, 7% by EVEs and 1% by weight is Moselkeramik (MOSL), 2% by EVEs and less than 1% by weight is central Gaulish/Lezoux black colour-coated ware (CGBL), 1% by EVEs and 1% by weight Cologne colour-coated ware (KOLN) and 6% by EVEs and 1% by weight mica-dusted wares. There are two sherds of central Gaulish samian ware (SAMCG) Dragendorff 37 and 31.

East Gaulish black colour-coated ware from Trier (MOSL) dominates the fine ware group. At least six vessels are present, five being indented beakers with folded rounded and long narrow indentations <P24> and <P25> and one being a plain globular beaker <P26>. All are directly comparable to examples from New Fresh Wharf (Richardson 1986, 119–21, 1.124, 1.127, 1.130, 1.38), as is the CGBL ware beaker (cf ibid, 115, 1.100), the KOLN barbotine-figured beaker, and the fine mica-dusted wares (sherds from a jar and a beaker) in an unsourced, possibly imported light-red fabric <P27>.

A complete mica-dusted *Firmalampe* <S35> from B[113]

(Fig 74) is also identical to a lamp from the New Fresh Wharf group (Richardson 1986, 132–3, 1.224). Both lamps are in a London mica-dusted fabric (LOMI) of the late 1st to mid 2nd century AD and their occurrence in groups dated a century later suggests that production or use of these lamps continued far longer.

The only mortarium sherd in the group is in Oxfordshire white ware (OXWW), dated to *c* AD 180–400 in London. There are also several sherds of Dressel 20 amphorae in the late Baetican fabric (BAETL 8DR20), dated *c* AD 170–300 in London.

The group is near contemporary with the pottery from New Fresh Wharf dated *c* AD 210–45, and has similarities with slightly later mid 3rd-century groups from 8 Union Street (Marsh and Tyers 1978) and 10–18 Union Street (Rayner and Seeley in prep), both dated *c* AD 250–70. The combination of forms and fabrics, together with the absence of forms found in late 3rd-century groups such as BB1 flanged bowls, flared cavetto-rimmed jars and the large plain-rimmed dish (5J) variant with a sagging base, and of the late Roman indicator fabric Oxfordshire red/brown colour-coated ware (OXRC), supports a terminal date of *c* AD 270 at the latest. The suggested date for the assemblage is *c* AD 230–50.

A much smaller group of pottery came from backfill B[100] and consisted of 30 sherds. It is dated post-AD 220 on the presence of a BB1 jar with obtuse lattice decoration (Holbrook and Bidwell 1991, 96). Other BB1 forms include a later jar with cavetto rim (2F13), a shallow simple dish (5J) with a burnished pattern on the interior known as the 'Redcliff motif', and a Gillam form 226 bowl with burnished intersecting arcs (4G226 ARCS). There are two sherds of samian, a central Gaulish (SAMCG) Dragendorff 33 cup and an east Gaulish (SAMEG) Dragendorff 37 bowl. The group is also dated to *c* AD 230–50.

Open Area 10 (not illustrated) is represented by a new drain, located on the south-eastern part of the site but aligned at 45° to the earlier drains and buildings in the area. The drain

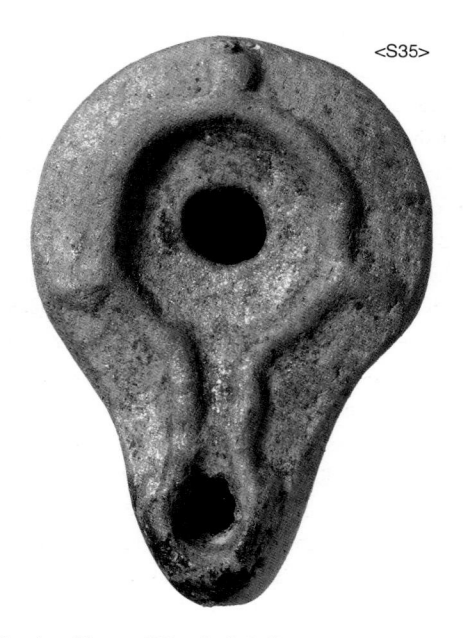
<S35>

Fig 74 Mica-dusted lamp <S35> (scale 1:1)

was backfilled after AD 350, based on the presence of Portchester 'D' ware.

3.3 The early medieval and medieval sequence up to *c* 1500 (period 5)

Activity south of Eastcheap

Pitting and soil horizons in Open Area 11

Three intercutting pits filled with 'dark earth' were found at the north-west corner of the site (not illustrated) and contained a preponderance of Roman finds which are presumed to have been derived from the soil used to backfill them. Much of the pottery from subsequent periods was also residual and included Late Saxon shell-tempered ware (LSS) dating from *c* AD 900, early medieval shell-tempered ware (EMSH), early medieval sand- and shell-tempered ware (EMSS), 11th- to 12th-century locally produced greyware (LOGR) and a coarse London-type ware (LCOAR) spouted pitcher. There are no imported or non-local wares present, and apart from the LCOAR spouted pitcher all forms identified are cooking pots.

A fourth, heavily truncated pit lay nearby and contained a similar 'dark earth' and mixed Roman and post-Roman finds. Fill B[178] included the articulated, partial remains of a lamb as well as a great many limb bones of sheep or goats. Eastcheap was an important centre for City butchers in the medieval period and was included as a butchers' area in the list of trades related to places in John Stow's 1598 survey of London (Stow 1603, 74), although it should be noted that much of the animal bone assemblage may have been redeposited from Roman contexts.

3.4 Post-medieval and modern evidence after *c* 1500 (period 6)

Further development along Eastcheap

Roadside property (B10)

The only surviving early post-medieval evidence at 13–21 Eastcheap was a truncated chalk foundation from a 17th-century building (not illustrated). A cesspit was attached to the side of the building, located towards the centre of 15 Eastcheap. Assemblages of pottery and tobacco pipes suggest that the pit was backfilled in the 18th century.

Excavation in the area of 13–15 Eastcheap was limited by the presence of 19th-century barrel vaults. The barrel vaulting was T-shaped, with one of the vaults perpendicular to the other. The vaults are presumed to be the cellars of the 19th-century pub whose facade was retained as part of the new development.

4

Thematic aspects and conclusions

4.1 The Roman culvert (S3) and terraced Building 2 at Monument House

The function and significance of the culvert (S3) and Building 2

Ian Blair

The late 3rd-century AD development represented by Building 2 and the underlying culvert Structure 3 was clearly part of a unified plan for the area. The culvert may have been designed to carry waste water from the building itself or from a spring line in the hillside to the north, which would otherwise have been 'trapped' behind the building foundations, beneath it and south to the Thames. However, the large size of the culvert suggests that it also served other buildings located on the higher ground to the north. Users may have included an unlocated bathhouse, but the culvert's projected alignment coincides with the east side of the 2nd-century AD forum, suggesting that it formed the lower end of an extensive drainage system which took waste and surface water from the forum buildings and adjacent streets and properties. The date of the culvert would mean that any association with forum drainage was probably as a later modification of an original system (Fig 75).

Only the south-east part of Building 2 survived but it probably had a symmetrical layout aligned east–west along the hillside terrace, with three room areas along its southern facade overlooking the Thames waterfront. The access shaft at the upper end of the extant culvert would therefore have been located in a central position within the building, perhaps in a central courtyard or atrium.

The Monument House culvert and access shaft comprise the only substantial subterranean Roman drainage system known from Londinium, and there is no evidence to suggest that the town had an extensive subsurface network for either water supply or disposal. The settlement lacked an aqueduct, with most fresh water for domestic and industrial use abstracted from wells. Although a few short runs of wooden and ceramic water pipes have been recorded in and around Cornhill, it is generally accepted that there was no overall distribution system (Merrifield 1965, 146; Blair et al 2006). Large capacity 1st- and 2nd-century AD wells served by mechanical bucket-chains have been found at Blossom's Inn (GHT00) to the west of the Walbrook stream and at 12 Arthur Street (AUT01) near the bridgehead (Blair and Hall 2003; Blair et al 2006), and it is possible that these facilities distributed water locally, perhaps along timber troughs, though no surviving evidence has been found. The vast majority of known Roman storm drains and sewers also took the form of timber drains along roadsides and across other external areas, flowing into canalised streams or directly to the Thames.

Most of the water that flowed through open ditches and subterranean timber drains and culverts would have been waste or run-off intended for disposal, and this is undoubtedly the function of the Monument House culvert. Culverts large

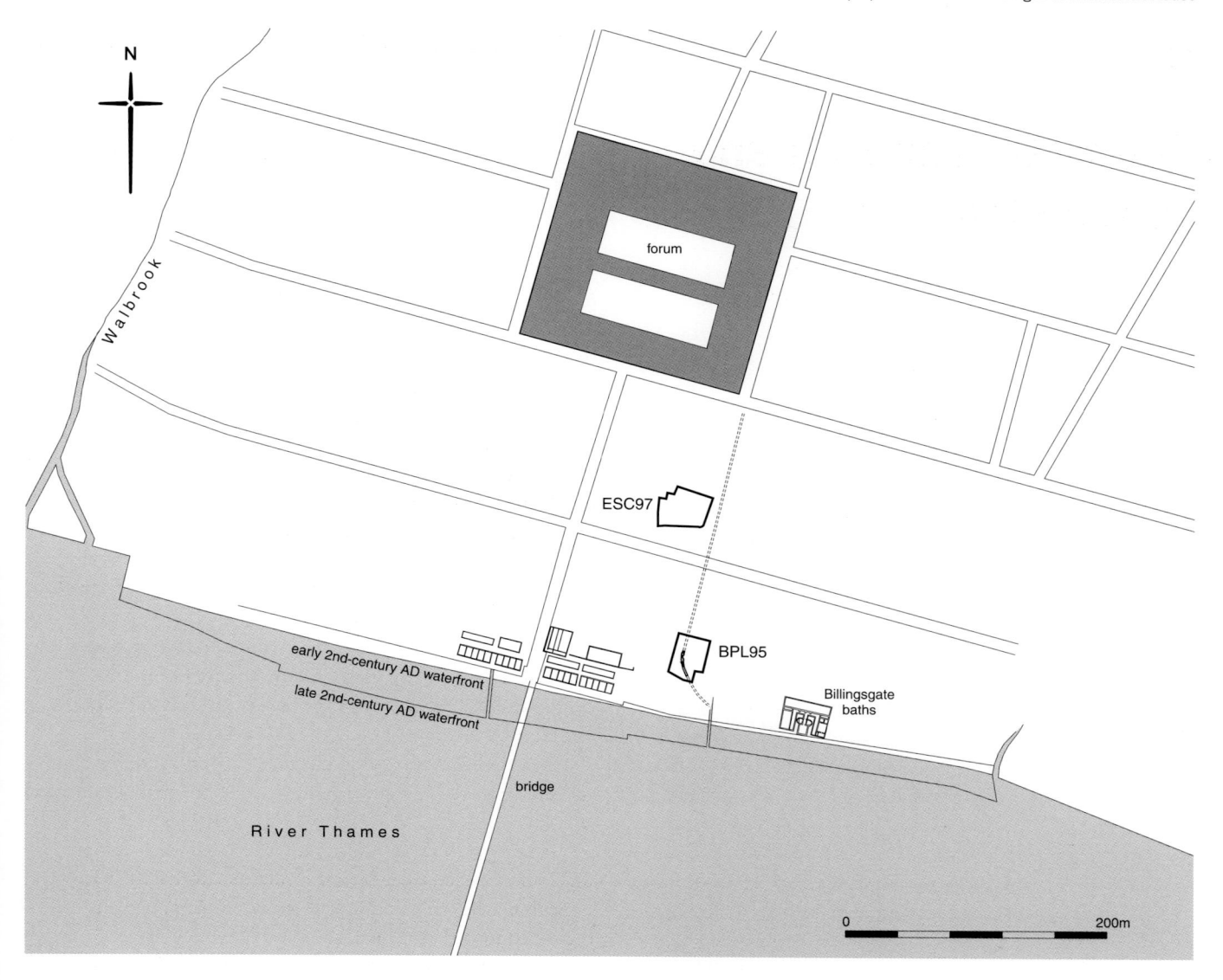

Fig 75 The alignment of the Roman culvert recorded at Monument House, shown in relation to the forum-basilica and the Thames waterfront (scale 1:5000)

enough to access and maintain were a rarity in Londinium. Examples of much smaller, buried timber box-drains, some with tile arches where they passed beneath terraced walls or buildings, have been found at several locations, particularly along the hillside behind the waterfront, where they were designed to carry surface run-off and spring-line water south to the Thames. Most roadside drains were built of timber, although a late 2nd-century AD tile culvert flanked the south side of the main east–west road at 1 Poultry (Hill and Rowsome in prep).

An apparent foundation burial beneath a Building 2 mortar floor and 'ritual' Camulodunum form 306 bowls found in the fills of the culvert (S3) (see discussion below) may indicate that the 3rd-century AD development at Monument House had a particular religious significance. The offering of votives to a range of water deities, many of which were adopted from Celtic mythology into the pantheon of Roman gods, was commonplace at sites close to a source of flowing water such as a spring or a well. However, although there was a preponderance of Camulodunum form 306 bowls from the culvert, there was a marked absence of coins and other finds

usually associated with votive sites. The deposition of the ritual bowl forms may represent a 'closure' deposit linked to superstition over the disuse and abandonment of the culvert.

The importance of the Camulodunum form 306 bowl

Robin P Symonds

The late Roman pottery assemblage from the period 3 phase 2 culvert (S3) disuse fills A[587] and A[641] at Monument House included examples of Camulodunum form 306, eight of which are illustrated as <P28>–<P35> (Fig 76). The bowl type is a simple bell-shaped bowl with a plain, thickened rim and an often badly finished base. It is, however, a form type with one of the most unusual distribution patterns of any Roman type found in London. The simplicity of the form is likely to be related to its function. The vessels are always broken and may have been deliberately smashed as part of a ritual or ceremony. The distribution of the type can be roughly divided into three

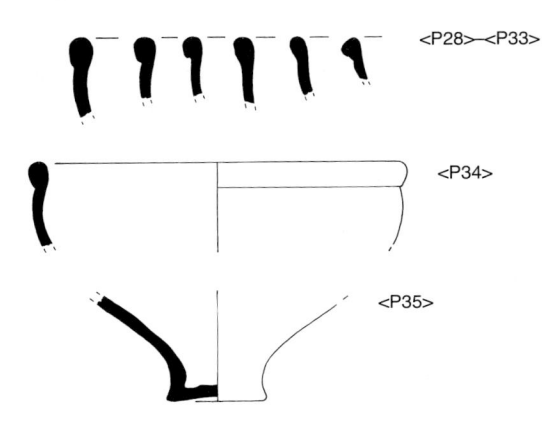

<P28>–<P33>

<P34>

<P35>

Fig 76 Camulodunum form 306 bowls <P28>–<P35> (scale 1:4)

categories: (1) sites where it is the predominant vessel shape in just one or a few localised assemblages; (2) sites where the form occurs abundantly in one or just a few assemblages, but does not entirely dominate those assemblages; and (3) sites where the form occurs in small numbers.

Out of almost 300 sites, 107–115 Borough High Street (107BHS81) in Southwark (Yule 1982; Rayner and Seeley in prep) accounts for 65.3% of the form in the MoLAS database, when measured by sherds. The form was also recorded in extraordinary numbers at three other London sites not listed in the database. These are the District Heating Scheme in Southwark (Hammerson 1988, 212–13), Billingsgate Buildings 'group Z',

Lower Thames Street (Green 1980, 72–3) and the temple of Mithras at Bucklersbury (Groves 1998, 103, 185). It was also common at the Butt Road cemetery at Colchester (Essex) (Symonds and Wade 1999). In all of the aforementioned 'category 1' assemblages Camulodunum form 306 is either the predominant form or the second most common form.

Whereas the last of these assemblages belongs unquestionably to the 4th century AD, the London assemblages seem to belong mainly to the early, middle or late 3rd century, with the exception of the Mithraeum vessels, the bulk of which are dated to the 'mid- to late fourth century' (Shepherd 1998, 184). In all these instances the abundance of the form is such that it seems likely it can be associated with some ritual activity observed in the vicinity, although it is only in the case of the Colchester examples that there is a definite link with funerary rites. There is some evidence for the use of the Camulodunum 306 form in ritual activities across the Empire – almost identical examples have been found at Apulum in central Dacia, in large favissa pits associated with a probable sanctuary dedicated to Liber Pater (Haynes in prep), although this is a 'category 2' site, where the form is abundant but not predominant (Table 1).

London 'category 2' sites are 2–10 Throgmorton Avenue, EC2 (TGM99) and Monument House (BPL95). Some comparative figures derived from the MoLAS database are shown in Table 1 and Table 2. The tables include figures for Northgate House, 20–28 Moorgate EC2 (MRG95), the largest and most important 'category 3' site, where the Camulodunum

Table 1 *Camulodunum form 306 bowls as a percentage of the total pottery assemblage at Monument House and selected other sites*

Site	Rows[1] 4C306s	Rows (total)	Rows (%)	Sherds 4C306s	Sherds (total)	Sherds (%)
107BHS81	13	648	2.0	924	2410	38.3
TGM99	25	3378	0.7	204	6254	3.3
MRG95	8	7748	0.1	17	30547	0.1
BPL95	35	1007	3.5	107	1822	5.9
Subtotal	81	12781	0.6	1252	41033	3.1
Other sites	101	178511	0.1	115	433685	0.0
All sites	182	191292	0.1	1367	474718	0.3

[1] Rows can be defined as the number of records in the MoLAS Oracle database, each of which contains all examples of each unique fabric, form and decoration combination; in practice, rows function in a very similar manner to 'minimum numbers of vessels'

Table 2 *Camulodunum form 306 bowls as a percentage of the total pottery assemblage in contexts where it is present at Monument House and selected other sites*

Site	Rows 4C306s	Rows (total)	Rows (%)	Sherds 4C306s	Sherds (total)	Sherds (%)
107BHS81	13	224	5.8	924	1346	68.6
TGM99	25	512	4.9	204	1318	15.5
MRG95	8	203	3.9	17	564	3.0
All BPL95	35	273	12.8	107	500	21.4
Strat BPL95	14	185	7.6	74	385	19.2

form 306 occurs in small numbers, apparently not concentrated in one or just a few assemblages. Of the 50 sites in the database where the form was found, 10 or more sherds of the form were found at only 8. Both 2–10 Throgmorton Avenue and 20–28 Moorgate are sites near to, or associated with, pottery production in the Moorgate area (Seeley and Drummond-Murray 2005), although there is no evidence for production of this particular form at 20–28 Moorgate.

A total of 89.7% of the 204 sherds at 2–10 Throgmorton Avenue are in an unsourced oxidised ware, and a further 8.3% are in a fine reduced ware fabric, whereas 97.9% of all the other 1211 sherds in the database are in reduced sandy grey ware. Such a high incidence of oxidised and fine grey examples at the site, and the fact that many of the examples are badly burnt, suggests possible production of this form in the Moorgate area.

Another 'category 3' site is the 'mithraeum' at Colchester (Essex), where the Camulodunum form was found in what may be a ritual context, but with few examples present.

Sedimentation in the Roman culvert

Jane Corcoran

Undisturbed sediment within the culvert (S3) was sampled at six locations, using nine monolith tins. A detailed method statement and report on the findings forms part of the site research archive and is only briefly summarised here. The sediments sampled in each tin were cleaned and described using standard sedimentary criteria (Gale and Hoare 1991) and their units were allocated to different facies, allowing comparison of deposits between profiles. A total of five facies types A–E were identified across all the profiles. From the earliest, these were: (E) initial sedimentation; (D) sediment accumulation during alternating turbulent/flowing and receding/still water conditions; (C) sediment settling out of still or slow-flowing water; (B) sediment deposited and winnowed by flowing water with little human input; and (A) localised and faster sedimentation and some winnowing.

Two main phases of sedimentation are visible in almost every profile. Phase 1 was a basal waterlain sequence (facies groups E to B) characterised by sediments sorted by fluvial processes, with scarce artefactual material that has undergone water transport and rolling for some time. Phase 2 was an upper diamict (facies A) of poorly sorted silty gravel with frequent artefactual material. The lower part of facies A is sandier and may have been winnowed by flowing water during or after deposition, while the upper part was regularly above water level and not strongly influenced by fluvial processes.

Phase 1 sediment (facies E–B): Phase 1 is made up of two distinct depositional stages: an early stage characterised by the deposition of fine clay-silts and a later stage when the surface of these clay-silts was eroded and redeposited with sandy sediments, characteristic of faster-flowing water. The duration of each stage is not known, but the relatively small amount of the lower clay-silt suggests that water was flowing fairly constantly and quickly in the early stage, carrying fine particles and most

larger clasts with it, although it is likely that very few larger clasts would have been carried into the culvert while the manhole shaft opening was above the level of material accumulating within the shaft itself. The manhole shaft may have been regularly cleaned out, but the bedded, sorted nature of the sediment suggests that it was not cleaned during the waterlain phase of sedimentation. Phase 1 could therefore have continued for as long as there was not sufficient input of sediment to choke the system.

Phase 2 sediment (facies A): The second phase of sedimentation is distinguished by the probability of a greatly increased sediment influx and a greater input of artefacts. Facies group A may have accumulated through a gradual build-up of material carried downstream during higher flow events, or by material input directly into the culvert from above, if openings existed or were cut during this phase of accumulation. The lack of depositional or post-depositional sorting implies different processes to those in phase 1, with less fluvial influence. The upper deposits do not appear to have been sorted to any extent. The use of the culvert may have changed by this time, maintenance of silt traps to prevent sedimentation may have lapsed or new openings into the culvert may have allowed more material to find its way into the channel.

Tidal influence: It is likely that during high tides saline water would have flowed into the culvert from the Thames, although diatom analysis was not undertaken to confirm this. Tidal ingress may have been associated with deposition of material and ponding-back of the outflow. This situation would cause increased precipitation of clay-sized particles, which flocculate to silt-size and become too heavy to be suspended in saline conditions.

4.2 Conclusions

Peter Rowsome

Research findings

The excavations at Monument House and 13–21 Eastcheap provided important new archaeological information which was analysed according to revised research aims developed during post-excavation assessment of the two sites (Blair 2000; Sankey 1999).

The evidence of early Roman terracing at the two sites adds to our understanding of the development of the sloping ground between the Thames and Cornhill. The Monument House evidence is particularly notable, however, for two sets of structures and their associated finds assemblages: a 3rd-century AD drainage culvert and 15th-century buildings destroyed in the Great Fire.

The Roman culvert recorded at Monument House is the only known example of a large, subterranean storm drain or sewer from Londinium, and it is now preserved *in situ* beneath the new development. It was designed to flush dirty water into the Thames but the source of that water is not certain. The culvert may have provided drainage from the forum-basilica 200m to the north or have solely served the overlying stone building or an unidentified building nearby. In either case, the provision of a dedicated underground culvert may only have been justified for a property which was a large consumer of water, such as a bathhouse or some other high-status public building.

The development of tenements north of Cat Lane from the 15th century until the Great Fire included buildings to the south and east of a courtyard to the east of Botolph Lane which may have been associated with Lombard's Place to the east. The cellars of the buildings survived and included significant structural details, many relating to early 17th-century renovations. Destruction debris contained the most important assemblage of finds so far recovered from a Great Fire deposit, including decorated tiles and ironwork from the stock of an ironmonger or hardware retailer along with objects from his household.

Future research questions

The recent work will help inform the development of new research goals for future excavation and study of existing archives, with research questions related to the *Research framework for London 2002* (Nixon et al 2002).

The route of the 3rd-century AD culvert recorded at Monument House can be conjectured north and south, allowing provision to be made for its excavation, study and preservation at development sites along its path. Study of the culvert can contribute to general research into Londinium's water supply and drainage, answering *Roman research priorities* such as *Development – the chronology and character of settlement R3 and – the built environment R4* (Nixon et al 2002, 31–4). The late medieval buildings and the Great Fire finds assemblage add to understanding of the growth of 15th- to 17th-century London in terms of its material culture and economy. Further comparative study of key finds assemblages should answer *London after 1500 research priorities* including *Economy L9 and L10* (Nixon et al 2002, 73–6).

The findings from the two sites can address research themes *Development - infrastructure TD4, Economy – distribution and consumption TE2 and TE3* and *Continuity and change – material culture TC4* (Nixon et al 2002, 82, 89) and will contribute to synthetic research into the wider settlement.

5

Specialist appendices

5.1 The Roman pottery

Robin P Symonds (Monument House); Beth Richardson with Louise Rayner (13–21 Eastcheap)

The Roman assemblage from Monument House totalled 1829 sherds, with much of the material recovered from residual situations in post-Roman contexts. The pottery assemblage from 13–21 Eastcheap amounted to 1978 sherds. A wide range of fabrics were identified in the assemblages, the majority of which are types commonly recorded in City groups. Detailed reports form parts of the research archive, with selected evidence summarised in the chronological narrative. Full lists of the fabric, form and decoration codes are available from the archive. Details of the illustrated Roman pottery, listed by <P> number, are given in Table 3.

5.2 The medieval and post-medieval pottery

Lyn Blackmore (Monument House); Roy Stephenson (13–21 Eastcheap)

A total of 1850 sherds of medieval and post-medieval pottery was recovered from the Monument House site, of which 1502 are of medieval date. The assemblage from 13–21 Eastcheap was much smaller, with more material dating from the post-medieval period, and was not taken beyond assessment. Reports on the assemblages form part of the site research archives, with selected evidence integrated with the chronological narrative. Full lists of the fabric, form and decoration codes are available from the archive. Details of the illustrated pottery, listed by <P> number, are given in Table 4.

Although much of the pottery from Monument House is residual, the predominantly early medieval composition of the group partly reflects the early activity at New Fresh Wharf and Billingsgate. The main period of deposition fits with the first significant activity at Seal House and Swan Lane (late 11th to mid 12th century: Steedman et al 1992; Vince 1985, 86–9; Vince 1991; Vince 1992, 141; Schofield and Dyson in prep). This suggests that the pottery, which is entirely domestic in character, reflects the urbanisation of the area that accompanied the construction of waterfronts 6–10 at Billingsgate. Similar groups of this date have been recovered from the nearby site of Governor's House (Blackmore 2001) and elsewhere along the waterfront.

The most interesting aspect of the post-medieval assemblage is the presence of three complete pots buried at the foot of three different staircases in Buildings 6 and 7. The tradition of burying votive offerings beneath buildings goes back to the Roman period (Merrifield 1965, 54, 277, no. 287). The only possible medieval examples from London are two complete Saxo-Norman pots buried beneath the floor of Building 23 at Gateway House,

Table 3 Details of the illustrated Roman pottery from sites A (Monument House) and B (13–21 Eastcheap)

Cat no.	Site/context	Site: period/phase	Site: land use	Form	Fabric	Fig no.
<P1>	A[709]	A:2ph1	A:S1	Camulodunum 8C186 amphora	CADIZ	6
<P2>	A[224]	A:2ph1	A:S2	cup ?6	FMIC	6
<P3>	A[515]	A:2ph2	A:B1	necked jar 2T	VCWS	8
<P4>	A[515]	A:2ph2	A:B1	lid 9A	LOXI	8
<P5>	A[200]	A:3ph1	A:B2	rouletted and stamped decoration ROU, STD	NVCC	22
<P14>	B[113]	B:4	B:OA6	shallow simple dish 5J3	BB1	73
<P15>	B[113]	B:4	B:OA6	shallow simple dish 5J3	BB1	73
<P16>	B[113]	B:4	B:OA6	everted-rimmed jar 2F	BB1	73
<P17>	B[113]	B:4	B:OA6	round-rimmed bowl 4H5	BB2F	73
<P18>	B[113]	B:4	B:OA6	round-rimmed bowl 4H5	BB2F	73
<P19>	B[113]	B:4	B:OA6	jar 2F OL	BBS	73
<P20>	B[113]	B:4	B:OA6	jar 2F VL	BBS	73
<P21>	B[113]	B:4	B:OA6	round-rimmed bowl 4H5	AHFA	73
<P22>	B[113]	B:4	B:OA6	everted-rimmed jar 2FX	AHFA	73
<P23>	B[113]	B:4	B:OA6	jar 2W	SAND	73
<P24>	B[113]	B:4	B:OA6	indented beaker 3 END	MOSL	73
<P25>	B[113]	B:4	B:OA6	indented beaker 3 RND	MOSL	73
<P26>	B[113]	B:4	B:OA6	globular beaker 3K variant	MOSL	73
<P27>	B[113]	B:4	B:OA6	beaker 3 UND	MICA	73
<P28>	A[587]	A:3ph2	A:S3	Camulodunum bowl 4C306	SAND	76
<P29>	A[587]	A:3ph2	A:S3	Camulodunum bowl 4C306	SAND	76
<P30>	A[587]	A:3ph2	A:S3	Camulodunum bowl 4C306	SAND	76
<P31>	A[587]	A:3ph2	A:S3	Camulodunum bowl 4C306	SAND	76
<P32>	A[587]	A:3ph2	A:S3	Camulodunum bowl 4C306	SAND	76
<P33>	A[587]	A:3ph2	A:S3	Camulodunum bowl 4C306	SAND	76
<P34>	A[641]	A:3ph2	A:S3	Camulodunum bowl 4C306	SAND	76
<P35>	A[587]	A:3ph2	A:S3	Camulodunum bowl 4C306	SAND	76

Table 4 Details of the illustrated medieval and post-medieval pottery from site A (Monument House)

Cat no.	Site/context	Site: period	Site: land use	Form	Fabric	Fig no.
<P6>	A[577]	A:4	A:B3	globular jar	RHGR	27
<P7>	A[464]	A:4	A:OA4	waisted baluster jug	LOND EAS	27
<P8>	A[422]	A:4	A:OA4	frying pan	KING	27
<P9>	A[183]	A:5	A:OA5	basket-handled bowl	CBW	30
<P10>	A[387]	A:5	A:OA5	decorated jug	LCALC	30
<P11>	A[148]	A:6	A:B6	deep two-handled jar	PMFR	36
<P12>	A[149]	A:6	A:B7	rounded two-handled jar	PMSRG	36
<P13>	A[104]	A:7	A:OA9	stoneware Bartmann jug	FREC	40

Cannon Street (Blackmore 2002, 35). Other medieval finds differ in that they are mainly from churches, usually placed in a cavity between the walls (Merrifield 1969, 100).

Complete pots were buried beneath the doorsteps of houses in the Netherlands and Germany in the post-medieval period (Merrifield 1969, 101), but in London the known finds were, until recently, from churches and institutions. One was placed in the foundations of the gatehouse at Aldgate, which is dated to 1607, while another was buried beneath the Wren Tower at St Mary Aldermanbury. Both are described as brown-glazed cooking pots (Merrifield 1969, 100–1). A large Woolwich redware jar found in 1954 in a well at Gateway House (ER207) and a complete pot found at St Stephen's church, Coleman Street, may have had a similar function.

The finds from Monument House belong to a growing number of similar pots from domestic contexts dating to between 1580 and 1666. Others include two *in situ* examples from post-Dissolution but pre-1680 contexts at Spitalfields (SRP98; Jeffries 2002) and two more found in Lamb Street, Spitalfields (SQU94, BHF97). The rims of these pots were flush with the floor, suggesting that they were not foundation offerings as such. They could have been covered by a lid and have contained something to ward off evil spirits, like a witch bottle (Maloney 1980). They may also have had a more practical function and possible uses include storage, or some medicinal or alchemical purpose. Several later medieval recipes survive which required pots to be buried and sometimes left over a period of time. In many cases two pots were involved, with an upper one draining into a lower one that was buried in a small pit (Moorhouse 1981, 117–18). The placing of such equipment by a staircase, however, seems improbable. The Spitalfields finds were interpreted as soakaways (Jeffries 2002), but the base of at least one of the Monument House pots is complete and could not have provided drainage without overflowing. A more plausible function of the pots may be as traps for vermin.

5.3 Accessioned finds

Jackie Keily (Roman) and Geoff Egan (medieval and post-medieval) (Monument House); Jackie Keily (13–21 Eastcheap)

Introduction

Important individual finds from the two sites are presented as part of the chronological narrative. The catalogues below are restricted to the illustrated finds from each site. A more detailed report and catalogue for each site forms part of the research archive.

A total of 452 accessioned finds were recovered during the course of excavation at Monument House, including 25 coins. Analytical work on the Monument House findings was concentrated on the Great Fire assemblage, presented in the chronological narrative. At 13–21 Eastcheap a total of 110 accessioned finds were recovered, most of them from Roman contexts and including 14 coins.

Characteristics of the site assemblages

At Monument House the earliest Roman activity produced few accessioned finds. Those that did survive are dominated by vessel glass, possibly a reflection of poor preservation conditions for both metals and organics.

The redevelopment of the site in the mid 3rd century AD is reflected in the increased number of accessioned finds present, particularly a high number of objects of personal adornment. A more normal pattern in Roman urban assemblages is for fasteners and fittings, a rather broad category, to dominate. The dominance of items of personal adornment may indicate that a bathhouse lay nearby, though the only object associated with personal hygiene was recovered from 'dark earth'. The construction fills associated with the culvert produced the two most interesting accessioned objects: the enamelled brooch and belt plate. The latter may have military associations (Bateson 1981, 55). The origin of both the brooch and the belt plate is unknown, and while they may be British a Continental origin cannot be ruled out (ibid, 99–107, 108–9). Usage and disuse fills within the culvert and manhole contained few finds.

The overall Roman accessioned finds assemblage from Monument House is quite sparse. The absence of evidence for industrial activities may be notable but little is indicated about the status of the site.

The few medieval non-ceramic finds are diverse, with several textile-working items – a small group of Saxon loom weights and an unusual find of a pair of woolcombs <S6>. A fragment of a stone mortar is a category of object usually associated with institutional sites or affluent dwellings.

The majority of the accessioned finds from 13–21 Eastcheap are Roman in date and the assemblage is rather limited, being largely domestic in nature and mainly comprising vessel glass. The majority of the finds date to the 1st to 2nd centuries AD and most are quite fragmentary. Very little metalwork survived as a result of the poor preservation conditions. The relative lack of medieval or post-medieval registered finds may have been primarily owing to truncation.

The glass assemblage comprises a range of domestic vessel and window glass broadly dated to the late 1st and 2nd centuries AD. The earliest fragment is a mid 1st-century AD beaker base <S33>. Most vessels are naturally coloured, though two small fragments are amber-coloured. There is very little higher quality colourless glass, the only identifiable forms being drinking vessels, an indented beaker B<42> and the base of a facet-cut beaker B<8>. The forms represented are generally utilitarian, made up of containers such as bottles, storage jars and phials with a few fragments of jugs or flagons. A number of small fragments of finer tablewares, such as beakers and bowls, were also found. A complete but flattened globular jar <S34>, possibly an unguent jar, is burnt.

The site produced six fragments of window glass. One of these, possibly a large part of a single pane now broken, is also burnt and the fragments fused together <S39>. All the window glass fragments belong to the earlier Roman cast glossy/matt type, with distinctive rounded edges. In addition to the vessel glass, there is one glass bead <S32>.

Catalogue of illustrated finds from the two sites

Monument House

PERSONAL ADORNMENT

<S1> Copper-alloy belt plate (Fig 19)
A<386>, A[416]; period 3, S3 Complete; L 45mm, W 10–16mm. Tapering rectangular plate with hinged fitting at narrower end for missing buckle. The plate is decorated with an enamel design of heart-shaped leaves. The background contains traces of blue enamel, while the colour of the enamel on the leaves is indecipherable. The form of these leaves is reminiscent of those found on seal boxes of the 2nd to 3rd century AD (Cool and Philo 1998, 100, fig 37, no. 493; Crummy 1983, 103, fig 106, nos 2523 and 2525), mosaics (for example, Neal 1981, figs 63 and 73; Toynbee 1962, figs 209 and 214) and other objects (for example, Bateson 1981, fig 8A and C). Enamelled belt plates are known from Caerleon (Monmouthshire) (Webster 1992, 122–3) and other military sites in the north and south-west of Britain (Bateson 1981, 55). This example is of a type that dates to the 2nd century AD and it may have been made in Britain, although a Continental origin cannot be ruled out (ibid).

<S2> Copper-alloy brooch (Fig 19)
A<296>, A[416]; period 3, S3 Near complete; Diam (including lugs) 28mm. Disc brooch with six peripheral lugs and a large raised central panel with enamelled decoration. The enamelling is in the form of a *millefiori* chequer-board comprising small white squares or quatrefoils on a ?red ground. The lower surrounding rim is

slightly recessed and may have been originally enamelled also. The edges of this central panel and of the brooch itself are knurled. The rear of the central panel has a small central recess with a raised rim, a feature noted on other similar brooches (Hattatt 1985, 148, no. 543). Hinged pin now missing. Dates to the 2nd century AD. A similar example, although without enamelling, was found at Billingsgate in the City of London (ibid).

HOUSEHOLD UTENSILS

<S3> 'Airlie' cup (Fig 19)
A<277>, A[416]; period 3, S3
Rim fragment from an 'Airlie' cup.

<S4> Glass bowl (Fig 19)
A<279>, A[416]; period 3, S3
Part of a bowl with an out-turned, fire-rounded rim, colourless glass.

HEALTH AND HYGIENE

<S5> Copper-alloy cosmetic set (Fig 23)
A<342>, A[192]; period 3, OA3
Incomplete; L 52mm. Small spoon; bowl missing; straight handle, widening at the top to a circular plate surmounted by a suspension loop.

MISCELLANEOUS

<S6> Pair of woolcombs (Fig 31)
A<397> and A<450>; period 5, OA5
Although corroded, the first is the more complete, with a basal sheet frame L 156, W 48, H 21mm; spikes protrude 78mm above this in two rows at c 10 per 60mm (cf Walton Rogers 1997, 1720–3; Goodall 1993, 182–3 nos 1415–29). The discovery of a pair is most unusual.

THE GREAT FIRE ASSEMBLAGE AND TOBACCO PIPES

<S7>–<S30>, period 6, OA9;
<S31>, period 8
Selected finds from the Great Fire assemblage and later periods are described and illustrated as part of the chronological narrative (Chapter 2.4).

13–21 Eastcheap

PERSONAL ORNAMENT

<S32> Glass bead (Fig 72)
B<71>, B[285]; period 5, OA9
Complete; L 18.5mm, H 11mm. Annular, natural blue-green glass; the central hole asymmetrical.

HOUSEHOLD UTENSILS

<S33> Glass beaker (Fig 67)
B<2>, B[317]; period 2, OA3
Incomplete; natural green blue beaker with a thick flat base with an internal dome. Mid/late 1st century AD; ?Isings 34.

<S34> Glass jar (Fig 69)
B<43>, B[155]; period 4, OA7
Complete; a small natural green blue burnt jar, its shape distorted by the heat. Possibly an unguent jar for holding bath oils; 1st to 3rd century AD; Isings 68.

<S35> Ceramic lamp (Fig 74)
B<67>, B[113]; period 5, OA6
Complete; L 74.5mm, H 28mm. Firmalampe of Loeschcke Type X, with open nozzle channel and no handle. The lamp is poorly moulded with three very blurred unpierced vestigial lugs on the rim and the whole object is somewhat lop-sided. There is a small central filling hole in the discus, and sooting around the wick hole in the nozzle. Mica-dusted fabric, probably local (LOMI); probably 2nd century AD.

WRITTEN COMMUNICATIONS

<S36> Copper-alloy ?seal box (Fig 69)
B<74>, B[119]; period 4, OA7
Incomplete; L 27mm, W 23mm, Th 9mm. A small rectangular box, with a bar hinge at one end and with three round perforations on one surface. The sides are slightly bevelled. The hinge arrangement is unusual for a seal box.

FASTENINGS AND FITTINGS

<S37> Copper-alloy mount (Fig 71)
B<32>, B[135]; period 4, OA8
Near complete; Diam 58.5mm. A plain circular plate, with a small central hole; there are four rivet holes around edge and three globular-headed nails remaining.

<S38> Copper-alloy ?fitting/mount (Fig 71)
B<19>, B[154]; period 4, OA8
?Incomplete; L 42mm. Circular-sectioned object with swelling at mid point and pointed terminal. Possibly part of a strap tag or scabbard runner, the upper part lost. Similarities with a terminal thought to be from a scabbard runner or a strap tag from South Shields (Durham) (Allason-Jones and Miket 1984, 197, no. 3.649).

MISCELLANEOUS

<S39> Window glass (Fig 72)
B<73>, B[285]; period 5, OA9
Natural green blue; glossy/matt; rounded edges. Up to seven layers of glass burnt and fused together; possibly from the same pane of glass.

FRENCH AND GERMAN SUMMARIES

Résumé

Cet ouvrage porte sur deux fouilles situées au nord-est de London Bridge, entre la berge et Cornhill au nord.

Monument House s'étire sur un terrain en forte pente à environ 120 m de la tête du pont. L'activité la plus ancienne de quelque importance était représentée par plusieurs zones d'extraction de graviers, du Ier siècle apr. J.-C. Ces carrières furent comblées et le terrain nivelé pour construire des bâtiments en bois à la fin du Ier ou au début du IIe siècle.

Un siècle plus tard, une vaste construction maçonnée fut établie sur la pente, dotée d'un drain enterré s'écoulant vers le sud. Un puits d'accès situé à l'extrémité nord de la canalisation contenait une trappe de limon en bois à sa base. Deux trappes pareilles mais plus petites à l'intérieur du drain comportaient une poutre datée de la fourchette 176-221 apr. J.-C. Des bols rituels furent découverts dans le comblement du drain, qui pouvait partir d'un bâtiment public situé au nord ou bien appartenir à un système d'évacuation des eaux usées partant du forum et de la basilique et se dirigeant vers la Tamise, au sud. Le bâtiment en terrasse et le drain restèrent en service jusqu'au milieu du IVe siècle et furent scellés par des « terres noires ».

La réoccupation du site prit la forme de deux fonds de cabane successifs établis au Xe siècle. Les parois du second, construits de madriers entre poteaux, furent détruits par un incendie dans le courant du XIe siècle. Les occupations ultérieures inclurent deux bâtiments adjacents du XVe siècle, établis sur les côtés sud et est d'une cour, qui ont pu faire partie de Lombardes Place. Sur la terrasse inférieure, au sud, une construction longeait Cat Lane, un étroit passage qui courait le long du côté nord du Cimetière Supérieur de l'église St-Botolphe.

Les caves de ces bâtiments furent reprises vers la fin du XVIe siècle, avec l'insertion de sols en brique et de nouveaux escaliers d'accès débouchant dans la cour. Ces constructions furent détruites par le Grand Incendie de 1666 et le mobilier qui leur était associé présente de nombreux objets rares, comme un ensemble important de pièces en fer, un manteau de cheminée richement orné et des carreaux de pavement et de revêtement mural.

Une vaste courte fermée établie après le Grand Incendie était associée à une belle demeure située à 32 Botolph Lane, reconstruite en 1670 par Arnold et Samuel Beake, membres d'une riche famille de marchands néerlandais. La maison fut démolie en 1906 mais la cour subsista jusqu'aux travaux engagés en 1998.

Le **13-21 Eastcheap** est situé environ 100 m plus au nord, sur le terrain plus élevé de Cornhill. Des travaux de terrassement du début de l'époque romaine y furent repérés mais il n'existait aucune trace de bâtiments contemporains ni de l'incendie associé à la révolte de Boudica (60-61 apr. J.-C.), détecté sur des sites proches. Des vestiges postérieurs à cette épisode furent observés ainsi que des bâtiments en terre et bois appartenant à la fin du Ier siècle apr. J.-C. La céramique comme l'ensemble du mobilier découvert étaient de nature domestique et incluaient une pièce en verre intact, peut-être un vase à onguent. Une partie des constructions fut recouverte par un dépotoir comportant une grande quantité de coquilles d'huîtres.

Une épaisse couche de débris brûlés peut être associée avec l'incendie dit d'Hadrien, des environs de 125 apr. J.-C. Les constructions ultérieures présentaient des canalisations en bois et des fondations de constructions maçonnées en calcaire sablonneux (« ragstone ») du Kent. De grandes quantités de céramique et d'ossements animaux, des IIIe et IVe siècles, furent prélevés dans les comblements des drains et des fosses.

L'occupation ultérieure à l'époque romaine fut fortement tronquée, malgré la conservation de fosses médiévales isolées, dont beaucoup contenant des « terres noires » et du mobilier antique redéposé. La faune découverte dans ces fosses peut être associée à la fonction de boucherie qu'a tenue Eastcheap au bas Moyen Âge.

Zusammenfassung

Dieser Bericht legt die Funde und Befunde von zwei Fundplätzen nordöstlich von London Bridge zwischen Flussufer und Cornhill im Norden vor.

Monument House lag an einem steil abfallenden Hang ca. 120 m vom Brückenkopf entfernt. Die früheste noch erkennbare Nutzung des Platzes trat in mehreren Kiesgruben des 1. Jhs. n.Chr. zutage. Diese wurden verfüllt und die Stelle planiert, um im späten 1. und frühen 2. Jh. die Errichtung von Holzhäusern zu ermöglichen.

Im späten 2. oder frühen 3. Jh. wurde ein großes Steingebäude am Abhang erbaut, in das ein südwärts verlaufender unterirdischer Abwassergraben integriert war. Ein Einstiegsschacht am Nordende des Abzugsgrabens barg an seinem Boden eine hölzerne Schlammfanggrube. Zwei kleinere Schlammfanggruben innerhalb des Abzugsgrabens lieferten ein Bauholz, das in die Zeit 176–221 n.Chr. datiert. Rituelle Schalen wurden in der Füllung des Abzugsgrabens entdeckt, der eventuell aus einem öffentlichen Gebäude im Norden kam oder als Teil eines Kanalsystems Abwasser vom Forum-Basilika-Komplex nach Süden in die Themse leitete. Das terrassenförmig angelegte Gebäude und der Abzugsgraben blieben bis zur Mitte des 4. Jhs. in Gebrauch und lagen unter einer Schicht der so genannten „dark earth".

Die Wiederbesiedlung des Platzes stellt sich uns in zwei aufeinander folgenden Grubenhäusern aus dem 10. Jh. dar. Die Pfosten-Bohlen-Wände des jüngeren Baus wurden durch ein Feuer im 11. Jh. zerstört. Spätere Anwesen beinhalteten zwei aneinandergebaute Gebäude des 15. Jhs. an der Süd- und Ostseite eines Hofes. Diese mögen einen Teil von Lombardes Place gebildet haben. Das tiefer liegende Gebäude auf der südlichen Terrasse flankierte außerdem Cat Lane, eine enge Gasse, die entlang der Nordseite des Oberen Kirchhofs der St. Botolphs-Kirche verlief.

Die Keller dieser Gebäude wurden im späten 16. Jh. neu gestaltet, indem Ziegelböden und ein neuer Treppenzugang zum Hof geschaffen wurden. Während des Großen Feuers von 1666 kam es zur Zerstörung, und die damit in Verbindung stehenden Fundkomplexe enthalten viele seltene Objekte, u. a. eine große Gruppe von Eisengegenständen, ein aufwendig ornamentierter Kaminsims und sowohl Boden- als auch Wandfliesen.

Ein großer geschlossener Hofkomplex, der nach dem Großen Feuer angelegt wurde, stand in Verbindung mit einem vornehmen Haus in 32 Botolph Lane, das 1670 von Arnold und Samuel Beake, Angehörigen einer reichen Kaufmannsfamilie aus den Niederlanden, wiedererbaut wurde. Im Jahre 1906 wurde der Bau abgerissen, der Hof aber blieb bis zur Neugestaltung von 1998 erhalten.

13–21 Eastcheap liegt ca. 100 m weiter nördlich auf etwas höherem Terrain des Cornhill. Frührömische Terrassierungen des Hügelhanges wurden hier nachgewiesen, aber keine Spuren von Bebauung oder der Brandschicht aus der Zeit des Boudica-Aufstandes (60–61 n.Chr.), wie sie von nahe gelegenen Fundplätzen bekannt sind. Fragmentierte Reste von Befunden aus der Zeit nach dem Aufstand und Holz-Erde-Bauten aus dem späten 1. Jh. n.Chr. kamen zutage. Keramik und andere Funde besaßen zivilen Siedlungscharakter und enthielten ein vollständiges Glasgefäß, möglicherweise ein *unguentarium*. Einige der Gebäude waren überdeckt von einem Abfallhaufen, der große Mengen von Austernschalen barg.

Eine ansehnliche Schicht verbrannter Reste könnte mit dem „hadrianischen Feuer" von ca. 125 n.Chr. in Verbindung stehen. Die nach-hadrianische Bebauung wies holzverkleidete Abwasserkanäle und Fundamente von Steingebäuden aus einem sandigen Kalkstein („Kentish ragstone") auf. Große Mengen von Keramik und Tierknochen stammen aus den Kanal- und Grubenfüllungen des 3. und 4. Jhs.

Die Schichten, die der römischen Periode folgten, waren stark gestört, obwohl einige isolierte mittelalterliche Gruben überlebt hatten. Viele enthielten „dark earth" und römische Siedlungsfunde. Die Tierknochen lassen sich vielleicht durch die Rolle von Eastcheap als Schlachtzentrum während des späten Mittelalters erklären.

BIBLIOGRAPHY

Manuscript sources

Corporation of London Records Office, London (CLRO) (now part of the London Metropolitan Archives)

HR Husting Rolls: deeds and wills enrolled in the Court of Husting

Guildhall Library, London (GL)

MS 59 register of the parish church of St Botolph Billingsgate
MS 1239/1–2 churchwardens' accounts of St Mary at Hill, 1422–1526

Printed and other secondary works

Alcock, N W, and Galinou, M, 2006 *The Beake House revealed: the history of a Dutch merchant's house, 32 Botolph Lane, London*, London Topographical Record, London

Alcock, N W, and Hall, L, 1994 *Fixtures and fittings in dated houses 1567–1763*, CBA Practical Handbook in Archaeology 11, York

Allason-Jones, L, and Miket, R, 1984 *The catalogue of small finds from South Shields Roman fort*, Soc Antiq Newcastle upon Tyne Monogr Ser 2, Newcastle upon Tyne

Atkinson, D R, and Oswald, A, 1969 London clay tobacco pipes, *J Brit Archaeol Ass* 32, 171–227

Bateson, J D, 1981 *Enamel working in Iron Age, Roman and sub-Roman Britain: the products and techniques*, BAR Brit Ser 93, Oxford

Betts, I M, 1991 Medieval and later building material from Billingsgate Fish Market car park, Lower Thames Street (BIG82), unpub MoL rep

Betts, I M, 1994 Appendix: medieval floor tiles in London churches, in Schofield, J, Saxon and medieval parish churches in the City of London: a review, *Trans London Middlesex Archaeol Soc* 45, 133–40

Betts, I M, in prep The building materials, in Bluer, R, and Blatherwick, S, *Great houses, moats and mills on the south bank of the Thames: medieval and Tudor Southwark and Rotherhithe*, MoLAS Monogr Ser

Bird, J, Graham, A H, Sheldon, H L, and Townend, P (eds), 1978 *Southwark excavations 1972–4* (2 vols), Joint Publ London Middlesex Archaeol Soc/Surrey Archaeol Soc 1, London

Blackmore, L, 2001 The pottery, in Brigham, T, and Woodger, A, *Roman and medieval townhouses on the London waterfront: excavations at Governor's House, City of London*, MoLAS Monogr Ser 9, 35, London

Blackmore, L, 2002 The pots buried beneath the cellar floor of Building 23, in Elsden, N J, *Excavations at 25 Cannon Street, City of London: from the Middle Bronze Age to the Great Fire*, MoLAS Archaeol Stud Ser 5, London

Blair, I, 2000 Monument House 30–35 Botolph Lane, 29–31 Monument Street, London EC3: an archaeological post-excavation assessment and updated project design, unpub MoL rep

Blair, I, and Hall, J, 2003 *Working water: Roman technology in action*, Museum of London

Blair, I, Spain, R, Swift, D, Taylor, T, and Goodburn, D, 2006

Wells and bucket-chains: unforeseen elements of water supply in early Roman London, Britannia 37, 1–52

Bluer, R, and Brigham, T, with Nielsen, R, 2006 Roman and later development east of the forum and Cornhill: excavations at Lloyd's Register, 71 Fenchurch Street, City of London, MoLAS Monogr Ser 30, London

Brigham, T, 1990 The late Roman waterfront in London, Britannia 21, 99–183

Brigham, T, and Watson, B, 1996 Current archaeological work at Regis House in the City of London (part 2), London Archaeol 8(3), 63–9

Brigham, T, and Woodger, A, 2001 Roman and medieval townhouses on the London waterfront: excavations at Governor's House, City of London, MoLAS Monogr Ser 9, London

Brigham, T, Watson, B, and Tyers, I, with Bartkowiak, R, 1996 Current archaeological work at Regis House in the City of London (part 1), London Archaeol 8(2), 31–8

Britton, F, 1987 London delftware, London

Bromley, J, 1960 The armorial bearings of the guilds of London, London

Cal Close R Calendar of the close rolls, 1892–1975, London

Cal Pat R Calendar of patent rolls (65 vols, 1291–1509, 1547–63), 1893–1948, London

Cool, H E M, and Philo, C (eds), 1998 Roman Castleford: excavations 1974–85: Vol 1, The small finds, Yorkshire Archaeol 4, Wakefield

Crummy, N, 1983 The Roman finds from excavations in Colchester 1971–9, Colchester Archaeol Rep 2, Colchester

Dam, J D van, 1991 (1988) Nederlandse tegels, 2 edn, Amsterdam

Davies, B J, with Hall, J, and Milne, G, 1992 An absolute chronology, in From Roman basilica to medieval market: archaeology in action in the City of London (ed G Milne), 60–72, London

Davies, B J, Richardson, B, and Tomber, R S, 1994 The archaeology of Roman London: Vol 5, A dated corpus of early Roman pottery from the City of London, CBA Res Rep 98, London

Davis, A, in prep The plant remains from Regis House, City of London EC3, unpub MoL rep

Dumbrell, R, 1992 Understanding antique wine bottles, Woodbridge (reprint)

Dunwoodie, L, 2004 Pre-Boudican and later activity on the site of the forum: excavations at 168 Fenchurch Street, City of London, MoLAS Archaeol Stud Ser 13, London

Dunwoodie, L, Harward, C, and Pitt, K, in prep Roman fortifications and urban development on the eastern hill: excavations at Plantation Place, City of London, MoLAS Monogr Ser, London

Dyson, T, 1990 King Alfred and the restoration of London, London J 15, 99–110

Dyson, T, 1992 The early London waterfront and the local street system, in Steedman, K, Dyson, T, and Schofield, J, Aspects of Saxo-Norman London: Vol 3, The bridgehead and Billingsgate to 1200, London Middlesex Archaeol Soc Spec Pap 14, 122–31, London

Eames, E S, 1980 Catalogue of medieval lead-glazed earthenware tiles in the Department of Medieval and Later Antiquities, British Museum, London

Egan, G, 1998 The medieval household: daily living c 1150–c 1450, HMSO Medieval Finds Excav London 6, London

Fries Museum, 1971 Antwerps plateel, Leeuwarden

Gale, S J, and Hoare, P G, 1991 Quaternary sediments: petrographic methods for the study of unlithified rocks, London

Giorgi, J, in prep Cereal supply, processing and distribution in Roman London, unpub MoL rep

Godfrey, W H, 1962 A history of architecture in and around London, London

Goodall, I H, 1993 Reports on various iron finds, in Margeson, S (ed), Norwich households: medieval and post-medieval finds from Norwich Survey excavations, 1971–8 (ed S Margeson), E Anglian Archaeol 58, 124–33, Norwich

Gotch, J A, 1914 (1901) Early Renaissance architecture in England: a historical and descriptive account of the Tudor, Elizabethan and Jacobean periods, 1500–1625, 2 edn, London

Gowland, R L, and Chamberlain, A, 2002 A Bayesian approach to ageing perinatal skeletal material from archaeological sites: implications for the evidence for infanticide in Roman Britain, J Archaeol Sci 29, 677–85

Green, C M, 1980 The Roman pottery, in Jones 1980, 39–79

Grew, F, 1984 Small finds, in Thompson, A, Grew, F, and Schofield, J, Excavations at Aldgate, 1974, Post-Medieval Archaeol 18, 91–128

Groves, J, 1993 Ceramic studies, in Milne, G, and Wardle, A, Early Roman development at Leadenhall Court, London, and related research, Trans London Middlesex Archaeol Soc 44, 114–50

Groves, J, 1998 The pottery: general discussion, in Shepherd 1998, 102–6

Hammerson, M J, 1988 Roman pottery, in Excavations in Southwark 1973–6, Lambeth 1973–9 (ed P Hinton), Joint Publ London Middlesex Archaeol Soc/Surrey Archaeol Soc 3, 193–294, London

Harben, H A, 1918 A dictionary of the City of London, London

Hattatt, R, 1985 Iron Age and Romano-British brooches, Oxford

Hawkes, C F C, and Hull, M R, 1947 Camulodunum: first report on the excavations at Colchester 1930–9, Rep Res Comm Soc Antiq London 14, London

Haynes, I (ed), in prep Excavations at Apulum 1998–2003

Hill, C, Millett, M, and Blagg, T, 1980 The Roman riverside wall and monumental arch in London: excavations at Baynard's Castle, Upper Thames Street, London, 1974–6 (ed T Dyson), London Middlesex Archaeol Soc Spec Pap 3, London

Hill, J, and Rowsome, P, in prep Roman London and the Walbrook stream crossing: excavations at 1 Poultry and vicinity, City of London, MoLAS Monogr Ser, London

Holbrook, N, and Bidwell, P T, 1991 Roman finds from Exeter, Exeter Archaeol Rep 4, Exeter

Horne, J, 1989 English tin-glazed tiles, London

Horsman, V, Milne, C, and Milne, G, 1988 Aspects of Saxo-Norman London: Vol 1, Building and street development near Billingsgate and Cheapside, London Middlesex Archaeol Soc Spec Pap 11, London

Horwood, R, 1813 Plan of the Cities of London and Westminster, the borough of Southwark, 3 edn, reproduced in Margary, H, 1985 The A–Z of Regency London, Margary in assoc Guildhall Library, Kent

Isings, C, 1957 Roman glass from dated finds, Archaeologica Traiectina 2, Groningen

Jeffery, P, 1996 The parish church of St Mary at Hill in the City of London, Ecclesiological Soc, London

Jeffries, N, 2002 Spitalfields pottery assessment (SRP98), unpub MoL rep

Jenning, C, 1974 Early chests in wood and iron, Public Record Office Museum Pamphlet 7, London

Jones, D M, 1980 Excavations at Billingsgate Buildings 'Triangle', Lower Thames Street, 1974 (ed M Rhodes), London Middlesex Archaeol Soc Spec Pap 4, London

Jones, P E (ed), 1970 The Fire Court: Vol 2, London

Littlehales, H, 1904–5 The medieval records of a London City parish (St Mary at Hill), 1420–1559, Early English Text Society, Original Ser 125 and 128

Lloyd, N, 1949 (1931) A history of the English house, 2 edn, London

Lobel, M D (ed), 1989 The British atlas of historic towns: Vol 3, The City of London, from prehistoric times to c 1520, Oxford

Lyne, M A B, and Jefferies, R S, 1979 The Alice Holt/Farnham Roman pottery industry, CBA Res Rep 30, London

Maloney, C, 1980 A witch bottle from Duke's Place, Aldgate, Trans London Middlesex Archaeol Soc 31, 157–8

Marsh, G, and Tyers, P A, 1978 The Roman pottery from Southwark, in Southwark excavations 1972–4 (eds J Bird, A H Graham, H Sheldon and P Townend) (2 vols), Joint Publ London Middlesex Archaeol Soc/Surrey Archaeol Soc 1, 533–82, London

Melling, J K, 1995 Discovering London's guilds and liveries, Princes Risborough

Merrifield, R, 1965 The Roman city of London, London

Merrifield, R, 1969 Folklore in London Archaeology: Part 2, Post-Roman period, London Archaeol 1(5), 99–104

Mills, P, and Oliver, J, 1962–7 The survey of building sites in the City of London after the Great Fire of 1666 (1667–73), London Topogr Soc Publ, London

Milne, G, 1985 The port of Roman London, London

Milne, G, 1986 The Great Fire of London, London

Moorhouse, S, 1981 The medieval pottery industry and its markets, in Medieval industry (ed D W Crossley), CBA Res Rep 40, 96–125, London

Musson, J, 2000 Plasterwork: 100 period details from the archive of Country Life, London

Neal, D S, 1981 Roman mosaics in Britain, Gloucester

Neve, R, 1726 (1703) The city and country purchaser, and builder's dictionary, 2 edn, London, reissued in facsimile Newton Abbot, 1969

Nixon, T, McAdam, E, Tomber, R, and Swain, H, with Rowsome, P, 2002 A research framework for London archaeology 2002, London

Noël Hume, I, 1977 Early English delftware from London and Virginia, Colonial Williamsburg Occas Pap Archaeol 2, Williamsburg

Norton, C, 1993 The export of decorated floor tiles from Normandy, in Medieval art, architecture and archaeology at Rouen (ed J Stratford), Brit Archaeol Ass Conference Trans 12, 81–97, London

Ogilby, J, and Morgan, W, 1676 'Large and Accurate Map of the City of London', reproduced in Margary, H, 1976, 'Large and Accurate Map of the City of London' by John Ogilby and William Morgan, 1676, Margary in assoc Guildhall Library, Kent

Oswald, A, 1975 Clay pipes for the archaeologist, BAR Brit Ser 14, Oxford

Pearce, J, and Vince, A G, 1988 A dated type-series of London medieval pottery: Part 4, Surrey whitewares, London Middlesex Archaeol Soc Spec Pap 10, London

Perring, D, 1991 Roman London, London

Pitt, K, in prep Excavations at 41 Eastcheap, City of London, Trans London Middlesex Archaeol Soc

Pluis, J, 1997 De Nederlandse tegel: decors en benamingen 1570–1930 [The Dutch tile: designs and names 1570–1930], Leiden

Price, J, and Cottam, S, 1998 Romano-British glass vessels: a handbook, CBA Practical Handbook in Archaeology 14, York

Rackham, J, 1994 Economy and environment in Saxon London, in Environment and economy in Anglo-Saxon England: a review of recent work on the environmental archaeology of rural and urban Anglo-Saxon settlements in England (ed J Rackham), CBA Res Rep 89, 126–35, London

Ray, A, 1973 English delftware tiles, London

Ray, A, 2000 Spanish pottery 1248–1898, London

Rayner, L, and Seeley, F, 2002 in Drummond-Murray, J, and Thompson, P, with Cowan, C, Settlement in Roman Southwark: archaeological excavations (1991–8) for the London Underground Limited Jubilee Line Extension Project, MoLAS Monogr Ser 12, London

Rayner, L, and Seeley, F, in prep, Roman pottery, in Cowan, C, Wheeler, L, and Westman, A, Roman Southwark: origins, development and economy, MoLAS Monogr Ser, London

Richardson, B, 1986 The pottery, in Miller, L, Schofield, J, and Rhodes, M, The Roman quay at St Magnus House, London: excavations at New Fresh Wharf, Lower Thames Street London 1974–8 (ed T Dyson), London Middlesex Archaeol Soc Special Pap 8, 96–138, London

Rowsome, P, 1996 The Billingsgate Roman house and bath – conservation and assessment, London Archaeol 7, 415–22

Rutter, J, and Davey, P J, 1980 Clay pipes from Chester, in The archaeology of the clay tobacco pipe: III, Britain: the north and west (ed P J Davey), BAR British Ser 78, 41–272, Oxford

Salzman, L F, 1967 (1952) Building in England down to 1540: a documentary history, rev edn, Oxford

Samuel, M W, 1997 Moulded stone, in Thomas, C, Sloane, B, and Phillpotts, C, Excavations at the priory and hospital of St Mary Spital, London, MoLAS Monogr Ser 1, London

Samuel, M W, in prep The architectural stone, in Sloane, B, Excavations at the nunnery of St Mary de fonte clericorum, Clerkenwell, London, MoLAS Monogr Ser, London

Sankey, D, 1999 13–21 Eastcheap, London EC3: a post-excavation assessment and updated project design, unpub MoL rep

Schofield, J, and Dyson, T, in prep London waterfront tenements 1200–1750, MoLAS Monogr Ser, London

Scott, E, 1999 The archaeology of infancy and infant death, BAR S819, Oxford

Seeley, F, and Drummond-Murray, J, 2005 Roman pottery production in the Walbrook valley: excavations at 20–28 Moorgate, City of London, 1998–2000, MoLAS Monogr Ser 25, London

Seymour Lindsay, J, 1970 Iron and brass implements of the English house, rev edn, London

Sharpe, R R (ed), 1889–90 Calendar of wills proved and enrolled in the court of Husting, London, AD 1258–1688 (2 vols), London

Shepherd, J D, 1998 *The temple of Mithras, London: excavations by W F Grimes and A Williams at the Walbrook*, Engl Heritage Archaeol Rep 12, London

Steedman, K, Dyson, T, and Schofield, J, 1992 *Aspects of Saxo-Norman London: Vol 3, The bridgehead and Billingsgate to 1200*, London Middlesex Archaeol Soc Spec Pap 14, London

Stow, J, 1603 *A survey of London* (ed C L Kingsford) (2 vols), 1908 repr 1971, Oxford

Straker, V, 1984 1st- and 2nd-century carbonised grain from Roman London, in *Plants and ancient man: studies in palaeoethnobotany* (eds W van Zeist and W A Casparie), Rotterdam, 323–9

Symonds, R P, and Wade, S M, 1999 *Roman pottery from excavations in Colchester, 1971–86* (eds P Bidwell and A Croom), Colchester Archaeol Rep 10, Colchester

Toynbee, J M C, 1962 *Art in Roman Britain*, London

Turner, M, 1999 *Eltham Palace*, London

Tyers, P A, 1996 *Roman pottery in Britain*, London

Tyler, K, and Willmott, H, 2005 *John Baker's late 17th-century glasshouse at Vauxhall*, MoLAS Monogr Ser 28, London

Valentine, E, 1968 *Rapiers: an illustrated reference guide to the rapiers of the 16th and 17th centuries, and their companions*, London

Vince, A G, 1985 The Saxon and medieval pottery of London: a review, *Medieval Archaeol* 29, 25–93

Vince, A G, 1990 *Saxon London: an archaeological investigation*, London

Vince, A G, 1991 Early medieval London: refining the chronology, *London Archaeol* 6, 263–71

Vince, A G, 1992 Finds catalogue, in Steedman et al, 139–42

Walton Rogers, P, 1997 *Textile production at 16–22 Coppergate*, The Archaeology of York 17/11, York

Watson, B, Brigham, T, and Dyson, T, 2001 *London bridge: 2000 years of a river crossing*, MoLAS Monogr Ser 8, London

Webster, J, 1992 Belt fittings, in *Roman Gates Caerleon: the 'Roman Gates' site in the fortress of the 2nd Augustan legion of Caerleon, Gwent* (eds D R Evans and V M Metcalf), Oxbow Monogr 15, 119–25, Oxford

Williams, T, 1993 *The archaeology of Roman London: Vol 3, Public buildings in the south-west quarter of Roman London*, CBA Res Rep 88, London

Whittingham, L, 1983 Metal objects, in Ellison, M, and Harbottle, B, The excavation of a 17th-century bastion in the castle of Newcastle-upon-Tyne, 1976–81, *Archaeol Aeliana* 5, 199–201

Yule, B, 1982 A 3rd-century well group, and the later Roman settlement in Southwark, *London Archaeol* 4(9), 243–9

Yule, B, 1990 The 'dark earth' and late Roman London, *Antiquity* 64, 620–8

INDEX

Compiled by Margaret Binns

Page numbers in **bold** refer to illustrations
Street names and locations are in London unless specified otherwise

B Building
O Open Area
R Road
S Structure

Alden, John 21, 48
Alfred, King 3, 17
All Hallows church, Lombard Street, floor
    tiles 36
animal bones
    Roman 7, 16–17
    medieval 23, 23–4, 25, 28, 61
    post-medieval 33
12 Arthur Street (AUT01) 62

Babington, Zachary 48
Beake, Arnold 22, 48–9
Beake, Samuel 48
Becke, John 21–2
belt plate, enamelled, Roman 13–14, **14**, 69
Billingsgate
    bathhouse (BIL75 and BBH87) **2**, 3
    Dutch wall tiles 40
    landing place (BIG82) **2**, 3
    medieval settlement 17–18
Billingsgate Buildings, pottery 64
Billingsgate Buildings (TR74) **2**, 3
Billingsgate Ward School 49
Blossom's Inn (GHT00) 62
bone objects
    Roman 14, 17
    medieval 25
bones see animal bones; fish bones
107–115 Borough High Street (107BHS81),
    pottery 64
Botolph Lane
    excavation site 1, **2**
    medieval development 3, 17–22
    natural slope 6
    post-Great Fire development 48–9
    Saxon settlement 17
32 Botolph Lane, Wren's House 49, **50**, **51**
Boudican revolt (AD 60–1) 3
Brereton, William 40
bricks
    Flemish-type 27, 29
    Tudor-type 29
bridgehead, Roman 3
brooch, Roman, enamelled copper-alloy 13,
    14, **14**, 69–70
butchery, medieval 61
Butt Road cemetery, Colchester (Essex),
    pottery 64

Canonbury Tower, Islington, ceilings 41
Cat Lane (R1) 3, 18, 25, **26**, **27**
ceiling plaster, Tudor 40–1, **40**
cesspit, medieval see Monument House,
    Structure 8
child burial, Monument House 16, 63
clay tobacco pipes
    Chester pipes 52, **52**
    dating of 52
    makers 53
    Monument House B8 50
    Monument House B9 51, 52, **52**
    Monument House B12 53
    Monument House OA9 47–8, **48**
    Monument House OA11 52
    Monument House S10 51
coins, Roman 16, 17, 54, 55, 56
Colchester (Essex), 'mithraeum' 65
conventions
    graphical **5**

textual 4
cooking vessel, iron 44, **44**
copper-alloy objects
    Roman
        enamelled brooch 13, 14, **14**, 69–70
        finger ring 13
        mount and fitting 57, **59**, 70
        ring 8
        seal box 57, **58**, 70
        spoon 17, **17**, 70
Cornhill, Roman occupation 3
crucible, Roman, ceramic 17
culvert, Roman see Monument House,
    Structure 3

'dark earth' 3, 17, 61
District Heating Scheme, Southwark,
    pottery 64
domestic equipment, ironware 45–6, **45**, **46**
drains
    Roman 58, 59, 61, 62–3, 65–6
    see also Monument House, Structure 3

Eastcheap
    butchery area 61
    documentary sources 3
13–21 Eastcheap (ESC97)
    accessioned finds 69, 70
    Building 1 (B1) 54, **55**
        pottery 54
    Building 2 (B2) 54–5, **56**
        pottery 55
    Building 3 (B3) 55, **57**
    Building 4 (B4) 55–6, **57**
        finds 55–6
    Building 5 (B5) 56
    Building 6 (B6) 56, **57**
    Building 7 (B7) 57, **58**
    Building 8 (B8) 57, **58**
    Building 9 (B9) 58, **58**
    Building 10 (B10) 61
    chronology 4
    drains 58, 59
    location 1, **2**, **3**
    Open Area 1 (OA1) natural deposits 54
    Open Area 2 (OA2) 55, **56**
    Open Area 3 (OA3) cut feature 55, 56,
        56, 58
        glassware 55, **56**, 69
    Open Area 4 (OA4) oyster shells 56
    Open Area 5 (OA5) 56, **57**
    Open Area 6 (OA6) drains 58, **58**
        backfill 59–61
        pottery 59–61, **60**, **61**
    Open Area 7 (OA7) Hadrianic fire debris
        57
    Open Area 8 (OA8) 57–8
        finds 57–8, **59**
    Open Area 9 (OA9) cut feature 58–9, **58**
        finds 58–9
    Open Area 10 (OA10) drain 61
    Open Area 11 (OA11) 'dark earth' 61
    period 1, geology and prehistory 54
    period 2 phase 1 (early Roman c AD 50–
        125) 54
        pottery 54
    period 2 phase 2 (late 1st century AD)
        54–5
        pottery 55
    period 2 phase 3 (early 2nd century AD)
        55–7, **57**
        pottery 55, 56
    period 3 phase 1 (Hadrianic fire horizon)
        57

    finds 57, **58**
    period 3 phase 2 (post-Hadrianic
        rebuilding) 57–9, **58**
        finds 58–9, **59**
    period 4 (late Roman) 59–61
        dating evidence 61
        pottery 59–61, **60**, **61**
    period 5 (medieval up to c 1500), 'dark
        earth' 61
    period 6 (post-medieval and modern) 61
    terracing of ground 54
41 Eastcheap (EAE01) **2**, 3, 54
enamelled objects
    Roman
        belt plate 13–14, **14**, 69
        brooch 13, 14, **14**, 69–70

fire debris
    Roman 6–7
    see also Great Fire (1666)
fireplace mantelpiece, Monument House,
    B7 32–3, **32**
fish bones
    Roman 7
    medieval 27, 28
fishmongers, documentary evidence 18
floor tiles
    medieval
        Dieppe tiles 35–6
        Low Countries type 32, 36
        Penn tiles 32, 35
    post-medieval
        Antwerp tiles 36, **36**
        delftware factories 38
        London tiles 37–8, **37**, **38**
        Low Countries type 33, 34
        Pickleherring delftware factory 38
        Spanish 36, **36**
footwear, iron patten 41–7
forum-basilica, Roman 3, 57, 62, **63**
foundation deposits
    Monument House
        B1 7, **9**
        B2 16, 63

Gateway House, Cannon Street 67–8
geology 6, 54
glass
    Roman 69
        'Airlie' cup 13, **14**, 70
        bead 59, **59**, 70
        beaker 55, **56**, 70
        unguent jar 57, **58**, 70
        vessel glass 13, **14**, 56, 69, 70
        window glass 59, **59**, 69, 70
    post-medieval, wine bottle 47, **47**
goffering iron 46, **46**
Governor's House, pottery 67
graphical conventions **5**
gravel
    natural deposits 6, 54
    see also quarrying
Great Fire (1666) 3–4
    destruction debris 35–48, 66
        clay tobacco pipes 47–8, **48**
        glassware 47, **47**
        ironware 41–7, **42**, **43**, **44**, **45**, **46**, **47**
        plaster mouldings 40–1, **40**
        pottery 35, **35**
        tiles 35–40, **36**, **37**, **38**, **39**
Hadrianic fire (AD 125) 3, 56
    debris horizon 57
historical background 1–4
horn working, waste 28
Horwood's map (1813) **52**

ironware
    Great Fire debris 41–7
        ?cooking vessel 44, **44**
        domestic equipment 45–6, **45**, **46**
        footwear 45, **45**
        goffering iron 46, **46**
        iron ?lid 47, **47**
        iron and bone rod for ?knife 46, **46**
        keys 41, 43, **43**
        military equipment 46, **46**

    mounted locks 41, **42**
    padlocks 41–3, **43**
    round grate 45, **45**
    security equipment 41–4, **42**, **43**, **44**
    waffle tongs 45–6, **45**
    window catch 41, **42**

Knole (Kent), fireplace 33

Lamb Street, Spitalfields (SQU94), buried
    pots 68
lamps, Roman 60–1, **61**, 70
Lobel map (1550) 3, **22**
locks, Great Fire debris 41–4, **42**, **43**, **44**
Lombards Place 31, 66
    see also Monument House, Building 7
Londinium
    bathhouses 3
    drainage system 62–3, 65–6
    forum-basilica 3, 57, 62, **63**
    military enclosure 3
    waterfront developments 3
    see also Roman period
loom weights, Saxon 24, 69
Love (Lovat) Lane 17
Lundenwic 3

maps
    16th-century 3, **22**
    17th-century 4, **49**
    19th-century **52**
medieval period
    settlement 3
    see also tenements
military equipment, Great Fire debris, iron
    46, **46**
Mitre Tavern 47
Monument House (BPL95)
    accessioned finds 69–70
    Building 1 (B1) 7–8, **8**
        pottery 7, 8, **8**, **9**
    Building 2 (B2) 8–10, **9**, 14–16, 62
        abandonment 17
        child burial 16, 63
        finds 16
        pottery 16, **16**
        robbing of 14, **15**, 16, 22
        secondary structural activity 16
        wall plaster 16
    Building 3 (B3) 23–4, **23**, **24**
        fire debris 24
        loom weights 24
        plant remains 24
        pottery 23, 24
    Building 4 (B4) (Tenement 1) **26**, 27
        robbing deposits 27, 28
    Building 5 (B5) 28
    Building 6 (B6) (Tenement 2) **26**, 27, 30,
        31
        cesspit see Structure 8
        destruction in Great Fire 35
        modifications (early 17th century) 32
        pot inset in floor 32, **32**, 33, 67–9
        pottery 29, 32, **33**
        rebuilding (late 15th to early 16th
            century) 28–9, 31–2
        soakaway 29
    Building 7 (B7) (Tenements 1 and 2
        combined) 29–31, **30**, **31**, 32–4
        animal bones 34
        fireplace mantelpiece 32–3, **32**
        Great Fire debris see Open Area 9
        modifications (late 16th to early 17th
            century) 32–4, **34**
        pots inset in floor 33, **33**, 67–9
        pottery 33, **33**
        room A (cellar) 30–1, **30**, **31**, 33, **33**,
            35
        room B (cellar) 30–1, **30**, **31**, 33–4,
            34, 35
        staircase 34, **34**
        sump in floor 33–4, **33**
    Building 8 (B8) 49–50, **50**
        clay tobacco pipes 50
        pottery 49–50
        well 50
    Building 9 (B9) 50–1, **50**

cellar backfilling 52
cesspit 51
clay tobacco pipes 51, 52, **52**
pottery 50–1
wall tiles 51
Building 10 (B10) **50**, 51
Building 11 (B11) gateway 52
Building 12 (B12) 52–3
clay tobacco pipes 53
chronology 4
culvert *see* Structure 3
location 1, **2**
Open Area 1 (OA1) natural deposits 6
Open Area 2 (OA2) 7
animal bones 7
pottery 7
Open Area 3 (OA3) 17, 22–3
finds 17, **17**, 22–3
Open Area 4 (OA4) **23**, 24–5
pit fills 25
pottery 25, **25**
Open Area 5 (OA5) **26**, 28
animal bones 28
cobbled courtyard 28
plant remains 28
pottery 28, **28**
robbing cuts and pit fill 28
woolcombs 28, **29**
Open Area 6 (OA6) 29
Open Area 7 (OA7) courtyard **30**, 31, **31**
Open Area 8 (OA8) ?courtyard **30**, 31
Open Area 9 (OA9) Great Fire debris
35–48
clay tobacco pipes 47–8, **48**
glassware 47, **47**
ironware 41–7, **42**, **43**, **44**, **45**, **46**, **47**
plaster mouldings 40–1, **40**
pottery 35, **35**
tiles 35–40, **36**, **37**, **38**, **39**
Open Area 10 (OA10) courtyard 49
Open Area 11 (OA11) quarry pits 51–2
period 1, geology and prehistory 6
period 2 phase 1 (early Roman *c* AD 50–
125) 6–7
animal bones 7
plant remains 7
pottery 6, 7, **7**
period 2 phase 2 (after *c* AD 125) 7–8
pottery 7, 8, **8**, **9**
period 3 phase 1 (3rd century AD) 8–16
plant remains 14
pottery 12–13, 14
see also Structure 3
period 3 phase 2 (late Roman
abandonment) 16–17
animal bones 16–17
'dark earth' 17
pottery 16, 63–5, **64**
period 4 (Late Saxon and early medieval
to the late 13th century) 22–5
animal bones 23–4, 25
documentary evidence 17–18
plant remains 25
pottery 22–3, 23, 24, 25, **25**
period 5 (later medieval, 14th and 15th
centuries) 25–8
documentary evidence 18–22
pottery 26, 27, 28, **28**
period 6 (post-medieval to Great Fire)
28–48
pottery 29
period 7 (post-Great Fire) 49–52, **50**
documentary evidence 48–9
period 8 (19th century) 52–3
Road 1 (R1) *see* Cat Lane
Structure 1 (S1) 6–7
Structure 2 (S2) 7
pottery 7
Structure 3 (S3) culvert 8–14, **9**, **10**, **11**,
62–3, 65–6
abandonment 16–17, 63
access shaft 10–11, **11**, 15, 62
construction method 10, 11
finds 12–14, **14**, 16–17, 63
plant remains 14
pottery 12, 14, 16, 63–4, **64**
preservation *in situ* 1, 65–6

ritual significance 16, 63–5
route of **63**, 66
sedimentation 14, 65
silt traps 11, **11**, 12, **13**, 14, 65
subterranean 11–14, **12**
usage 14
Structure 4 (S4) 17
finds 17
Structure 5 (S5) **23**, 24
pottery 24
Structure 6 (S6) Tenement 3 boundary
wall 26, **26**, **30**
pottery 26
Structure 7 (S7) well 29, **30**, **31**, 50
Structure 8 (S8) cesspit **26**, 27, **27**
pottery 32
remodelling (late 15th century) 31–2,
32
Structure 9 (S9) drain **30**, 31
Structure 10 (S10) cesspit **50**, 51
pottery 51
see also Wren's House
20–28 Moorgate (MRG95), pottery 64–5

Neve, Richard 40
New Fresh Wharf (NFW74) **2**
pottery 60, 61, 67

Ogilby and Morgan map (1676) 4, **49**
oyster shells, Roman 56

Pagett, William 47
Peninsular House (PEN79) **2**, 3
Philpot Lane 3
pipes *see* clay tobacco pipes
Plantation Place (FER97) 3, 55
plant remains
Roman 7, 14, 17, 18
Late Saxon 24
medieval 28
Plas Mawr, Conway (Conwy), ceiling 41
plaster mouldings
Tudor ceiling 40–1, **40**
see also wall plaster
Pottergate, Norwich (Norfolk), fire debris 41
pottery
Roman 67, 68
Alice Holt/Farnham ware (AHFA) 12,
14, 16, 59, 60, **60**
black-burnished-style ware (BBS) 56,
59–60
black-burnished ware 1 (BB1) 16, 56,
59–60, **60**, 61
black-burnished ware 2 (BB2) 8, 59,
60, **60**
Camulodunum 186 amphora (CADIZ)
6, **7**
Camulodunum form 306 bowls 12,
14, 16, 63–5, **64**
central Gaulish/Lezoux black colour-
coated ware (CGBL) 60
central Gaulish samian ware (SAMCG)
8, 60, 61
Cologne colour-coated ware (KOLN) 60
Dragendorff 24/25 cup 54
Dragendorff 27 cup 8
Dragendorff 31 60
Dragendorff 33 cup 61
Dragendorff 37 60, 61
Dressel 20 amphorae 61
early Roman micaceous sandy ware
(ERMS) 6, 54
fine micaceous reduced ware (FMIC)
7, **7**
fine micaceous reduced ware cup
(FMIC 6) 58–9
grog-tempered ware bead-rimmed jar
(GROG 2A) 55
Highgate Wood ware B (HWB) 7
Highgate Wood ware C (HWC) 7, 55
Hofheim cup 14
la Graufesenque samian (SAMLG) 7,
54
lamp 60–1, **61**, 70
late Baetican fabric amphorae (BAETL
8DR20) 61

London mica-dusted fabric (LOMI) lamp
60–1, **61**, 70
London oxidised ware (LOXI) 7, **8**, **9**, 55
Lyon colour-coated ware (LYON) 54
mica-dusted ware 60, **60**, **61**
mortaria 13, 14, 61
Moselkeramik (MOSL) 12, 14, 16, 60,
60
Much Hadham oxidised ware (MHAD)
16
Nene Valley colour-coated ware (NVCC)
16, **16**
north French/south-east English
oxidised ware (NFSE) 7
Oxfordshire red/brown colour-coated
ware (OXRC) 14, 61
Oxfordshire white-slipped red ware
(OXWS) 14
Oxfordshire white ware (OXWW) 61
Portchester D ware (PORD) 16, 61
pre-Flavian 5
south Gaulish samian ware cup
(SAMLG 6) 55
Sugar Loaf Court ware (SLOW) 54
unsourced imported colour-coated ware
(CC) 16
unsourced oxidised ware (OXID) 13
unsourced sand-tempered ware (SAND)
6, 12, 14, 16, 59
Verulamium region coarse white-slipped
ware (VCWS) 7, 8, **8**
Verulamium region white ware (VRW)
7, 56, 60
votive pot 55
Saxon, Late Saxon shell-tempered ware
(LSS) 22, 23, 24, 61
medieval 67, 68
baluster jugs 25, **25**, 26, 28
coarse London-type ware (LCOAR) 61
coarse Surrey-Hampshire border ware
(CBW) 28, **28**
Dutch redware (DUTR) 26
Earlswood-type ware (EARL) 25
early medieval sand- and shell-
tempered ware (EMSS) 22, 24,
26, 61
early medieval shell-tempered ware
(EMSH) 23, 61
early Surrey ware (ESUR) 22–3
globular jar 24, **25**
Kingston-type ware (KING) 25, **25**, 28
late medieval Hertfordshire glazed ware
(LMHG) 28
locally produced greyware (LOGR) 61
London-type ware (LOND) 24, 25, 26
Mill Green ware (MG) 25, 28
northern France green-glazed ware
(NFM) 25
Rhenish greyware (RHGR) 24, **25**
Saintonge ware (SAIN) 25, 28
Scarborough ware (SCAR) 25
shelly-sandy ware (SSW) 24, 25
south Hertfordshire-type greyware
(SHER) 25, 28
waisted baluster jug 25, **25**
post-medieval 67–9
Britton type I 51
Cheam whiteware (CHEA) 29
Chinese porcelain (CHPO) 51
coarse Surrey-Hampshire border ware
(CBW) 29
Dutch redware (DUTR) 32
early post-medieval calcareous redware
(PMREC) 29
early post-medieval redware (PMRE)
29, 32
English stoneware (ENGS) 50
Frechen stoneware (FREC) 35, 51
Frechen stoneware (FREC) Bartmann
jugs 35
Frechen stoneware (FREC) bottle with
applied medallion 35, **35**
post-medieval fine redware (PMFR) 32,
33
post-medieval redware (PMR) 35, 51
pots inset in floors 32, **32**, 33, **33**,
67–9

Saintonge ware (SAIN) 32
Siegburg stoneware (SIEG), funnel-
necked beaker (*Trichterhalsbecher*)
29
slipped and green-glazed post-medieval
redware (PMSRG) 33, **33**
slipped post-medieval redware (PMSR)
35
Staffordshire mottle-glazed ware
(STMO) 51
Staffordshire salt-glazed stoneware 50
Staffordshire white dipped stoneware
(SWSL) 51
Surrey-Hampshire border whiteware
(BORD) 35
tin-glazed ware 35, 51
Valencian lustreware (VALE) 32
Proctor, William 47
Pudding Lane
Great Fire 3–4
Roman waterfront (PDN81) **2**, 3

quarrying
Roman 7
medieval 24–5
Queenhithe 17

rapier, iron 46, **46**
Reformation 18
Regis House (KWS94) 3
ritual activity
Camulodunum form 306 bowls 63–5
see also votive offerings
Road 1 (R1) *see* Cat Lane
Roman culvert *see* Monument House,
Structure 3
Roman period
Boudican revolt 3
bridgehead 3
decline 3
drainage system 62–3, 65–6
Hadrianic fire (AD 125) 3, 56, 57
see also Londinium
roof tiles
Roman 6
medieval 25

St Botolph Billingsgate 3
churchyard 18, 20–1, 26, **26**, 49
floor tiles 32, 35
St Dunstan's Hill 17
St George Eastcheap 18
St Mary at Hill 17
Tenements 1 and 2 bequeathed to 18,
19, 20, 21
St Mary Clerkenwell, nunnery fireplaces 33
Saxon period, settlement 3, 17
Seal House 67
security equipment, ironware 41–4, **42**,
43, **44**
site A *see* Monument House (BPL95)
site B *see* 13–21 Eastcheap (ESC97)
Spitalfields (SRP98), buried pots 68–9
Storay Steps Warehouse 49
Stow, John 61
Sutton House, Hackney, fireplaces 33
Swan Lane 67

Tabard Inn 3
tegulae 10, 17
tegula mammata 6
temple of Mithras, Bucklersbury, pottery 64
tenements 18–22, 66
Tenement 1
documentary evidence 18–19
see also Monument House, Building 4
Tenement 2
documentary evidence 19–20
rebuilding 28–9
see also Monument House, Building 6
Tenements 1 and 2 combined
documentary evidence 18, 19, 20,
21–2
inventory (1485) 20
inventory (1646) 22
see also Monument House, Building 7
Tenement 3 (later St Botolph's

churchyard) 20–1
  see also Monument House, Structure 6
terracing
  natural 6
  Roman 3, 65
    13–21 Eastcheap 4, 54
    Monument House B2 8, 62–3
tesserae 14, 16, 57
2–10 Throgmorton Avenue (TGM99),

pottery 64–5
tiles *see* floor tiles; roof tiles; tegulae;
    tegula mammata; wall tiles
trades, tenements 18

8 Union Street 61
10–18 Union Street 61

votive offerings 55, 63, 67–8

see also ritual activity

waffle tongs, iron 45–6, **45**
wall plaster, Roman 16, 17, 55–6, 57–8
wall tiles
  post-medieval
    documentary evidence 40
    Dutch 38–40, **39**
    London tile 51

Low Countries 40
  intrusive (18th century) 40
West Escape Shaft, Bridge Street (LBA95)
    60
West Stow (Suffolk), pottery 59
window glass, Roman 59, **59**, 69, 70
wine bottle, mid 17th century 47, **47**
woolcombs, medieval 28, **29**, 69, 70
Wren's House 49, **50**, **51**